Love and Fury

A MEMOIR

MARGIE ORFORD

Jonathan Ball Publishers
JOHANNESBURG & CAPE TOWN

All rights reserved.
No part of this publication may be reproduced or transmitted, in any form or by any means, without the prior written permission of the publisher or copyright holder.

Text © Margie Orford (2024)
Cover image © Gallo Images
Published edition © Jonathan Ball Publishers (2024)

Published in South Africa in 2024 by
JONATHAN BALL PUBLISHERS
A division of Media24 (Pty) Ltd
PO Box 33977
Jeppestown
2043

ISBN 978-1-77619-088-1
ebook ISBN 978-1-77619-089-8

Every effort has been made to trace the copyright holders and to obtain their permission for the use of copyright material. The publishers apologise for any errors or omissions and would be grateful to be notified of any corrections that should be incorporated in future editions of this book.

*To protect the privacy of certain individuals, names have been changed.

jonathanball.co.za
x.com/JonathanBallPub
facebook.com/JonathanBallPublishers

Cover by Sean Robertson
Design and typesetting by Melanie Kriel
Printed and bound by CTP Printers, Cape Town
Set in Sabon LT Pro

For my daughters ♥

To Unravel a Torment You Must Begin Somewhere
– Louise Bourgeois

LONDON

NAMIBIA

NEW YORK

CAPE TOWN

IN TRANSIT

LONDON

Acknowledgements 278
About the author 280

LONDON

one

The flat at the top of a Dickensian house I moved into in the autumn of 2018 had two poky bedrooms – one for me; a rotation of daughters would share the other – but the living room had a panoramic view of Hampstead Heath, the only wild place left in London. Other writers had stayed there before me, my elderly landlords told me when I went to lunch with them. Famous writers wrote famous books at the very table they had decked with a bowl of olives, a salad and a basket of stale bread.

'You'll be happy here,' they said, gesturing towards the serene Heath where the leaves were turning russet and gold.

I agreed. I looked forward to settling. To making their home mine. To finishing a book at their table. It was arranged. Money was exchanged for keys to the eighth place I had lived in during the three vagrant years since I packed the clothes I could fit into a large red suitcase and fled Cape Town in 2015.

The next day I dragged that case up four flights of narrow stairs and put it next to my books and bin bags stuffed with bedding. I set about scouring a decade of other people's grime from carpets, windows and walls. I washed the mismatched crockery, cutlery, pots and pans crammed into the kitchen cupboards. I scrubbed floors, stripped walls of the landlords' looming pictures, packed away their ornaments and winnowed the furniture down to the bare minimum.

I rearranged plants, books, cushions, furniture. I hung the three small oils I had brought from South Africa – a landscape with aloes in vivid red bloom, a portrait of my Granny Margaret as a cherubic baby and one of me as a fat-cheeked toddler in blue dungarees. Those paintings had hung in all twelve houses I had lived in as a child, and they made yet another place that wasn't mine home.

I threw out the old bills and takeaway menus jamming the drawer in the dining table to make space for the papers one needs to prove to the authorities that one is who one says one is – my passports, my daughters' too, our birth certificates, my divorce papers, tax records.

A photograph fell out. *London, 1988*, scrawled on the back. I picked it up and turned it over and there we were, me and my ex-husband, my children's father, in a photo booth. I am wearing a neon-pink scarf and black-and-silver starburst earrings that always got tangled in my hair, I'm looking straight at the camera, and at myself thirty years later transfixed by the remembered sensation of Aidan nuzzling my ear. His eyes, laughter in them, are also turned towards the camera. Seeing us looking at me gave me vertigo.

It had been taken the year before we married. I was twenty-four then, too young to know a wedding is as much a beginning as it is an ending. That marriage is the institution in which, generation after generation, women are forged. That it is both sanctuary and prison. That success can look like failure and failure like success. That marriage can be a place where loneliness hides in plain sight. I shoved that picture containing our optimism and naivety to the back of the drawer.

That first night in my new bed with its freshly laundered sheets, I could not sleep. When the blackbirds called the dawn, I got up, made coffee, and looked out at the Heath. The clouds were pink and the sky orange above a slender spire surrounded by tall trees. My first wedding in the hot June of 1989 took place under one of those trees, on one of those lawns. Had that been my first step in the direction leading to where I was now, looking for a way to disappear?

For months, I'd been trying to write a suicide note, but my '*writing*', which I regard as separate from me – something life- and death-giving, beneficent and tyrannical as the Furies, those ancient goddesses of life, death and vengeance – vetoed me.

Now I see their tactics, the Furies' and the writing's. But then I could not, so it bewildered me when I sat down to draft my farewell note – calm because I was doing something – that questions of form would swirl. What would it say? What reasons does one give? What reasons does one need to put a stop to things, this thing that is oneself, one's self, *my* self? I wished to set her/me free – to turn to air. To escape. But I could not find the right words. Writing was the one thing I knew how to do, but when I needed it most it abandoned me. It made me desperate. And mad.

'Dearest, I feel certain that I am going mad again ... ' Virginia Woolf wrote in the suicide note addressed to her husband. I did not hear voices like she did; I heard muffled silence; felt my lack of ballast.

I tried copying hers, but I had no *'dearest'* to address. Must one stay alive simply because there is no one to write to? There was a void, and I was falling, but try as I might, try as I did, over and over, I could not write my own note and it seemed unethical to plagiarise someone else's death.

So, I cast about for a way to leave life in a manner that would not disturb anyone, as a mother tiptoes away from a sleeping baby. But babies wake and cry for the mother's return. I knew because I have had three, all grown and nest-flown now, but still my babies.

I considered giving my life away. Donating it as if it were a spare organ – a kidney, say. But what (here the doubt crept in) would I be donating? This worried me. Would the recipient be able to make something of the extra time (my time) or would they become as mad as I have been?

To know, I would have to better understand this tenacious life of mine. I would have to go out into the world again and look for what I had not been able to see before. It was a raw November day and in the grip of this lucid insanity, I put on my coat and gloves, spiralled down the stairs and stepped into the street.

A hundred paces ahead was a path onto the Heath. I took it, and plunged into the trees, searching for the place where we had eaten our optimistic wedding feast. Looking for the grassy slope where we'd sipped champagne under a gnarled oak. But the trees had grown or died back, and I could not find the place. I could not find myself either.

The rain started, scudding over the muddy ground, driving me away. Once inside, I retrieved my pen and notebooks, tearing out pages of 'To whom it may concern' death notes.

I have had to be quiet and patient long enough for the shy night creatures of the mind to slip out of their shadows so I could befriend them.

This book kept me alive; I will give it that.

two

'How can you two not have met?' asked Karen, introducing me to Aidan in the noisy university cafeteria five minutes before our first lecture. 'You know all the same people.' She dashed off to class, but I lingered. Aidan tore his doughnut in two, and his copper bangles jangled as he held half out to me. When I took it, his warm, sugary fingers touched mine and I could imagine wanting more.

'Do you want to see *Battleship Potemkin*?' I asked. 'I'm doing English and Film Honours, so we're watching Hitchcock and all these old silent Russian movies.'

'I do,' said Aidan. He walked down University Avenue with me while I explained my theories about the male gaze, acquired from that week's reading list.

'I love film,' he said. How I wanted his eyes on me.

That was 1987 and Aidan was studying architecture, which was how we worked out he knew my sister – her boyfriend was doing the same degree. Aidan met Melle when she stopped her car on the highway below the university at rush hour, blocking the traffic in both directions because a golden mole was trying to cross. Aidan ensured that Melle was not run over as she shepherded the panicked animal across four lanes of traffic. I could picture her – fearless, protective, her blonde hair whipping about in the southeaster.

'That's my sister for you,' I whispered as I smuggled him into the darkened projection room. The film had already started so we broke off, but there was electricity where our forearms, laid casually on the armrests, touched.

The first night we spent together we had gone to a fancy dress party – me as Cyndi Lauper's 'Girls Just Wanna Have Fun', him as Godzilla. The morning after, we went to Camps Bay as the sun rose, and it was decided, in that wordless way of the Eighties, that we were together.

I loved having someone to meet after lectures, go to the beach with, make breakfast for on Sundays. The routine of romance steadied me and gave me a sense of belonging. A year later, after we graduated – him an architect; me whatever it is people with English Literature degrees are – he was called up. He had done his two years of conscripted military service on the Namibian border, but all white men were being summoned to do what were euphemistically called 'camps'. The South African army had invaded the black townships that ringed South African cities. There, from their armoured vehicles, they shot to kill, intent on crushing the insurrection against the apartheid state. There was no political fence to sit on. To avoid the army, Aidan, like many of the men of his generation, left the country.

He wrote to me from London, his elegant handwriting filling aerogrammes with his longing for me, for the softness of my skin and my funny stories, describing a Grace Jones concert, the friends he'd seen there. He filled the margins with witty sketches, all rendered with a few sure strokes of black ink – cavorting dogs, a tiny drawing of St Paul's, children in a park. Those miniatures, his glimpses, made me long for him and for the tranquillity of the London he captured in his drawings. Our correspondence was more intimate and eloquent than any conversations we'd had. I found it easier to love people when I was not with them – something I'd learned from boarding school.

His invitation to join him was the promise of a life elsewhere. South Africa's hold on me was strong, but it was impossible in 1988 to imagine an end to its undeclared civil war. The leaden heaviness lifted when I resigned from my job as a salesgirl in a dress shop, giving away everything except the clothes I could fit into a single suitcase, and fled to London where, in the accidental city of my birth, together with a tall, sheltering man, I was sure to belong.

Aidan was waiting for me at the station in Kensal Rise in west London on the wet evening of my arrival in November 1988. Our kiss was awkward. It had been three months and I had forgotten how tall he was, but he took my bag and I fell into step beside him. Our conversation went in fits and starts as if we were improvising our lines. He told me about his job at an architectural firm, that he'd made plans to meet up with some people I knew at the pub on Friday after work. I said a pub sounded nice. I told him his family was well when Melle and I visited them on their apple farm outside Cape Town. We'd driven along the N2. There were bulldozers crushing the zinc shacks along the highway. I saw a little boy with a red toy truck clutched to his chest running across a stretch of sand between pyres of black smoke rising from a razed settlement. We closed the windows, but still we choked on the stench of burning rubber, I told him as we turned into Bathurst Gardens.

The house where Aidan rented a room was halfway down the street. It had stained glass in the front door, which cast lozenges of yellow light on the path. There was a phone in the hallway, a book next to it for recording calls so that the monthly bill could be tallied and shared. The people we would be sharing with were in the kitchen. 'Hey,' said one, an American, pointing to Aidan, 'that dude has been looking forward to having you here!' The other two, English, offered tea. 'Maybe a bit later,' I smiled, and followed Aidan up the narrow stairs.

He opened the door into his bedroom, now ours. It was the front room on the first floor, and it had a bay window. In the middle of it was the bed. A huge futon on the floor, with duvet and pillows covered in bachelor-pad black. At the foot was a small television set. I walked over to the window, opened the curtains, and looked down the desolate ribbon of street lined with identical houses. Aidan came and put his arms around me, and we went to bed to find a way back to each other.

That Christmas, the trees were skeletons against the ashen sky, while the snow shone on Hampstead Heath. We threw snowballs, laughing because we could not feel our fingers. New Year 1989 the water froze, but we bundled up and walked along the canals from Kensal Rise to Camden Town where, among the cheap punk T-shirts, tartan miniskirts and fishnets, we ducked into a photobooth and took pictures of us clowning. I snipped up the set of four photographs, posting one to my parents, one to Aidan's, and one to my sister. Those photo-booth pictures were a rite of relationship passage, a tacit announcement we were no longer two but one. Aidan-and-Margie to his friends and relations; Margie-and-Aidan to mine.

Among the reasons Aidan had fallen for me were the stories I told, especially my travel tales from 1986: hitchhiking from Lake Van in the far east of Turkey to Amsterdam, where I crashed my bicycle in front of a gay S&M club and had Mercurochrome dabbed on my wounds by musclemen in leather shorts and gimp masks; having my palm read in Marrakesh. He wanted to travel with me, and we'd had every intention to do so, but we were marooned.

Somehow, together, we had fallen into an inertia of coupledom. Our far-flung plans vanished into pubs on Fridays, art galleries on Saturdays, and Sunday lunches in large homes in the leafy parts of London with friends of our parents. It was as if the M25, the city's ring road, was a cordon we could not escape.

three

In January 1989 my savings ran out, so I registered with an employment agency. The man who took my details told me South Africans were popular. We were hard-working and self-reliant, he said. Not nannied by the state, like in Britain. I did not disagree with him. He whipped through the records and references I had given him. He was glad to see I had a first-class degree. He would send off my CV and samples of my writing to advertisers, publishers and magazines.

Sure enough, there was interest. An advertising agency or a publisher or a magazine – exactly which, I am no longer sure – shortlisted me for a position so junior there was nothing beneath it. The interview would be at the grand building on the Thames where the company had its offices.

I was ushered into the boardroom where two women in suits sat at an oval table. They had their backs to the window, so I could not read their faces, and they had my CV in front of them.

'You have a good turn of phrase,' one said, pointing a manicured finger at photocopies of my student articles. They asked me questions about the research I had done, the interviews, the writing. It was like an exam, and I thrived, drilled from childhood to debate my father, to hold my own, to listen and to respond to the facts. They seemed impressed. I was pleased. The one on the left made notes in the folder with my name on it. The one on the right leaned forward and said she'd been to Oxford and read the Romantics. 'What do you think of them?' she asked.

'I love "Daffodils" and "Westminster Bridge", but the "caverns measureless to man" is my favourite,' I said. 'I was studying Coleridge when I was arrested.'

'Arrested?' The notetaker riffled through my transcripts, as if looking for something she had missed. 'What for?'

Fool that I was, I rushed on, not for a moment thinking she might think I was a criminal. 'Protesting against the State of Emergency.

You see, the police had the power to arrest anyone, to detain without trial. By that time thousands of people were in detention; I was nothing special.'

The interview woman put her pen down. I saw the ice in her eyes, but it was too late for me to stop.

'I was studying for my final exams when a friend came by and told me to come to campus with her. There's no arguing with Miriam, so I went. When we got there, we joined the others and faced off the riot police across the road. I remember the loudhailer: "You've got five minutes to disperse!" But we didn't move, cops surged towards us, and we ran. I turned and saw four coming at me, one pulling ahead of the others, and then I passed out. When I came round a cop was telling me to get up. But my legs didn't work, so he pulled me up and walked me as if I were his drunk girlfriend. Other students were being loaded into a van, but he put me into a car. I remember a policeman drumming his fingers on the steering wheel. They took me to the police station, and from there we were all taken to Pollsmoor.'

They both looked blank.

'That's the maximum-security prison where Mandela was taken after Robben Island.'

The two women exchanged glances. 'And what was it like in there?'

'A nightmare,' I said. 'The police shouted at us to get out. There were floodlights, six-metre walls with razor wire, guards with Alsatians straining at their leads. The prison services didn't know what to do with a bunch of white girls, but they soon figured this out. We were in solitary for a few days, and then all of us, twenty-one or more, were in a cell for eight people.'

'That's where you wrote your finals?' said the one with my transcripts.

'I did,' I said. 'There was such a fuss about us white students getting arrested that the Minister of the Interior granted us permission to write exams. Only three of us gave it a go, but at least we were given our books. The Romantics – the daffodils, and Blake's rose with the worm.'

The Oxford woman didn't smile.

'So, you don't have a criminal record?'

'No,' I said. 'They charged us with crazy things, but the judge dismissed these.'

The way they looked at me, they would never call me back, I knew that, but we said goodbye as if they might.

Out on the street, fighting its tide of rushing people, buffeted by passers-by, I burned with shame. Thousands were in detention and the police were shooting people in the townships every day. There was no heroism in an accidental arrest. I had made a story of it, but had been unable to convey to the two women, shoulder pads as crisp as if they were soldiers in a firing squad, the terror I'd felt as the door of the cell slammed shut. The sound a bullet in my back. My cell was two paces long, its width that of my outstretched arms. My trousers sagged, the belt taken so I would not be able to hang myself.

This was not something I had considered before, but the thought of suicide, now that it was there, was alluring – a silver flash, a fish diving for freedom in dark water.

Feeling insubstantial, I turned down another busy road. I understood that the law, and what is right, are two separate things. I had been shaped by a place where they were in opposition to each other. Unlike those two women, I thought. By then I did not know where I was and I was desperate to get home, but when I tried to read the street signs the letters jumbled, and I could not decipher the names of any of the streets. I pulled my coat closer as I hurried down another street I did not recognise.

My cell had been colder than this, and empty apart from a bulb behind a metal grille, a toilet without a lid, and a bed with a folded grey blanket on it. I had wrapped the blanket around my shoulders. It released the smell of the woman who had been there before me. I lay on her bed and closed my eyes, but it had been impossible to sleep.

A bag arrived with my name on it in Miriam's handwriting. I hugged it close as if it were my friend herself. Inside was a pair of new sheepskin slippers, a size too big but so soft, and a froth of white lace. A party dress for a party girl. I put it on and, Madonna's 'Like a Virgin' playing in my head, pirouetted. There was also soap, face cream, shampoo, tampons and lipstick. I didn't have a mirror in my cell, but I applied the red lipstick, and, for a moment, felt defiant.

I dropped to the floor and tried to do push-ups the way real political prisoners did, but my arms, not seeing the sense of what I was making them do, refused to lift me.

I made a jaunty tale of those failed exercises and of the whack-whack-whack of our guard-invigilator's rifle butt on the desks when we wrote exams. That was at the party friends had organised to celebrate my release – beers, hugs, cigarettes, compliments on how great I looked, on how thin I was. 'I couldn't eat,' I said with a laugh. 'I threw everything up.'

'It makes a good story, doesn't it, Margs?' said a friend, the expression in his eyes speculative – or bored. That shut me up. I did not know how else to make sense of what had happened, except by fashioning my terror and fury into a tale. Fortunately, there was dancing and I could escape with the The Clash thrashing out 'London's Calling'.

Everything was over as if it had never happened. Except it had not been a jaunt and it wasn't over. The girl who went through those prison gates was different to the woman who came out, and I did not always recognise her.

The doctor who checked my pulse and blood pressure said I was in perfect physical nick, but was I coping mentally? He was the only person who asked that question. I wanted to fling myself into his arms and tell him how I struggled with time, with making it pass. Tell him it was as if I was caught in invisible quicksand. That ever since those two security policemen had interrogated me, one standing so close that I could feel his hot breath on my neck, I'd had nightmares in which men, grim-faced and skeletal as Giacometti sculptures, chased me – so I did not, could not, sleep, and I was so tired I thought I would go insane. I opened my mouth to say this, but all that came out was, 'I'm fine.'

I could not speak to this worried-looking man. His niece had been in solitary confinement for months. We prisoners had talked to her when filing past her window on our way to the exercise yard, but the wardens told us that was forbidden. The next day we sang to her, our voices soaring above the concrete walls. When we went past the next day, workmen were welding a metal sheet over her window. Because of our singing, she was immured in darkness. So what could I possibly have to complain about mentally?

Afterwards, whenever our digs were empty, I'd lie on my bed and stare at the ceiling. When my last exam came round I intended to get up, get to work, but instead I watched motes of dust glide up and down the afternoon rays that shone through a slit in the curtains. Which I was doing when a motorbike pulled up outside. I opened the front door, and a friend was standing there with a helmet in his hands. He held it out to me and said, 'I've come to take you for a ride.'

The houses of Cape Town soon vanished as we rode through fynbos and blooming proteas. At Cape Point the waves pitched at the jagged black rocks where the continent knifed into the southern Atlantic. My eyes narrowed against the tormenting wind, and as we sat looking, we passed each other the half-jack of whiskey he had brought with him.

It was dark when we left, the moon a gleaming crescent bobbing in the churning sea beside us. I felt better. All I needed to make time pass was to keep moving because then I felt alive. A week later, I left South Africa, and for a year I did not stop moving. I did not mean to return, but by the end of 1986 I was adrift in a sea of homesickness – the name I then gave to the despair I felt – and so I returned, met Aidan in 1987, and followed him to London.

All this circularity, this restless movement without purpose, had resulted in me interviewing for a job I wanted but could not really imagine doing. Lobbing that hand grenade of a tale across that boardroom table foreclosed a particular kind of future for myself. I had ensured that whatever it was I was doing in London would be temporary.

That cold, frantic girl turning down wrong London street after wrong London street in 1989 did not know why she seemed unable to settle in England. It is only now, after moving myself half to death, that I understand I did not know how to feel at home in a what seemed like a safe place with a predictable future. Nothing felt familiar. Nothing felt like home. I could not attach. The safety felt dangerous. The predictability made me want to die.

four

February 1989 brought astonishing drifts of snowdrops. In March the daffodils gleamed yellow in the exposed earth skirting the path where Aidan and I were walking. We had visited an English friend and her baby earlier. I felt at home in the busy, friendly mayhem of my friend's house – her mother, brothers and sisters coming and going. I loved the tumult and how a baby made the family and the house busy and purposeful. When I held the little girl in my arms, my loneliness receded and my heart stilled, but for all the words I was capable of marshalling about any topic flung at me, I could not acknowledge, let alone articulate, the yearning I felt for a baby of my own.

There was no feminist language then, or none that I knew of, which accommodated the desire for maternity. I had been so determined not to be dragged down among the women, where I would lose myself in the invisible labour of cooking, cleaning, caring, that attending to my desire for a child was like looking at one of the Gorgons. It turned me to stone, so I looked away and pretended it wasn't there.

There is no way to say something out loud that you can't say to yourself first. And so I was silent. But the body knows what the mind doesn't, and it has its own ways of getting what it wants, and I had gone off the pill. I told Aidan it made me nauseous and that my breasts hurt, which was the truth. I said hormones made me blue and that was true too. I was blue. The tears I had not shed in South Africa had risen to the surface since I had been in London. They would appear when I rattled along on the Underground to work. Come when I drifted through the crowds in St James's Park, an invisible foreigner in the strange and ordered country where I had been born but which was as unfamiliar to me as the moon.

Up ahead was the entrance to London Zoo. Flocks of children, women with prams and men with them because it was Sunday were buying tickets and King Cones. On a whim we bought tickets and ice creams and went in. Arm in arm, we walked past the reptile house, the zebras and their soggy faux savannah, the cage where the big baboons glowered at a group of boys who leapt about grunting. People clustered around the chilly elephants, but on we went towards the rhinoceros racing up and down her enclosure. Spectators leaned over the metal paling protecting her from them, teenage boys shouting how ugly she was, how big, how clumsy, such a dinosaur, such a fat slag. I leaned against the paling too, but I said nothing, as if my silence would set me apart from those others.

Thud-thud-thud she went; not so much a sound as a tremor in the earth. My heart thudded in unison with the rhino as she charged down the narrow concrete culvert, oblivious to the taunts and catcalls from the watching crowd. Oblivious to the Coke can bouncing off her rump.

Her flanks were bleeding – her hipbones and shoulders rubbed raw where she knocked the concrete barrier as she ran. Fifty paces north, turn, the same fifty paces south: the length and breadth of her shrunken world. When she turned, I locked eyes with her, but she did not see me, she did not see anyone. Her small fierce eyes were fixed, her gaze turned towards the immense distance within herself where she retreated because there was no escape. The crowd found it hilarious. They laughed at how she ran, their lumbering prisoner, and curled their cruel pink tongues around their ice creams.

Sorrow for this tortured animal filled my throat, but I could not turn away from the sight of her suffering. Aidan folded me against his chest and his heartbeat drowned out the din of the world. He led me out of the zoo. We walked back along Regent's Canal, and the sunlight danced on the dirty water where a pair of swans made elegant turns.

five

Don't throw up on him, I commanded myself. The morning tube into Central London was packed. The man wedged in next to me smelled of aftershave, toothpaste, fried eggs and deodorant sprayed onto unwashed armpits. It turned my stomach. I gripped *The Satanic Verses,* wrapped in a brown paper bag because of the fatwa against Salman Rushdie, my knuckles white. If the sweaty man next to me did not move soon, I would need the bag. The train stopped. The doors opened, the man left and I could breathe.

Another man approached. 'I'll be sick on you if you sit here,' I hissed. He backed away from me, as people do from the mad. Thank god, because that pocket of air got me to the next stop.

I eddied along the stream of people flowing up into the fresh April air. The nausea receded as I walked across Trafalgar Square, past the anti-apartheid protestors encamped outside South Africa House since 1986, the bronze lions, Nelson on his column, before turning into Spring Gardens. I pushed open the heavy brass doors of the British Council and took the lift to the top floor, where I was temping in the Press Office. I picked up a pile of newspapers from the mailroom. They rustled when I opened them, with their traces of faraway.

Those newspapers made me yearn for the thrill of living by my wits in foreign tongues. For the freedom I had felt when I slipped the traces of South Africa for the first time. When it got cold in Northern Europe, I had gone south and fallen for a blond Italian in Lisbon. We'd gone to Morocco together. He'd said, 'Come to Merano with me', but I lost my travelling nerve at the Algerian border and returned to South Africa. We wrote to each other for a while but that had petered out. Reaching for my razor-sharp scissors with my right hand, I felt a pang for that abandoned future.

Mine was the most junior of junior positions, but I loved it. I was a human search engine. My task was to read all English-language newspapers, from the Far East to the West. I started with the Hong Kong papers, then the rest of Asia, Australia, New Zealand. After Pakistan and India came the Soviet Union and the Middle East. When Africa was done, I turned to Europe. After that I skipped to the Americas, parsing those papers, only a day or two out of date, for the British Council's small glories and its efforts at winning hearts and minds in former colonies and other places where influence mattered. I clipped out stories that mentioned the British Council in a world changing as the Cold War thawed. I snipped out the stories mentioning English books, art, films and television.

Why aren't you doing this? a voice in my head whispered as I read the journalists' bylines. *Why are you cutting out other people's stories? Why aren't you writing?*

I'd written before. At sixteen, I wrote to *Fairlady* magazine, prompted by a scene in *An Officer and a Gentleman*, a film where white World War II soldiers who tried to stop a black officer from dancing with a white woman were roughed up and thrown out. When the couple resumed their turn on the dance floor, the Cape Town audience clapped. It gave me hope to see those on-screen racists sent packing. So, I wrote and was published on the Letters page. I felt a swell of joy when I saw my words in print.

At university, I wrote for the student newspaper. By the time I was in second year, every article was vetted by lawyers to get it past the ever-present censors, which showed me the power of words to unsettle tyranny.

Small commissions came my way after I graduated, and while they all engaged my intellect, none captured my heart. These were the pieces in the portfolio that the navy-blue women in the fancy office had looked at and liked. It had not included my short fiction and poetry. That was work I showed no one because it frightened me.

I tried, without yet having read Angela Carter, Kathy Acker or Tsitsi Dangarembga, who would one day show me how, to capture the turbulence of the body. I tried to write its desires, excesses and subjugations, but I could not think of this intimate woman's writing as political. I had written love stories that acknowledged cruelty and fear. I had put the body at the centre of a tale and tried to express the passions that had gripped me. But I had failed. The savage censor in me tore up my pages, revolted by the self that appeared on the page – naked, wild, vulnerable.

Writing, like sex, carries with it disruption, furtiveness, shame and power, but I vowed not to write until I could write about things other than myself. But what else did I know? So, instead of finding out, I stopped, losing my writing nerve before I began. I felt that self-inflicted loss as an impotence, but instead I had cut something off. It was a castration. There is no word for female impotence or castration. Women are, if one goes along with Freud, a wound, but I was not sure I agreed. Writing and sex, creativity and love should be entwined, but I did not yet know how to weave them together. It felt then as if it had to be one at the expense of the other: writing or sex, creativity or love.

I put my scissors down and took my pile of clippings over to my pink-shirted boss. He thanked me without looking up and so, my work done, I returned to my desk and looked out of the seventh-floor window, waiting out the end of the working day. Looking out over the slate roofs I saw a flock of pigeons swirl in the wind. The unpredictable movement made me think of the man I had fallen in love with at nineteen.

He had blown me off course when he caught my eye at a nightclub. He sat opposite me, and I lit a cigarette. He had taken the box of matches from me, struck a match, and put it back into the box. It burst into flame, but he grabbed my hands to stop me from putting out the conflagration. I never wanted to let him go, so I took him home and put myself in his hands. When he slept, I caressed his shoulder, mesmerised by the tattoo of a scorpion, its tensile tail poised in readiness to strike.

He stayed for a year. It was thrilling, but I was off-kilter with a falling that never seemed to stop. I could not think, not with that tumult of feeling, and I could not work properly. Mind or body – that was the choice because I did not know how to inhabit the middle ground. I chose the body, a wild leap that made me afraid, as did the intensity of my desire to lose myself, to give myself over to him. He liked the 'click' that his new flick-knife made. He persuaded me to stand with my back to our bedroom door. He took the measure of me through dark, narrowed eyes.

'Don't move,' he said. The blade whizzed past the top of my head. He took it out of the wood. It flew past my arms, my waist and my hips. A deft, daft game, but I trusted him. I had no fear, standing there with my arms spread out against the door. He never harmed me, but still, I cannot explain why I stood there; why I believed that the knife would not pierce me; why I did not care if it did. I relinquished myself because he asked me to. I would have done anything for him, which is why I broke it off in the end.

I was not able to tolerate being that trusting, so I ended things. It was love that undid me. Love stole a woman from herself. I could not bear how love unravelled logic, undid controls, made me abject. He slipped past my defences, disarmed me, made me stand before him, undefended. When I lost the studded leather belt he made for me, as narrow as an asp around my waist, I cried, though by then I was with someone safer, less savagely transformative, whom I could live alongside intact, separate, myself.

The five o'clock flurry signalled the end of that working day. Everybody downed pens, picked up bags, put on coats, jammed into lifts, and scattered across Trafalgar Square. By then my nausea had returned. Despite having had sex for weeks without contraception, I had not thought about conception, but the evidence was stacking up; so I went into the chemist at the entrance to the Underground, asked for a pregnancy test, and blushed as I paid. I shoved it into my coat pocket as I took the escalator down to the crowded platform. More people arrived, jostling me along until there was nowhere further to go.

'Train's late,' a voice announced over the public address system. 'Body on tracks.'

Around me, tongues clicked in annoyance at the inconvenience. An accident or a suicide, no one knew. We shifted and muttered on the platform, trying to work out how to make our onward journeys to circumnavigate this inconvenient corpse.

six

It was after eight when I reached the pub where I was meeting Aidan and some friends. 'Sorry I'm late,' I said. 'Body on tracks.' Everyone laughed at my imitation of the cold, calm voice. I slipped in next to Aidan and he placed a warm hand at the base of my back. Somebody poured me a glass of white wine, but I did not drink it.

It was past eleven when we paid our portion of the bill and we left. I said nothing about the test in my coat pocket as we walked home, but that did not stop me from feeling that I was about to float away.

Night was tilting towards the dawn when I eased myself out of the bed so as not to wake Aidan. I felt my way to the grubby communal bathroom. Half asleep, bladder full, I unwrapped the pregnancy test and read the instructions: Urinate on stick. Wait.

I urinated. I waited. And, as if by magic, a line materialised on the plastic strip. One blue line appeared, then another. I was pregnant. My unquiet heart was no longer alone. I turned my mind's ear inwards, listening. The numbness inside me fled. I had a companion – a tiny accumulation of cells doubling and folding into a new person. My body was a sanctuary, providing protection and shelter. I ran my hands over my breasts, my still-narrow waist, my rounded hips, grateful to the potent body that had thrown me a lifeline.

What about your life, asked my mind's chilly voice, *your career, your writing?*

I will do all of that later, my exultant body replied, *I can do anything. I will do everything. I will come back to you.*

Never in my life had I felt such certainty. The drift was gone. The doubt was gone. The future was now. I knew what it would be. I was so certain. I would have this baby. This comrade-in-arms. I would not be like all the women who had gone before me. Women whose lives had been subsumed by men and children and their demands. Lives deferred and lost. I was a free woman. I would find a new way. I did not have to be dependent. I could choose what to do. I could choose who to be. I could circumvent the tyranny of biology. I felt as if I had robbed a bank and got away with it. I was elated. My body knew what it wanted, so it had rebelled and taken charge.

I made tea and took two mugs upstairs, setting Aidan's down with a sharp little click on his bedside table. He did not wake, so I opened the curtains and flooded our bedroom with spring sunshine. I waited until he had taken a sip of tea before I told him. I told him how certain I was about this baby. Certain in a way I had never been before. He looked at me with an expression of bewildered tenderness and asked what I thought we should do.

'Have the baby,' I said. 'There's no point talking about it. We could talk about it, but I can't make a different decision.'

I was going to have the baby. I had to. The certainty was in my body. In my cells. I could not argue with it. It was decided in a way that I, who usually thought so much, found strange. He was free to choose to be part of this or not, I told him. I could not bear the idea of coercing someone. I could only value love – only believe it was love – if it was freely given, without obligation.

He opened his arms to me. I went over and got into bed with him and it was such a relief to stop talking, to stop standing to attention, and to lie against his chest listening to his familiar heartbeat.

When Aidan got home at the end of that strange and secret day when it was only the two of us who knew we had made a new person, he told me he had ridden his bike straight into the back of a stationary truck on his way to work that morning. I laughed at the harmless accident. Laughter confirmed what had been decided that morning when he said he would be part of it all. I knew then, for all my bravado, that I would not have to do this alone, and I was happy.

I dreamed of my baby, and in the dream, one whose vividness has never faded, she appeared beside the bed I shared with Aidan. Until then, I had not thought of the embryo as separate from me, but there she was, beside my bed, gazing at me. When, in my dream, I opened my eyes and saw her face, the beautiful face – high, wide cheekbones and slanting eyes – that she has to this day, I smiled. 'Don't worry,' she said, 'I'm a girl and we'll do this together.' My fear of not being up to the task dissipated. Her dream words gave me confidence in our capacity to be mother and daughter.

seven

After I had been to the clinic, had proper tests done and told the kind-faced nurse I knew what my choices were and having this baby was decided, I phoned my parents in Windhoek, Namibia. 'Dr Orford's home.' My mother's doctor's-wife voice always startled me.

'Mum,' I said. 'It's me.'

'Darling! How lovely to hear you.' She switched to her mother-voice and shouted to my father, 'It's Margie! She's on the phone.'

I was so nervous I didn't say hello when he joined her on the line. 'I think you should sit down,' I said. 'I've got something to tell you.'

'You're pregnant,' said my mother.

'How did you know?' I asked, the wind taken out of my sails.

'You've done everything else.' My father laughed ruefully. I laughed with him, even though twenty-four was far too young to have 'done everything'. I didn't know what to say after that, but my mother must have said something because the conversation fitted-and-started back to life. When it found its way back onto a medical track, things steadied. My father would phone his old gynae professor at St Mary's Hospital in London. He took care of the Queen. Now he would take care of me.

My parents had never met Aidan. I had not taken him, or any other boyfriend, to Windhoek, but Melle would vouch for him; he'd helped her save that mole. I handed the phone to Aidan, and the three of them spoke. When that was over, he was going to phone his parents, but I was exhausted by the relentless morning sickness so I went to lie down.

I closed my eyes, turning my gaze inwards so I could see the little alien who now inhabited me. I clasped my hands over my flat belly. The small creature whose life depended on mine needed all my love, time and attention. She made sense of things. We were a team.

Aidan came in. 'My mother says if men aren't married to the mothers, they can lose touch with their children.' He sat next to me on the bed. 'She says I should ask you to marry me.'

I liked Aidan's mother. My own mother said the reason she agreed to marry my father was because of his wonderful mother, Margaret. I adored my grandmother. She and my grandfather's ordered marriage and their farm, Bosworth, the place I thought of as home even though I only visited there, was a world entire of itself.

The gentle way Aidan stroked my face reassured me. What he was offering me seemed to be a sanctuary. I held out my hand to him, and stepped into it.

Our wedding, to be held in June in a registry office, was hastily arranged. It did not enter my head to have a bridesmaid. I did not think to invite my sister and brother. My friends – lawyers and journalists – were in South Africa, busy with the struggle against apartheid. It seemed frivolous to invite them. So far to fly. So expensive. But Aidan's parents and my mother would come over. My father could not make it. His surgery list was already set; it was impossible to cancel those operations.

'It doesn't matter,' I assured him, although my throat was tight with tears. 'Ours isn't going to be the kind of wedding where there'll be walking down aisles. I'm keeping my name. I'm a feminist, Dad, I don't believe in one man giving me to another.'

Since I was twelve, I had rebelled against the idea of being a good girl, a good woman. Lives that seemed small, drab and narrow. I had given no thought to husbands or children, even though it was marriage which, in my then unexamined experience, made familial meaning. Looking back on that strange sleep-walking interregnum, all I can think is that I did not really take in what I was doing. What I was getting myself into.

The couples that made up my clannish family went everywhere together. More accurately, the women went where the men wanted them to go. It was a segregated world. There were strict, if unstated, rules about who provided what. The men made the money, and the women made the homes from which those family men went into the world in the morning and to which they returned at night. The making of the money was lauded. The making of the homes and of everything those homes made possible was rendered invisible in that process; the working men and their money appeared as if by magic.

Conflict and unfulfilled female desires were sequestered – or ridiculed. Ruptures in marital harmony were turned into oft-repeated jokes. My favourite was about the night my grandfather threatened to leave my grandmother. Granny Margaret rose from her chair in the sitting room, stalked through to the bedroom and returned with two suitcases, one in each hand. She held them out in front of her.

'Right, Jack,' she said, 'which one shall I pack – the red one or the blue one?'

He slid back into his rocking chair – and that was the end of his insurrection.

It took me decades to decipher the mix of desperation in my grandmother's brandishing of those two suitcases and the aggression in my grandfather's capitulation. I had no comprehension of how the institution of marriage, filled as it is with the ghosts of every bride there ever was, would bend me to its will.

eight

On a sunny weekday morning in May I went in search of a wedding dress, meandering down Portobello Market on my own. Caught up in the solipsism of pregnancy, I was not lonely, and my nausea abated. For the first time in weeks I was hungry, and there ahead of me was an Italian café with tables in the sun. I sat down and the waiter brought me sparkling water and a basket of bread. I dipped the bread into the olive oil, which slid down my chin. It was delicious and my empty stomach growled for more. I scanned the items on the one-page menu. I didn't know any of them – the only Italian food I knew was spaghetti bolognaise or lasagna drowned in white sauce topped with grated cheddar cheese burned to a crisp.

The waiter returned, his pad in one hand and a pen in the other, as if this customer was to be taken seriously. He arched an eyebrow in anticipation. I looked down at the menu, too shy to ask what the dishes were. My attention was caught by '*Caprese tricolore*'. The name made me think of revolution – the tricolour being, as I remembered, a kind of French revolutionary hat.

'I'll have this,' I said.

The waiter wrote it down and went away. He would bring me what I asked for; I would give him money, and that would be that. The tricky question of eating was made simple by the transaction that takes place in a restaurant, which strips food of emotion and disentangles it from desire, obligation and shame. I could eat there by myself and for myself, not with or for anybody else – a realisation that was a gift. I would not be afraid, as I usually was, as I suspect my father was, that if I spent money on something fleeting and pleasurable – a meal and a frock instead of property or shares – money would be finished, never to return, and I would be instantaneously so poor I would be homeless and starving to death the next day.

No. On that day, I experienced a rare feeling of peace, plenitude and competence, so I did not care how much the food cost. I felt at home sitting in a café watching tourists turn trinkets over, asking 'How much?' and 'Where from?'. I had the feeling I could belong in London because of the tiny seed of a baby making itself human around its giant fish-eyes and pulling me, its mother, into its orbit. That was enough.

The waiter brought a white platter and set it down in front of me with a flourish. It was a work of art. A colour wheel of food – swirls of red, white and green. The tomatoes, the cheese – the first time I met mozzarella – sliced avocado, arranged in a fan. Basil leaves, torn to release their summery smell, scattered across it all. The nausea was gone. The waiter picked up the thick linen napkin and draped it across my lap. I felt grown up enough to be a mother with such sophisticated food in front of me.

My mouth watered. I had not known I was starving. I ate every illicit expensive thing on my plate. I ordered an espresso. It was bitter but delicious.

Replete, I made my way through the market, pausing outside a shop, cloche hats draped with black netting in the window. A crocodile-skin handbag with a gold clasp brought to mind the evening bag I coveted, which my grandmother kept beside a box of brass-tipped bullets on top of the gun safe inside her bedroom cupboard.

A bell tinkled as I pushed open the door and stepped into the dim room. A woman with a beehive appeared from behind a velvet curtain. 'Hello, darling,' she said, perching on a stool behind the till while I riffled through racks of vintage clothes. I found a silk dress splashed with roses and held it against me.

'Go on, love,' the woman encouraged. 'Try it on.'

I did. The Marilyn Monroe cocktail dress transformed me into a vision of crimson sexiness. The waist was nipped. The back dipped low, revealing my shoulder blades. My collarbones were displayed too, delicate wings above the sweetheart neckline.

I turned sideways. The skirt fitted snug as a hand over my bottom, while in front the silk moulded itself to my infinitesimally convex belly, where the new person now lived. I looked a dream. The price made me gasp, but I forgot the money the second the transaction was done. The woman swaddled the dress in tissue paper.

The bell tinkled as I stepped back into the warm spring sunshine.

I opened the bag to peep at my red dress. I could marry. I could mother. I could be a woman in the world. I could be myself. Life on my own terms was certain in a frock that glamorous.

nine

My mother arrived a week before the wedding and set about organising with zealous efficiency. Food, drink, guests, a dress.

'I have one,' I said, slipping on my second-hand scarlet sheath.

'It's too tight for you,' and she patted my stomach.

'It isn't.' I pulled the zip closed. 'See, it fits me.'

'Darling,' said my mother. 'Let's get you something pretty. Something comfier for that tummy.'

I capitulated. It seemed such a small thing, a wedding dress. We took a taxi to Laura Ashley on the King's Road.

The shop was jammed with women in pairs, mothers and daughters, rummaging through the sales racks. I felt faint; there was no oxygen in there. No men either.

A shop assistant was summoned. Dresses swagged and lacy, floral and frilled were brought. I raised my arms, and one by one they were slipped over my head. I was zipped up in them. All of them were too big, too pale, too sprigged, too ghastly. None of them showed off my newly magnificent cleavage. All hung loose and ashamed over my belly and backside.

'Beautiful,' the saleswoman exclaimed at a cream confection, its layers of tulle stiffening the cotton skirt pocked with yellow, pink and blue flowers. The puffed sleeves were like paper frills in a butcher's display. I did not recognise myself, but what did that matter? It was only a day. Only a dress. Only a wedding.

'Very pretty,' said my smiling mother. 'Now, shoes.'

The nausea was unbearable by then, and I wanted to go home, but a pair of corpse-coloured Lady Di pumps were found to fit my swollen feet – and there I stood, kitted out for my wedding day.

There was a tube strike on the day of my wedding, a Friday, so my mother and I were up and dressed at the crack of dawn. Because we imagined London would be gridlocked, we set out by taxi so early that we arrived at the registry office an hour before it opened.

The only place open was a workman's caff. In we went, my bridal skirt rustling, and sat at a red Formica table. We ordered tea with bacon sandwiches which we ate surrounded by men in hard hats and neon-yellow jackets. At nine o'clock my mother paid the bill and, as we left, the workmen lifted their mugs of tea and toasted me, saying whoever the groom was, he was a lucky bloke.

My heart surged when I saw Aidan standing on the pavement, so handsome and shy in the silver suit he'd bought for the occasion. I took his arm, and we went into the registry office to be transformed by law from the separate selves we were into the entity of husband-and-wife. After the rudimentary ceremony, we were told we could exchange rings if we wished. Aidan gave me a ring. I gave him a silver bangle engraved with the date of our wedding.

'You may now kiss the bride,' said the smiling Justice of the Peace. We kissed. It was done. We were ushered out and our wedding party – stray cousins, people we knew from work and flat shares, South African friends living in London – followed us to a room where photos could be taken.

Aidan stood behind me, seated at a table with a vase of white chrysanthemums and a fake registry book, which an official said to pretend-sign for the photographs. I smiled, pen poised above the page, which was blank except for a doodled 'Kilroy Was Here' winking over a wall drawn brick by meticulous brick. After that we took a fleet of taxis to Hampstead Heath. Our guests spread blankets in the shade of the trees I would look for in 2018, but would not be able to find.

But under the hot June sun of 1989, we poured champagne into plastic flutes and toasted each other. A homeless man sidled over, and my mother, wielding a serving spoon and full of largesse, sent him away with a heaped plate. We feasted on ready-made picnic food my mother had bought from Marks & Spencer's. Afterwards, we napped in the sun.

In one of the wedding photographs, Polaroids stuck into a now disintegrating scrapbook, my new husband in his silver wedding suit touches the back of his head with his right hand, a thing he did when he felt self-conscious or was out of his depth. The elbows and knees poking through the suit are as bony as a boy's, even though he was twenty-eight at the time.

In another photo, the sun glances off the rose-gold wedding ring Aidan had bought from a Portobello pawn shop. My face is full of laughter, and pretty despite my not feeling this, feeling instead my belly against the seams of my dress, sensing the future taking hold and bearing me away.

ten

In October, at the beginning of my third trimester, we moved to a furnished two-up two-down sublet on the fourth floor of a grim council estate in Battersea. The lifts stank of urine, but the apartment, once we were inside, was welcoming. This was the first time we'd lived together on our own and it was like playing an elaborate grown-up version of house-house.

I rearranged the furniture and put the black-and-white coffee pot Aidan had given me for my twenty-fifth birthday on a shelf in the living room. The baby paraphernalia went downstairs into the small bedroom next to ours where I unpacked my clothes. I was sure I had packed my unworn red dress, but although I turned every bag out, there was no sign of it. It was as if everything wild in me had vanished with it.

After Aidan left for work, I shopped and cooked as if I was playing the role of wife in a sitcom. I did not feel myself at all, but I played the part exactly. It was as if I knew by instinct how to shop, chop, cook, tend to a man – but it was by training. I'd grown up in a home that revolved around the maintenance and servicing of my father and his work.

I had read Simone de Beauvoir's *The Second Sex*, so I had no excuse. I knew women are trained to be women, but I sank into wifedom with a startling lack of resistance. During the week I was on my own after Aidan went to work. It would not be accurate to say I was afraid of being alone because it wasn't fear; it was a strange feeling of suspension because all the undefined tasks of housewifery meant time slowed down. Seconds became minutes, minutes became hours, hours became days. Without work, the days felt indistinct.

I had asked the British Council about maternity leave, but I was a temp, so for me there was no such thing. It stung how obviously replaceable I was. There was an awkward farewell of chocolate cake and tepid champagne and a gift of three yellow rompers. I put them in the baby's room where there was a pile of infant clothes on the changing table. My mother had sent them to me as they had been mine when I was a baby. I picked up a hand-smocked romper and held it to my face. The smell of the fabric softener my mother used made me feel so lonely I put it down and fled upstairs.

In the living room were my law books, set out and waiting for me. In a fit of panic about my fate, I had registered to study law with a distance education university. My future had a baby in it, so I would need to make a proper living. As a lawyer I would be able to do good and earn money. English literature did not seem like a useful subject for doing good or for earning the money needed to pay for babies and, apart from how useful the law might be in the fight against apartheid, I felt entirely responsible for the life growing inside me.

I could not bear the thought of being dependent, of being a leech on my husband, of needing someone else to pay my and my baby's way. That filled me with horror and shame. Economic dependence was a trap I had watched women fall into. We were not free if we did not have our own money. How could I love a man if I depended on him financially? How could he love me? How could I stay if I was not free to leave? With this storm of existential anxiety raging through me, I sat down at the table and opened *The Law of Contract*. The words on the page in front of me did not coalesce into any kind of sense. The language was stiff and cold. I was unable to read it. I could not do the assignment, but how would I live if I did not earn?

I jumped up, put on my coat, and hurried down to the south bank of the Thames. The river's ebbing flow was soothing. The baby remained quiet when I slowed my pace. By the time I reached the second-hand book stalls under Waterloo Bridge, the sun was out, and a busker was playing Bob Marley's 'Three Little Birds'. With that sound of chirpy happiness surrounding me, I flicked through the paperbacks, finding a dog-eared copy of Nabokov's *Lolita*. I had read the novel in an English seminar, which the convening professor in his tight maroon velvet trousers had titled 'Tragedy of the Bedroom'.

Lo-lee-ta. I tapped her name out with my tongue. From the first page, Lolita is with you. That is how the narrator-abuser starts the book – putting his words in the reader's mouth. Lolita is eleven, turning twelve, the same age I was when the hard, tender little nipples appeared on my chest and, to my mortification, wrinkled my T-shirts. To mask them, a friend of my mother's bought me my first bra – hummingbirds and butterflies embroidered onto small, cream-coloured triangles – but this did not work.

I had ventured to bring something paltry into classroom discussions of the great novel – us seated in a half-circle radiating from the professor, who seemed preoccupied with the more ethereal-looking girls.

I did not tell of the body-shock of the headmaster's hands grasping at Lolita-aged me. A memory I put aside. An unexploded bomb of shame and violation I had buried, and then reburied each time it re-emerged, its grave too shallow, perhaps.

But I did remember – still remember – feeling sick and infinitely stupid when the velvet-trousered professor told me to argue that despoiled *Lolita* is a great and playful work of literature contrasting the old world with our brash new one.

The next book in the seminar was Tolstoy's *Anna Karenina*. Her ghastly suicide – flinging herself under the wheels of an oncoming train – haunted me. I thought of her then, and I still do, as a friend, someone who killed herself because of the double standards for men and women. Anna had no way of escaping the confines of being a woman in her time, caught in the cul-de-sac of femininity that ended in the coffin of marriage where, for the wife, independent life ceased. Freedom and motherhood in Anna's world could not co-exist. But men could continue being themselves in a world where, returning home, all their appetites would be anticipated – and satisfied. Marriage, I said to myself, I could do in a modern way, yet undefined, but I would find a way – to be a wife *and* to be myself.

I was turning away when I caught sight of a hardback edition of *Life is Elsewhere*. Milan Kundera! I had written a dissertation about him two years earlier. My heart gave a leap, as if I had bumped into an old lover, which in a way I had. A part of me held in abeyance came alive with the remembered pleasure of those pages. Everyone said he was just another misogynist, but I did not care. Kundera captured something about the helplessness of surrender – a kind of masochism of the spirit – that overcame his female characters in relation to men.

I loved him for writing this down, their abjection, so that I could read it and know I was not the only one afflicted.

I found more treasure: *The Unbearable Lightness of Being, The Book of Laughter and Forgetting, Laughable Loves* – novels that resisted Soviet totalitarianism. The oblique and playful way Kundera kept the individual's experiences at the centre of his writing, his creation of a realm of privacy beyond the prurience and control of a spying state, which was akin to apartheid with its cruelty and surveillance. Those Eastern Europeans championed the body in ways that undermined totalitarianism. There were lessons there. 'Get this published,' my supervisor, a charming poet, had urged me, but I did not believe this was possible. 'Go on and do your Master's.'

I promised I would, but how to continue with Eastern European literature and liberation now that I was pregnant and the Iron Curtain was being yanked open as if it were a lace doily? The axis of the world had tilted, and what I had thought I would write, read, study was now part of history's debris, and people were scrambling over the Berlin Wall to buy bananas. I looked up for someone to share my thoughts with, but there was no one except the stall owner and he was eyeing me with suspicion. I did not have money to buy books, so I put them down and continued along the embankment. There were iron-grey clouds shuttering the sky and, far below, the beckoning brown River Thames.

I turned away from the water's edge and plunged into the rush of strangers heading home with their collars turned up against the drizzle. I was lost. The city had become too vast, and I was fleeing from myself. The baby within me, disturbed by my agitation, kicked, and dived deeper into her amniotic ocean, away from the noise of trucks and sirens.

That morning I had, with my meal-planning housewife mind, which set the clock of household order tick-tick-ticking, decided to cook calf's liver for dinner. Plans for cooking, for purchasing an item for the house, for a clinic visit, were the things that got me through those strange days I spent marooned on the strange female island of pregnancy. I stood in the butcher shop on Battersea High Street.

'What can I get you then, darling?'

'I want that,' I pointed at the tray of glistening livers.

'How many you got to feed then, love?' His gloved hands hovering above the innards.

'Just two of us,' I said.

'Very good for you,' said the butcher. 'Plenty of iron. What you need, in your condition. Bye, love. Next!'

eleven

I took my package and hurried home. By some miracle the lift was working and I reached the fourth floor. Down the corridor – five, six, seven front doors – and there I was, back inside the flat. I went to the kitchen and put the liver on the counter, sliced two onions and melted a knob of butter in a pan. The onion rings sizzled and, because the windows were jammed shut, the kitchen fogged up.

My mother had always told me to use a lower heat than one would think for onions, so I turned the gas down and the onions cooked to perfection – soft, translucent, beginning to brown. I added salt and pepper.

Now to slice the liver. I eased it out of its paper wrapping and tipped it onto the chopping board. The texture was repellent. Smooth on the surface, the flesh fine-grained and too dense. Too obviously a filter. I picked up the sharpest knife but the liver, so deceptively supine on the board, resisted the blade. I hacked at it, got it into pieces and hurled it in with the onions.

Thyme. I picked the last curled leaves off the plant in the pot on the windowsill and added them. Simmer. When the liver was a rich brown all the way through, I added the sherry. It looked disgusting, but it smelled good. I boiled and mashed potatoes and sprinkled finely chopped chives over this and put it in the oven to keep warm. I put two plates, two glasses, two knives, two forks, two paper napkins, salt, pepper and serving spoons onto a tray, carried it through to the living room.

The table was covered with law books, their pages seething words I could not read. I grabbed them and all the futile notes towards essays I could not write and opened the rubbish bin and pushed them down among the onion skins and the butcher's bloody wrapper. *I would never be a lawyer, but one day I would write.* That thought was so distinct I wondered if I had spoken out loud. The baby, wedged uncomfortably tight inside me, drummed her feet against my ribcage.

A baby, murmured a sibilant voice in my mind, *is a legitimate desire for a woman. Writing – being in the world – is not.*

I had not been able to articulate to myself what I was setting aside to have this baby, which I desired without shame or limit. I could revel in the creative power of pregnancy because I knew it was nothing to do with *me*; it was what my young woman's body did. I could exult in the act of making a person, but not in the creation of things of the mind. I had to drive the writer underground; exile her so I could have this baby I felt shame for wanting so much. A different kind of shame, a feminist shame, but shame nonetheless in settling for the shelter of marriage. I paid for that protection by terminating my writing, trading it for a path mapped out by the arcane rules of my unconscious – it was not Aidan who had asked me to be a housekeeping zealot who cooked liver and crushed boiled potatoes as if they were the heads of my enemies.

The twist and stab of anger, briefly visible, dived back down to its depths, but on its way it threw its grenade into the right hemisphere of my skull. The pain uncoiled, twisting and knotting the muscles of my neck. I dug my fingers in where the skull reaches the vertebrae, but it was too late. A migraine – my comrade, bodyguard, hostage taker since my teens – reached its steel claw inside my eye socket, then gripped and squeezed.

The midwife had told me that the best thing for a headache was to sit in a darkened room and stretch my neck left and right. I did not take any medication because who knew what crossed the placenta. I washed my hands and returned to the living room. I sat in the dark and stretched, but it made no difference to the pain. So I clasped my hands around the tautening drum of my belly and waited.

It seemed years before I heard Aidan's key in the lock, but the sound brought me to my senses. By the time he was inside, I had switched the lights back on and was laying the table for dinner.

twelve

In the first week of December 1989 my thoughtful mother sent me a parcel addressed to Mrs Aidan Williams. The sight of that usurper's name – that wife, that being I never could or would be, stopped my breath as surely as if I had been buried alive. I crossed out that alias, scrawled 'Person unknown return to sender' across the front of the package in black felt tip, and shoved the parcel into the bemused postman's hands with a force that made him step back.

'You all right, love?' he asked.

'I'm fine, but I don't know who Mrs Aidan Williams is.' I slammed the door.

Lurking beneath that seemingly placid surface of my wifedom was a fury that frightened me.

Three weeks later I went into labour. It was dark outside, lights glittering on the frost when Aidan called a mini-cab and picked up my hospital bag, packed and ready at the front door, and I heaved myself into the car. He squeezed my hand. I was glad he was there.

In the labour ward we were ushered into a room with a clock on one wall and insipid watercolours on the others. The midwife got me onto the bed, reaching her hand inside me. 'Breathe,' she instructed.

'Why are they here?' I asked about the awful paintings.

'Why are what there, dear?' the midwife asked.

'The paintings,' I said. 'Why are they here?'

'To make the labour rooms feel like home,' said the midwife, withdrawing her hand. 'The consultant's wife does them.'

The pain of the next contraction seared me. I got off the bed and walked about the room, glaring at the consultant's wife's washes of peach and pale green. The flat landscapes mocked the hot glacier shifting in my pelvis, a skull bearing down with whip-crack agony that struck every three minutes.

'You're making slow progress, love,' said the midwife. 'You might want to think of pain relief.'

I refused.

'How about a bath, then,' she suggested, her comforting hand on my cheek. I let her strip me. 'Good girl,' she said as she sat me down in a plastic paddling pool.

'More hot water!' I demanded. I, too, could be a tyrant. They complied.

The warm water eased the pain. I wished I were a dolphin protected by a pod of females who would shoot my dolphin baby to the surface of the ocean to take her first breath. Time lost track of me – minutes passed, or perhaps it was years, before the midwife returned and got me out, a porpoise clumsy on dry land.

'No progress,' she announced, and time disintegrated.

I cut loose of the clock on the wall with its two spectral arms, one short, one long, chasing each other around the white moon face. *One, two, three, four* went the clock. *Five, six, seven, eight*. The midwives and the doctors and my husband were in the linear time of clocks; I was exiled in the non-time of a pain-wracked body that would not surrender its treasure.

'Give her an epidural.' A decisive male doctor voice.

They wheeled me into an operating theatre, placed me on a table as high as an altar, and turned me on my side. A needle went into my lumbar spine and the pain that had made me warrior queen of the battlefield of my body vanished.

'Get angry with the baby,' a midwife urged. 'Be angry and push.'

I'm not angry, I wanted to tell her, but I could not speak. How could I be angry when I felt only tenderness towards my child, who was resisting being thrust into the clamour of this brightly lit world?

'A Caesar?' asked the doctor.

I had a terror of a shiny scalpel slashing a bloody grin across my belly, so to say my 'No', I marshalled my strength and pushed.

Shit. I smelled its sharp hot shame stink. It was unbearable that these men – doctors, husband – could see me reduced to a grunting, suffering, speechless, defecating animal, with a doctor's hand, heavy and paternal, on my naked shoulder. His voice at the far end of his arm said, 'We are using forceps,' as he clamped my baby's head with the cold curved tongs and slipped her free.

Wrapped in a white blanket, she was held out to me, but I didn't take her. I couldn't lift my arms, so the midwife gave her to Aidan and I watched him fall in love with our daughter. He spread out her tiny, curled hands and, tears of reverence in his eyes, said, 'She has fingernails.' I loved him for that.

A cup of strong, sugary tea got my arms working. I took my baby and breathed her in, my heart leaping at her brand-new smell as we were wheeled to the post-partum ward where she and I stayed for four blissful days. There, she opened her pink mouth and latched, savage with hunger. When she was sated, she slept, and so did I. On Christmas Eve we went back to the flat and that was a shock.

My mother was going to come and help me when Aidan went back to work after New Year, but her father died the day she was meant to fly, and she couldn't come until later. The newborn time, which I had imagined filled by my organised mother, spread around me and the baby, pristine and silent as falling snow.

thirteen

By the time Rose was booked for her six-week vaccinations, my mother had come for the post-partum visit and gone again. The baby and I were alone. With so few things in my diary, the note for the clinic visit was a beacon in the darkness of February 1990's blank pages. I was so grateful to have somewhere to go that, on the day, I washed my hair and put on a black polo neck. The mini-skirt was still tight on my belly, but I wiggled the zip closed and put on mascara so my face didn't look so naked.

It was icy, so I wrapped Rose in so many clothes she was sweating by the time we got to the clinic – a drab, functional building filled with women rendered into a dishevelled uniformity by the motherhood I, in my student outfit, was resisting.

There we sat, a flabby army, our prams parked beside our plastic chairs, waiting for our names to be called so that we could take our infants to a nurse. She wrote name, date and birth weight into a small golden notebook before inserting needles into the tiny upper arms exposed at her behest. One after the other, the babies bellowed with pain and outrage until it was Rose's turn.

'There, there,' said the nurse. I swallowed the murderous fury I felt towards this woman who had hurt my baby – briefly and out of necessity.

I tried to console my infant so that I could concentrate on the contraceptive advice I was being offered. When the nurse was finished talking and I had all the advice I could ever want on the importance of post-partum intimacy, I strapped my crying baby into her pram and wheeled her home through the sleet on Battersea High Street. I took the lift to the fourth floor and counted the front doors down the corridor until I reached mine. It was eleven in the morning, and a Siberia of a day stretched ahead of us.

Rose was still crying when I lifted her out of the pram. Her cheeks were flushed and her body rigid with distress. I put her to my breast, but she arched her back and would not drink. I put her dummy into her mouth and she sobbed and sucked, but if I did not hold the dummy in, it would fall out and she would cry again.

'Sorry, baby,' I murmured. 'Sorry sorry sorry.'

She couldn't understand what I had done to her. Didn't know why her arm hurt so, why her whole body was aching and paining as her immune system reacted to the vaccines. I held her to me, but by then I was crying too.

When the Health Visitor had come round the first time, she had told me to go into another room if I felt desperate. Her visit had punctuated an endless day and I had looked forward to seeing her regularly, but during the second visit she told me she could see I was doing well, the baby was thriving and my husband didn't beat me. She said there were so many new mothers who weren't doing well and, because of cost-cutting, she would not come unless I absolutely needed it. I said I would be fine; I had lied.

I put the baby into her carrycot, closed the door to the sitting room and went to the kitchen, where the windows were filmed with condensation. It was like being in an aquarium. I put on the kettle.

The Health Visitor had told me no harm would come to the baby if I left her in a safe place and had a nice strong cup of tea when I did not feel right. I thought they must tell this to all the 'new mums', as they called the women in the maternal trenches, as if we were no longer people. As if 'mums' were a separate species.

I could not work out how to be a 'mum'. I did not know out how to inhabit the orderliness of England. The unfamiliarity and loneliness of it all. I had no idea how to live its neatly mapped-out life cycle. The steps – education, work, marriage, mortgage, reproduction, work – seemed so predictable, so compulsory, I might as well have bought a funeral plot and, at twenty-five, lain down in it and died.

I put a teabag into a cup and poured boiling water over it.

The Health Visitor had told me about going to the other room because after New Year, a mum – 'single' it said in the papers (the most dangerous kind of 'mum', apparently) – had thrown her twins out of the window of her twelfth-floor South London council flat one after the other before jumping after them.

I was on the fourth floor, so there wouldn't be much point. I took the teabag out and sipped the tea.

The baby's wailing grew louder. I found the Calpol and a needleless syringe, drew up five millilitres of the painkiller and went back to the living room. I dripped the livid red medicine into her mouth, but she was thrashing about with distress, and she choked and spat out the syrup over both of us.

I took her downstairs, intending to change her nappy, to put her in the black Baby-gro with red poppies, to brush her quiff of blonde hair. To shower myself with her watching me from her bouncy chair, then to dress, brush my own hair. To have the two of us looking pretty; not like two refugees slipping between the cracks of this city full of people with places to go, with friends and family to visit.

I got us dressed, but I did not get us out. Instead, I got into my unmade bed with Rose, and the weight of my sobbing baby on my chest stopped me from flying off.

It was dark when Aidan came home, his leather bag thudding when he dropped it in the hallway. The bedroom door opened and there, silhouetted by the light in the passageway, was a human being. I had forgotten what they were. He switched on the bedside lamp.

'What's wrong?' he asked.

I couldn't tell him about how worried I had been about the foreign woman who had bowled her babies out of the window.

He put his hand on Rose.

'She was crying.' I tried to smile at him. 'We were crying. The vaccinations.'

He sat on the bed. Rose was quiet, but her chest with its filigree of ribs beneath the skin was wracked by the aftermath of her sobs.

'I want to go back home,' I said. I was unable to say how frightened I was.

He lifted Rose off my chest, one hand cupping her bottom, the other a shield across her back. She was quiet, but his eyes were full of worry. He took her upstairs while he made supper. The idea of leaving London created a picture of the future. We would pack. We would move. That always gave me relief.

We all slept that night, and the next day, life was better. I fed the baby while Aidan was upstairs. I could hear him in the kitchen – the water flowing, the kettle whistling, the radio pips preceding the murmur of the news, then him tearing downstairs.

'Did you hear?' he asked.

'No. What?'

'Nelson Mandela is being released.'

'Wow,' I sat up. It was impossible to take in this news lying down. 'When?'

'Tomorrow,' said Aidan.

A weight lifted. Here was the future. Mandela was free, which meant we were all free. Aidan hugged me, and Rose, squashed between us, squeaked. We made more space for her.

'Everyone will think we decided to go back because Mandela was freed,' I said. 'They'll never believe it was because Rose and I cried all day.' We laughed at that, which made Rose smile.

Later, when I laid her down in her bassinet, her sky-blue eyes flickered and then closed. For a long time, I held my hand on her chest, its rapid bird-like rise and fall my anchor.

That evening and for days afterwards we talked about where the three of us would live. Aidan wanted to go back to Johannesburg, the city he grew up in, but Joburg was a warzone. There were elements in the security forces who did not want apartheid to end and so were backing murderous agents provocateurs. There were machete massacres of commuters on trains and in the mine compounds. I preferred Cape Town, but that would not do either – one of us winning, the other losing.

Namibia was our compromise. It was about to become an independent country. Unlike South Africa, which tipped towards civil war right up until the elections in 1994, the killing had stopped in Namibia. The war of liberation against the occupying South African army ended under a UN-brokered peace treaty in 1989. Sunburned, khaki-clad soldiers unclipped their bayonets, unfurled the orange-white-and-blue flag, climbed into their Bedford trucks, and drove back to Pretoria.

On 21 March 1990, Namibia became independent. The long bush war – the killings in Owamboland, a car bomb outside the Odeon Cinema in Windhoek, roadblocks, the talk of 'terrorists', military drills at school, the loaded revolver my father put next to the handbrake when we drove on Namibia's lonely roads – was behind us.

Us: I caught myself with that pronoun. Given the segregated histories of South Africa and Namibia, *us* was an irreducibly complicated idea, even though Namibia had changed its name, its flag and its official language. A line had been drawn. Everyone who stayed or returned, black or white, became a Namibian. It was a way of wiping the slate clean.

A new identity, a new nationality, a new way of life, released from the iron grip of apartheid, beckoned. Also, my parents lived there. It is a lonely thing if all you have is a threesome made up of two amateur parents and a baby – it felt like too few people and too quiet to be a family.

NAMIBIA

fourteen

Namibia's new flag, an exuberant mix of red, white and green with a yellow sun in the blue corner, was whipping from the flagpoles flanking the entrance to Windhoek's newly renamed Hosea Kutako International Airport when we landed there in May 1990. The sun was blowtorch hot when I stepped off the plane with Rose in my arms. My heart leapt with the joy of homecoming.

My parents were waiting on the other side of passport control, and the baby was admired and kissed and passed between her grandparents until she had had enough of the fuss and was given back to me. My father and Aidan stowed our mountain of luggage in the boot of the four-by-four. My mother and I climbed in the back and settled ourselves on either side of Rose; my father and his new son-in-law sat in front for the forty kilometres from the airport back to Windhoek, which is nestled in the mountains of the Khomas Hochland.

At first, we all spoke at once, over each other, new to each other, but by the time my father had pulled up in front of the house, the conversation, interrupted by a tumult of dogs, had found its way. My father and Aidan ferried the luggage into the kitchen while my mother introduced Rose to Leah Kasuto, the housekeeper who had made my mother's house run like clockwork ever since I'd gone to boarding school.

Leah handed the baby to her cousin, telling me in Afrikaans I was too young to know what to do with a house or a baby, so she had brought her cousin Magdalena Gaingos, now holding a cooing Rose in her arms, to help. There was no arguing with Leah, so I was matched with the woman, who turned out to be my age, and who'd make my as-yet future career possible. With three women to hold the baby, I was free to leave the happy homecoming chaos in the kitchen.

I wandered through the house my father had bought in 1974. I was ten when the boxes we schlepped from house to rented house were unpacked for the last time. Before that, while my father was qualifying as a gynaecologist, we had moved house twelve or thirteen times. My valiant mother could never remember exactly how many times, but it had been her job to magic those temporary houses into homes. First with me, born in London in 1964 and shipped to South Africa with them the following year. Then with Melle, born in Klerksdorp in 1966, together with a Labrador and a cat and, to complete the menagerie in 1968, my brother John, born four or five houses later in Cape Town.

Instructed by my father to 'look after your mother and the little ones', I would help pack and unpack, but if my toy seal was tucked under my arm, any new bed felt like home. My sister, like the cat, was disturbed by each move so, to pacify both, my mother would try to arrange the furniture exactly as it had been in the place we'd just left.

By the time we reached this house halfway up a hill and surrounded by veld in the centre of Windhoek, I no longer thought of home as a place where one stayed put. I would soon be sent to boarding school. It wasn't my mother's thing, but for my father, a farm boy, it occupied an idealised Boys-Own-Adventure place in his storytelling heart. And so, even as a ten-year-old arranging my belongings in my room with the old white-and-blue curtains its previous occupant had left behind, I was preparing to depart. That house always felt like a way station to an undefined elsewhere.

Now, all these years later, I opened the door to my childhood bedroom and surveyed the frayed curtains sprigged with dainty blue flowers, the books on the shelf, the single bed. Still hanging on the wall was a tenth-birthday gift from my mother's mother. An ordinary white bathroom tile with a figure painted on it: a self-sufficient little blonde girl with a lantern in her hand and the inscription 'Margaret Dreams Here' at her bare feet. I ran my fingers over the satin rosettes around the mirror. I had loved my horse more than anything except my new baby.

It was for that horse I had fought and won a year's reprieve from boarding school. Instead of leaving at thirteen, my first year of high school, I went at fourteen, stealing one more year of helter-skelter cross-country, galloping full tilt through the veld, flying over fallen trees and down dry riverbeds with other hardy white children. All our lessons were done in German, the language in which I learned to ride, the language of Namibia's first colonists who, between 1904 and 1908, took the land of the Nama and Herero people they decimated in the first genocide of the twentieth century. These local people had given the names to the small towns – Okahandja, Otjiwarongo, Outjo, Omaruru – where we went for riding shows, and their descendants cleaned our horses' stables.

I took the rosettes and put them into the dressing-table drawer. One more year at home, but after that I could not go on repeating 'No' to my father, who said how bright I was, who knew the value of going 'elsewhere' to be educated, whose best Sundays had been spent roaming the hills of 1950s Natal in a pack of schoolboys. Because he loved me, he suffered from this conflict. Because I loved him, I could not fight him forever. The only way I could save him from hurting me was to capitulate. Humiliated at being outmanoeuvred, I agreed to go a thousand miles away to school.

My father was right, in the ambiguous way fathers often are. The first day I entered the vaulted library at Herschel, an all-girls' private school in Cape Town, I did enter a heaven of sorts. With its walls of books and cushioned recesses in mullioned windows that kaleidoscoped the sunlight, I could hide, reading, for hours. But no matter how beautiful it was, I was confined, and I found the routine of bells and meals eaten en-masse a deafening tyranny.

I vowed to myself I would never be homesick, never ask my parents for anything, show nothing of the loss, and never return to Namibia. To do that, I swallowed something hard and bitter. I know now that hard, hot bitterness was fury, but once it was ingested, I lost touch with it.

Now, to be back with a husband and baby – the trappings of the conventional female adulthood and status I had repudiated – felt as ludicrous as the virgin birth.

I lay down on the narrow bed and stared at the white tile with its unsettling little girl that today hangs next to my London study's wisteria-draped window. I'd brought it back after a visit to my parents, with the thought that it was time I took those childhood dreams with me. When I look at it now, as I did that day in 1990, I feel my astounded young-self, full of hope and trepidation, back in that bedroom where time was suspended because I'd left it too early, my first home life incomplete. The girl who had not wanted to leave was still trapped, her development arrested. Lying there, I felt a burn in the marrow, and it was as if I was being possessed by the fourteen-year-old who had lived in that room ten years before.

The turbulence of my adolescence had taken place off-stage. Visits home had been regular, four a year, but school holidays are brief. In a family ill-suited to conflict, it was easiest to leave the woman I was growing into elsewhere and to show, when I was at home, a Peter Pan self that never changed, who never grew up. That was the only way to keep the unsatisfying but precious visits home uncontaminated, but it is not possible to rebottle the genie of a girl's development once it starts.

My father, who loved and missed me as I loved and missed him, would say with a note of yearning in his voice, 'She was perfect until she was twelve.' The tale my father always told to prove this – which I knew he would tell Aidan the next day if he did not tell him over dinner that night – was of my first return from boarding school, even though he had not been there himself to welcome me home. My mother disliked this story of misrecognition, as did I, but my father could not help himself from telling this story of metamorphosis, perhaps because change unsettled him.

'Your mother,' he would say, 'was waiting for you at the airport when she said to your grandmother, who was there with her: "Ooh, I'm glad I'm not meeting that little tart." But Granny Margaret looked closer at the apparition clad head to toe in purple, and said, "Darling, I think that little tart is your daughter."'

I loved my grandmother for recognising me, but it had troubled me that my mother did not see me through my peacock clothes, which marked the new self I'd had to assemble to survive the new world I had been sent into alone.

I discarded my old self after my first Cape Town party, to which I wore a white halterneck disco dress I had saved for months to buy. I had not cared that my high-heeled sandals bit into my ankles because they'd made me feel pretty and so grown-up – until the assembled teenagers, all strangers, and all dressed in their cool 1979 hippie pants and Indian tops, stared at me in the doorway, burning my skin with their derision, before turning away and resuming their conversations.

I knew, as any fourteen-year-old starting at her fifth school knows, that everything about me was wrong – the disco dress, the ringlets, the blue eyeshadow – because it exposed the effort I had made. I could not shed the dress, nor could I flee. I wanted to, despite the dangers of Cape Town's night streets. Girls got murdered, like the one from Walvis Bay in Namibia, and also, I did not really know where I was. All I could do was endure that endless party where not one person spoke to me. When I got back to school, I threw the sundress away and found some muslin trousers, a flowing top and feather earrings, which I wore to fly home: a reinvented Margie.

fifteen

The welcome-home dinner was eaten with Rose in her carrycot on the floor. There was roast lamb enough for ten people, although we were only four, and the conversation flowed, my father at its centre. Which schools Aidan had attended was ascertained and approved of. Boarding-school tales were exchanged. Aidan, a more reticent man than my father, had few; my father had many, and he told them with the perfect timing and humour of the raconteur he is. He told Aidan the story of the purple tart, and my mother was, as ever, tight-lipped. When that was over there was the tale of the letter requesting a special diet that I had forged, purporting to be my father writing to my headmistress.

'Her crime was uncovered immediately,' said my father, 'Because she wrote it on Herschel paper.' Everybody laughed, but I had found entrapment is impossible to digest. It settled below my ribs so I could not tell whether I was empty or full. Also, I did want to be thin. I wanted to disappear. I would grip my thighs and pull the flesh to make a thigh gap.

One girl, also a termly boarder, was a mistress of the anorexic arts that swept through the boarding house. She clasped her hands behind her back and twisted her arms and shoulders out of the way, and said, 'Imagine I was this thin.'

'But you'd have no arms,' I said.

She looked at me as if I was mad to worry about something as minor as arms. In the following months, I watched in fascinated admiration as her exquisite skeleton was slowly revealed – the sharp-edged vessel of her pelvis, the flat wing-tipped scapulae jutting over her towel, the trenches on either side of her clavicles, and the sharp triangular bones on the outside of her wrists. Oh, to be so vanishingly small, to be so narrow that one could slip between the bars keeping us in, protecting the world from our unruly bodies.

I tried to follow her lead, but I lacked her tenacity. I gave in and ate, substituting emptiness for the bloat of twenty pieces of toast or a tray of roast potatoes. Afterwards I dashed to the communal bathrooms and rid myself of everything that I did not want but had taken in. Purging was an act of rebellion and a liberation.

My mind would float me away as it later did, at university, where I was free in a wild, undirected way. But now, I was back at my mother's table, where there were second helpings for everyone, and a third for Aidan, whose appetite pleased my mother.

I cleared the plates, and my mother served perfect crème brûlée. Liqueurs were poured and my father checked with Aidan, as he did with anyone who entered his house, whether he had read the correct books on evolution, Charles Darwin, genetics. Aidan had not, and so my father, thrilled to have a new mind to mould, fetched them from his shelves.

Aidan took my father's pile of hardbacks, and I took the sleeping baby through the garden to the guest cottage that smelled of the creosote coating the thick ceiling beams. There was a cot in the corner and twin beds pushed together. I got into Aidan's and lay in his arms. The guinea fowl roosting in the branches above the roof settled as soon as the lights were switched off. When his even breathing told me Aidan was asleep, I climbed into my own bed.

I lay awake, looking through the open curtains at the velvet sky divided by the great wash of the Milky Way. In the distance a dog howled and then was silent. An owl called and I tried to adjust to the strangeness of having the sounds of my childhood punctuated by the steady breathing of a husband and the snuffles and tiny cries of a sleeping baby. The transformation – my capitulation to the domestic signalled by this return to my parents' home, a place I had made so much effort to escape – made it impossible to sleep.

There were traces in the room of the free woman I had been. Under the bed where we had shoved our empty suitcases were boxes of the books I'd collected at university, among them novels that capture how colonialism deranges people – *Nervous Conditions*, *The Grass is Singing*, all Bessie Head's novels, and all my papers. I had flipped through them before dinner, finding the aerogrammes sent to my parents while hitchhiking in 1986. Rereading these, I remembered my disregard for limits, and my ambition to go everywhere and know everything. It had been so much easier to be with the interchangeable strangers one meets in youth hostels, people to whom one owes nothing, than it was to be with the same people – my family to whom I owed everything – day after day.

I did not know then that obliviousness to risk was not courage; it was a way of countering numbness. All I knew was that I was at ease when I was in motion and restless when I was still. Lying in the quiet dark night, a wedding band encircling my ring finger, the words on the rustling pages were little ghosts whispering that I had lost my nerve. The thought of my own cowardice was a wildfire sweeping through me.

It was not unfamiliar, this feeling, this burning late at night while everyone else coolly slept. When I was young, I would leave my bed when the pressure became too intense and slip into the car port where, on the other side of the metal gate, lay the boundless night. The steel security bars had grown stealthily through the war years, as they would continue to do in the peace that followed, in the way briars grow around the time-suspended castles in fairy tales.

There, I would take off my clothes and cool my fiery skin on the steel gate that kept me in and the world out. I cannot say what I wished for during those fugue states – freedom, death, sex: those teenage things – because all thought ceased when I fused to the bars. No one ever came, but when my skin was cool and the bars were hot, I was released from the prison of myself, and I would put on my nightie, return to bed, and fall asleep.

The night sky paled in preparation for the first morning of the rest of our lives.

sixteen

At the end of 1990 we bought a low-ceilinged bungalow in Academia, a blue-collar suburb built in the 1960s on the outskirts of Windhoek. All the streets had been named after philosophers. So, there we were, me and Rose, driving home, turning into Plato Street, then Aristotle, turning left into Hegel and right into Bacon Street. I could not help but think of the final philosophy exam I had written in Pollsmoor Prison seven years before. I had picked the hardest question: 'Does the external world exist? Discuss', and written my answer – that I wasn't sure – as the rifle butt of the prison invigilator whack-whack-whacked against the desks. I was even less sure that day I pulled into the driveway and liberated Rose from her car seat so she could race through the water sprinkler on the lawn, shaded by purple jacarandas and tall acacias.

In Academia, where cars were lovingly washed on Saturday afternoons, the yards were divided by barbed wire fences. On Sundays the air was thick with dust and braai smoke; men talking rugby and hunting, in Afrikaans, and women yelling at children when the food was ready, '*Kom eet nou!*' On Mondays Aidan would leave me and Rose to go to work. It was as if I had sleepwalked out of the life I intended to lead: one where women wrote books and did things.

Some mornings, I would stand on the stoep and watch him leave. The segregated female world of suburban-housewife life hurt my head; a stabbing pain in my right temple that announced the onset of a migraine. I felt guilt at the invisible chains my fertile body had cast around Aidan. He had said it was my tales of daring travels that had seduced him, firing his imagination with the exotic places we would visit.

Yet Aidan seemed at peace with his oscillation between home and work and back home again. When he returned, he bathed Rose and read her bedtime stories and she loved him. Once she was asleep, we ate the food I cooked and drank wine and smoked cigarettes on the verandah. I never asked him if it was enough, afraid he would ask me in return. For me, it was not enough.

After Aidan turned the corner and disappeared into the world of men and life and work, I went indoors where the deadly trap that is the housewife's day lay in wait.

Both sets of parents had given us furniture and, when the boxes we had shipped from London arrived, I unpacked them. The coffee pot with its black daisies had broken en route, so it became a vase for veld grasses picked on visits to my father's weekend farm east of Windhoek. The bevelled mirror and a white wicker chair I had scavenged from a skip in London went into the bathroom. The bone-handled Sheffield bread knife I'd nicked from our last flat landed in the kitchen drawer. I unpacked the books last, putting them on the shelves that were out of a child's reach and out of my line of sight. But those books I had stopped opening accused me anyway. They had been my guides and I had abandoned them.

At eighteen, I found in them a political language that enabled me to express what I saw around me, but which I had struggled to name. At twenty-six, I had strayed – been led astray – by my female body and its desires and its conditioning, despite Simone de Beauvoir showing me how women are made and not born. Dog-eared copies of classics like *The Myth of Motherhood* and *Fat is a Feminist Issue* had unshackled a schoolgirl mind that encountered feminism, socialism, psychoanalysis and literature.

Feminism had been my way into politics. In Fresher's Week in 1983, I went to my first Women's Movement meeting and joined Fem Comm (Feminist Committee). Together, we discussed books destined to become classic texts of second-wave feminism. They gave me new ways of understanding the politics that define and control the bodies of women – in the personal sphere, too; in that consciousness-raising group, where we sat in a hairy-legged circle, we imagined what our liberated selves might be capable of. How marvellous to roam without fear, if we could only take back the night and make everyone understand that our bodies are ours and ours alone.

I had flourished in that women-only space. In theory, I had believed men should also attend. It was, after all, in the interests of all women for men to be feminists. But in practice, I had not wanted them there. The presence of men inhibited me. I was different when they were there. Sharper. Less at ease. More contrary. More eager to please. Some people said it was because I had gone to an all-girl's school, but I had enjoyed not having to pretend to be stupid as I had seen so many girls do in my co-ed Windhoek school. Men assumed themselves to be the centre of gravity around which women revolved, and I resented not only how naturally it came to women to anticipate their needs, but also how deft I was becoming at making these invisible.

That was how families – mine, at any rate – worked. The rhythm of my mother's day revolved around my father's work comings and goings. Her interests were tucked into the pockets of time when he was out of the house. It was the negative version of that woman's space in which I had thrived at university. I was replicating it because I did not know, or could not imagine, another way of doing married life, with all its shopping and cooking and keeping-up-appearances.

From the outset I was drawn to the politics of the female body – abortion law reform, rape centres, shelters for battered women and children. The violence done to women, physical and economic, felt personal, and it was through women's politics that I could understand the anti-apartheid slogan, 'An injury to one is an injury to all.' It was through women's testimonies that I could, momentarily at least, breach the iron curtain of race in southern Africa. My eyes were opened to the idea of women as a group who are oppressed – but what kind of group were women in apartheid South Africa? How could feminist solidarity bridge the divide between privilege, which was white, and poverty, which was black? Among that circle of Fem Comm recruits, not many had done much housework – especially those of us with our white stay-at-home mothers.

I, a newly minted housewife in Namibia, didn't do much housework either. I was idle and ornamental, tormented and bored in that segregated suburban life, where the actual work in my house, the labour of family, was done by someone else. There, in the private domain, the colonial system continued unchanged, as if the world of women existed outside of the political realm with its flags and anthems and Independence Days. Even as I sat looking at my books, Magdalena was in the kitchen, wrapping Rose in a towel, having wiped her own feet to prevent soiling the blue linoleum floor she'd just mopped.

My brother, John, four years younger than me and here for a visit, came to see me in the new house. I gave him a Windhoek Lager and he sat at my kitchen table opposite Rose in her highchair.

Popping the cap off the bottle, he said, 'I can't believe that my sister is living with a baby in a backwater.'

'I can't believe it either.' I placed the banana I had been slicing in front of Rose. 'But here I am,' I said brightly and opened a beer. 'So, cheers.'

We clinked bottles and smiled, but his words stung because the life I'd imagined for myself had slipped through my inattentive fingers.

It was not the place that was a backwater, it was me. My spirit had eddied into the shallows of domesticity and beached itself. I had let John down because I had let myself down by immuring my combative originality, which he'd always valued and loved. Yes, my brother's words stung – look how long I have remembered them – but they were a gift: he would not let me forget that I had once known other things and made other plans. His words gave me the backbone I needed then, as an oyster needs grit to make a pearl.

There was no rain in the summer of 1991/92. Month after month, the sky was a deathly blue and the sun flayed the leaves off the heat-crippled trees and scorched us if we forgot our hats. Cattle and wildlife died by the thousands. My firstborn and I scanned the empty sky, and then, just as we were all mad from drought, a cloud appeared, and then they all came, cumulating until there was no room left in the sky. The crackle in the air was palpable. Hope swelled, but we left the sheets on the line so as not to jinx it.

The dogs howled when the rain and wind came, teasing at first. Then a sudden gust grabbed at my skirt and whipped the trees and the washing into a frenzy. We slitted our eyes against the dust and held hands as lightning bolts half the size of the sky raced towards us, trailing thunder in their wake.

The first few drops fell, puffing up miniature dust devils, and the air filled with the intoxicating smell of rain. The gap between the flares and the thunderclaps decreased until they were simultaneous, and the storm – a wall of sound and water – was on top of us. Tilting our faces to the sky, we drank the rain in and whirled about as the soil turned to mud between our bare toes.

When the storm passed and the sun came out, flying ants hatched from the ground – a whirl of insects that flew up and mated and then died, leaving their transparent wings heaped in shimmers on the ground. Days later, green shoots pierced the earth and pink and white rain lilies nodded their pretty heads.

That was the year that my belly swelled with my second child, in the winter of 1992. Rose, two-and-a-half years old, put her ear to it, and listened for the little fish-baby swimming there in the darkness, but she refused point-blank to believe she too had once lived inside me.

seventeen

My waters broke late in August, a hot oceanic gush that pooled on the kitchen floor. I put the plates down and phoned my mother. She collected Rose, who frisked off with her overnight bag, all prepped to continue her lessons on the Latin names of trees with my father. I stayed home, waiting for the contractions – which started, sudden as a lash, at four the next morning. One after the other they came, without time for breath.

At the hospital my midwife placed her old-fashioned listening horn on my belly. The baby's heartbeat was steady. I breathed in and out, even as pain hammered at my cervix, cranking it open, but the baby was not presenting properly. Her neck flexed back, her face to the world. She could not be born unless the crown of her head came first.

'A Caesar,' said the doctor.

'No,' I shouted, but the pain took my refusal and turned it into a screech, raw and animal-like. I clutched my midwife's hand. She knew I would turn them all to stone if I could only look at them long enough.

The anaesthetist sauntered in and those medical man-witches, my enemies, looked down at me, exposed and panting, and conferred about cutting me open.

'Go sort out the theatre,' my midwife said. 'I'll wait with her.'

The second they'd left, she instructed: 'Face on the bed, arms crossed, knees under you, backside in the air. We don't have much time. But do it. Maybe the baby slips back enough to re-engage.'

I obeyed, and the slick otter-body slipped back far enough for her to tuck in her chin. The midwife and Aidan, one on either side of me, got me in a squat, and this time the hammer-blow contractions did their work.

The doctors returned, placed their hands, hairy as spiders, on the bed and announced the theatre was ready.

'The baby's crowning,' said the midwife. 'We do it here.'

Hatred flared off those men, interlopers into our women's world of birth.

I had triumphed.

My daughter slithered out and I reached for her, my beloved stranger, and laid her on my chest so she could hear my heart. It had been her heart too until the cord linking us was cut.

'Hello,' said Aidan, and his new daughter turned her black eyes towards him, gazing with the unnerving and all-knowing intensity of a newborn.

eighteen

Three days later we went home. I laid Grace on my bed. Her older sister sidled into the room and scrutinised the swaddled bundle. 'Shall we kill it now, Mummy?' asked Rose.

'No,' I said. 'We can't.'

'Why not?' Rose raised her eyes, piercing as a hawk's, to meet mine.

'That's not our job,' I replied.

'What's our job, then?'

'To look after her and to love her.'

Rose looked at me for some time, then she raised her shoulders and dropped them; the way the world is organised had at last been explained. She climbed onto the bed with me and the baby. She placed her hand on her little sister's chest for a moment then said, 'Okay, Mum. Let's do it.'

When my sister came to see us, she gave Rose her big-sister gift first. Only when Rose had unwrapped her toy horse and its foal did Melle reach into the carrycot. She opened the sleeping baby's hand, her green eyes luminous with love, and touched the tiny pink palm. Grace curled her fingers around her aunt's finger and clung on for dear life.

'She's minute,' said my sister.

'She's not *your* newt, Melle,' Rose shot back at her. 'She's *my* newt!'

We laughed, my sister and me.

My ears were attuned to when they cried out at night, my arms to the softening of their limbs as they fell asleep again, but nothing except their physical presence made sense. The baby's body slick when I bathed her, the sheen on my three-year old's blonde hair, the smell of them – dust, milk, warm skin. Those were the moments in which time made sense, one minute seamlessly connected to the next. For the rest, time was suspended as if it were amber, and I was trapped in it. I burned with the fiery love I felt for my babies – that was real – even as the melancholy that had taken root in my sixth month of pregnancy burst into malignant bloom.

Each morning was uncharted territory. Each day was a repeat, and yet each day had to be invented. It was hard to know what to do with those days, back then. The smell of my baby's neck when I picked her up, the gleam in her beady little eyes as she suckled: that was real, but the lassitude that descended filled me with mortification. The disconnect I felt frightened me, but there was no sign of either fear or shame in photos taken at the time.

I found one the other day. In that picture, taken in late 1993, Grace is a baby in my arms, and Rose is a little girl wrapped like a vine around my leg. I am smiling, a vision of fecund joy I did not feel. Looking at that picture thirty years later, I remember the fear I felt then. I felt like I was standing on a precipice, and it unbalanced me. To stop myself from falling, I threw myself into a frenzy of wifely activity and invited everyone I met to our new house. Windhoek in the early Nineties was in the first euphoric flush of independence. The small city was full of people returning from decades of exile, and newcomers – people excited about making up this new nation.

Friends from South Africa came to stay, journalists and filmmakers I had known from the life I had lived before – everyone wanted to document this phoenix rising out of an arid colonialism. They were there because Namibia was *the* news story: a civil war replaced with peace and democracy. Visitors would stop by for a night or two on their way to the Namib Desert or to Angola. When they arrived, I breathed in their mobility, their freedom, and the fog of loneliness would lift. I cooked elaborate feasts, and we ate at a big table under the trees while my children splashed in a paddling pool, but their stories of parties, music, shifting love affairs and the unfolding events in South Africa no longer included me.

When my friends returned from their news-gathering adventures, we would stay up late and talk about what they had seen and done. In the morning, they would refuel their vehicles and leave again. I yearned to go with them when, after breakfast, they took the long road south. Marooned in a suburb, I was a housewife entangled in the love trap of family, its invisible tentacles around my chest, neck, waist – and lips. A blind, strangling thing, monstrously maternal in its need to attach, envelop, smother.

This tentacled creature, this anxiety, had climbed inside me. It was hunkering down, making itself at home. I was afraid and I wanted it evicted, but I did not know how. I could not tell anyone about it, but everywhere I turned it was there, reaching out its arms, finding me in the dark, taking my air, turning ordinary tasks into ordeals.

One such ordeal was shopping. My trolley was humpbacked by the time I pushed it to the supermarket checkout. I could not work out what to do with the all the things I had shovelled off the shelves – *two kilos of rice, onions, garlic, Rice Krispies, cornflakes, mielie meal, castor sugar, eggs, disposable nappies, toilet cleaner, sliced carrots, whole carrots, oranges, orange juice, bin bags, cumin, turmeric, coriander, chilli flakes, lentils red and brown, coffee, sugar, shampoo, deodorant, bread for today, bread for freezing, milk, razors, pot scourer, mincemeat, tinned tomatoes, pasta, lasagna sheets, lemons, Windolene, Handy Andy, green washing-up liquid, fish fingers, yoghurt, yoghurt for babies, baby food, butternut, linguine, tagliatelle, spaghetti* – I hate spaghetti – *tomato paste, leg of lamb, lamb shanks, lamb chops, venison steaks, pork sausages, mustard, yellow washing-up gloves size medium, toilet bleach, Pears bath soap, green blocks of Sunlight Laundry Soap for hand-washing clothes, Woolite, cheddar cheese, grated parmesan, soda water, wine, beer, ginger ale, pegs, fabric conditioner, a pocket of potatoes, a pocket of onions, a watermelon, strawberries, apples, pears, bananas, bananas, bananas, bananas* because when there are babies there can never be enough *bananas*.

The cashier waited for me to unpack this mountain of food so that she could scan it. Once scanned, she would pass each item to the bone-thin packer at the end of the conveyer belt. He would then fill endless plastic bags with this tsunami of things that I would have to push to my car.

My car, baking in the sun for the eternity I had been in the supermarket, would be a furnace into which I would have to heave the bags before I got in and placed my hands on the blazing-hot steering wheel so that I could go.

Go? asked the voice in my head. *Where could I go?*

The women in the queue behind me were clicking their tongues. It was nearly lunchtime, and the husbands of Windhoek went home for lunch, expecting to be served promptly. Unable to tolerate those housewives a second longer I lifted my baby out, abandoned the laden trolley and dashed outside. I strapped my startled Grace into her car seat and drove home.

It was such a relief to have nothing to carry into the house except my handbag and a baby. When the glass of water I had poured shattered on the kitchen floor because my fingers had not held it properly, I swept the shards into the dustpan and threw them away so that no small bare feet would be cut when Rose returned from nursery school.

I fed the baby, and then I tucked her in to nap in the dog basket with Tigger, the shaggy Alsatian who loved Grace as much as she loved him. I was dizzy when I stood up, but I could not tell if I was hungry or not. I never knew. I had lost touch with my own appetite thinking of the alimentary canals of other people, and I felt ashamed of eating. My body, which no longer felt as if it was mine, belonged to an inverted Alice-in-Wonderland universe. It was either too small – not enough to provide the sex and the food required of it. Or it was too monstrously big to fit into the narrow domestic niche I found myself in.

nineteen

'Normal,' said the gynaecologist of my blood pressure and pulse.

'Normal,' I said when he asked me about menstruation, micturition, bowel movements, breast-feeding.

'Marital relations?' he asked.

'Normal,' I replied.

It was only when he asked me how I felt after he had fitted a new IUD that the mortifying tears came. The doctor smiled – I had crossed him, after all, during the delivery of my baby girl – then offered me a tissue and said I could tell him what was wrong. There was time.

'Time is the trouble,' I said. I no longer experienced my days as linear or purposeful. I was trapped in cyclical domestic time, I tried to explain, where there was no past and no future because the washing-up, cooking, eating, talking, sex, my period, were always on repeat.

He made a little speech about how it takes some young women a while to get used to a new baby and the responsibilities of managing a household.

I told him I loved the baby; I understood babies and their wildness; it was not the baby that was the trouble.

There were adjustments to be made, said the doctor. On he went. I drowned out his voice by picturing the paper knife on his desk plunged into his heart. It was only because killing him was illegal and I did not want to go to prison again that I sat on my hands and allowed him to live.

He went on talking and so I did not tell him about wanting to die when the afternoons took forever to get to the night.

I don't think I told him about the invisible concrete in the air that made it difficult to inch my arms, legs, body through the day.

I did not tell him that a chasm had opened, dividing the terrain of my self as tectonic plates divide continents. The 'I' of myself, which is what I thought of as the mind, was now separate from the 'me' of myself – the body.

I did not tell him I had to fight my hands so they did not swing the steering wheel of my car sharply to the right, hurling me off the bridges that spanned Namibia's dry rivers.

I did not tell him I felt as if I had been buried alive.

I did not tell him any of this, even when he ran out of things to say and stared at me across the no-man's-land of his desk. He would have laughed at me if I had tried to convey the danger of the gulf that lay between what I had once imagined I would be – a clever woman leading a life of the mind – and what I was – a bovine muted creature sprouting milk, reprising a role I had never for a moment imagined playing. Maybe I said something, maybe it was the tears, but the doctor said that post-natal depression was not something to ignore as he flipped open his prescription pad and scribbled. 'Prozac,' he said, handing it to me, 'one tablet a day. Take evening primrose oil too.'

I was afraid. I wanted to be content. I would have laid down my life for my babies. I would have broken the neck of anyone who tried to harm them with my bare hands. They depended on me, as did their father. I did as I was told.

I did not like how the Prozac made me feel, nauseous, numb, outside of myself, set apart from other people, muffled. I was told I needed to give the body time to adjust, but months passed and the despair was no different, even though I took those pills exactly as prescribed, because I wanted to inhabit life, not drift through it like an angry ghost. Like the ghost who'd haunted me at boarding school, the ghost of a girl who, in the 1920s, had burned to death in the dormitory where I slept. A boarder from far away, she and two companions had stayed an extra night after the end of term because of the timing of their trains. The three of them had played a game, dancing in a circle around a brass candlestick in their long white nightgowns, taking turns to jump over the burning flame. She had caught alight and burned to death, but had lived on in the attic.

I would steal up the narrow stairs and pick my way through the trunks, the skin between my shoulder blades prickling with her presence as I climbed out onto the roof and turned loneliness into solitude by smoking Camel cigarettes. When I was done, nauseous from the tobacco, I would make my way down again, and despite what logic told me, it was hard not to glimpse her flitting between the cobwebbed eaves. Once, as I went down long after lights out, I looked up those stairs vanishing into the dark attic, and there she was in her white nightie. 'I'm sorry,' I whispered. I could swear I saw her eyes flame.

That burning ghost girl came to my aid when there was a fire. It started late one night in the kitchen, which was below a wooden bridge linking the boarding house to a corridor of classrooms. The boarders, fleeing the sirens, came to a halt at the door at the end of the corridor. On the other side of the locked door was a broad flight of stairs leading to the safety of the outside world.

More and more girls arrived. The fire alarms went off, girls jostled, squashing us against the locked doors.

There was a key behind a pane of glass inside a red wooden box that said 'EMERGENCY'. Next to the box was a small hammer – but nobody took it down, and the key to our escape remained behind the glass. Nobody would help themselves, so they could not help one other.

We will die, I thought. We'll burn to death because no one would break the rule never to go outside. We will die because not one of those girls, not even the prefects who were there in loco parentis at night when there were no adults, would smash the glass and take out the key.

And then I knew *she* was there too. I felt her fury at being burned to death, at having to stay in that place forever. It was the ghost girl, I was certain, who walked me to the front of that scrum of girls. Who lifted my hand to take the red hammer off the wall. She drove the metal head into that pane of glass with such force that a shard cut my palm, but I did not care about the blood as I grabbed the key and unlocked the door and rushed outside with everyone.

We assembled under the ilex tree and our heads were counted. Everyone was there. The fire had been put out. We were cold by the time we trudged back up the stairs and, the doors double-locked, sent back to bed. For a while we lay there, whispering, until the others fell asleep.

When it was quiet, I thought about the prefects, the older girls, the ones in charge. Would they really have let us burn to death rather than smash the glass in front of a red box that held the key to our escape, the key to our lives? I think they would have. I think that is how so many girls are conditioned.

The next night I went through the attic out onto the roof and smoked under the starry night sky, but I did not feel her presence. She must have slipped out with us when we poured down the fire escape. There would have been no need for her to return because who would have thought to include her in the headcount?

She was free, that furious burning girl who had showed me how to save myself, and I was glad for her, bell-jarred as I now was in my suburban house with steel bars on the windows.

twenty

'*Asseblief, miesies* – please, madam,' mouthed the ragged boy pressing an armful of newspapers against my car window. It was late April 1994, and the Namibian newspapers were full of the story of Mandela and De Klerk and South Africa's first democratic elections. I grabbed the parking money next to the handbrake and rolled down the window, just enough to hand the boy the coins. The lights changed and the person behind me hooted as I took my copy of the *Namibian*. I shoved the newspaper into my bag and went to fetch Rose from nursery school. I strapped her into her car seat and drove home, listening to her regale Grace, her rapt twenty-month-old sister, with the morning's stories.

The fridge was empty except for a few eggs, which I scrambled for them. I fished the newspaper out of my bag and flicked through pages filled with South Africa's violence-wracked lurch towards and away from civil war. When the girls were finished eating, I settled them down for their nap and returned to the kitchen.

An article buried in the arts pages had caught my eye. 'A woman making history by making books', read the headline. I could hear from the muffled sounds coming down the passage that no afternoon sleeping was going on, but I didn't care. I was riveted by a profile piece about a woman called Jane Katjavivi.

Jane was British, but she had come to Namibia with her exiled husband when he returned just before independence. Soon after her arrival, she had founded a small independent publishing house, New Namibia Books, so that the people of Namibia could see themselves reflected in literature. Books about the north of the country, where the long war for independence had mostly been fought, and where the local people were subjected to martial law.

Many people had died; thousands had fled the conflict, yet there had been no public reckoning with the atrocities of Namibia's past. There were many wounds to heal, many stories to tell of the war. It was over, but the violence and its effects endured. To make a future, shared storytelling was needed. I read what she had to say about the healing power of writing. That we needed to tell the tales of the past to better shape the future. Jane had opened up a vital literary space.

I sat up straight, my mind clear. There was nothing wrong with my head, I knew; it was my circumstances I had got so spectacularly back to front. Pills were not going to heal me. What I needed was work. Real work. Being part of the world, part of this project of world-building, would fix me. This woman I did not yet know opened that window in my mind and let the light in. My inertia, the sense of parasitic uselessness the housewife life had given me, dispersed. I had to be part of what that woman was doing. I had to help find the words that would fix things.

I called New Namibia Books. A woman answered, and I asked to speak to the publisher. 'This is Jane Katjavivi,' said the voice with its clipped English accent.

'This is Margie Orford,' I said.

'How may I help you?' she asked.

'I need to work for you,' I said.

She was silent, so on I rushed. I had written for the student newspaper at the University of Cape Town. I felt compelled to write, to bear witness to injustice. To change things by writing. I had done this before. 'It wasn't much,' I said, 'but in my second year at UCT, I'd got myself elected to the Arts Students Council to do something about the absence of black and women writers on our reading lists.'

'We're working on a shoestring budget,' came the reply.

'Please,' I said. 'Show me what you do.'

'Right. I'll see you tomorrow morning,' she said, a smile in her voice.

Every single article of clothing was on the floor by the time I settled on the teal-green dress I had tried on first. The minute Magdalena arrived, I put Grace in her arms and dashed out. The morning traffic was slow, but I arrived half an hour early for what I thought of as my interview.

At the allotted time I went in, and after offers of coffee, which I refused, and minimal small talk, which I fluffed, Jane showed me around. She handed me a pile of illustrated children's books she had published – Namibian stories set in the landscapes I knew from my own childhood. Next were textbooks. There was so much work to be done, she said, overhauling the apartheid education system book by book. She showed me some work in progress, the first drafts of memoirs by struggle veterans.

'This is the work I want to do,' I said, holding a pile of page proofs in my hands. 'These are the stories – Namibia's stories – that I want to be part of.'

'I've hired a science editor for a new series of schoolbooks,' she said. 'I can't afford anyone else now.'

The non-existent job I had made up in my head was the lifeline that would stop me from going under. 'I'll do anything,' I said. 'I can read. I can write. I can edit. I can do research. I'll make new schoolbooks for children. Just give me a chance.'

Her eyebrows arched as she studied my face and I suspected that she, also a wife and a mother, understood domestic drowning.

'All right,' she said. 'I was planning to do English textbooks too. Next Monday morning, then. At eight?'

I hugged her. Thanks to her, I was going to fix myself. I was going to fix the world. I was going to do this with books. When I got home, I threw away those numbing little pills and negotiated a new way of working with Magdalena – and there I was, all set for my future life's work.

twenty-one

I knew nothing about publishing, educational or otherwise, and so, after a few months of feeling our way in the dark, the new science editor and I were sent for a fortnight of training at Heinemann Publishers in Johannesburg. During the day I had no time to think about anything. We were given an exhilarating crash course in curriculum design and social redress, in commissioning and materials testing, in production schedules and copy-editing, in teacher training, and in distribution and marketing. We visited schools full of nervous optimism about the new South Africa where new ways of teaching and learning were being tested. We made plans for what we would do in Namibia and how we would collaborate, and then, my sense of self restored by two weeks of busy solitude, I flew home.

At the airport on my return, Aidan hugged me and whispered I had been missed. It was wonderful to have my daughters wrap strong little arms and sturdy legs around my body, a body that had relished two weeks of uninterrupted sleep. As I settled into the car, I took my world-woman self and scaled her down sufficiently to fit back into the smart blue briefcase my mother had given me before I'd left. From it, I again took out my mother-sized self.

The truth is, being contained in the back seat of the car, pinned down by my children's bodies, their hands searching under my clothes for skin to caress, was bliss. It was also true – I thought as the veld whizzed by and we kept a lookout for kudu and baboons – those two weeks with nobody to attend to, nobody to interrupt me, nobody asking for food or comfort, had been bliss too. Being away and being alone had restored my sense of self. I had been able to think and to write.

I wanted both. I could be both, but not at the same time: world-woman and home-woman are too different, but if I could only keep those two dimensions parallel to each other, I could make it work. I would just have to move between those universes. I put my arms around my girls and pulled them close. I could do it. I had spent my life moving between places, which had taught me that the solution to any difficulty – whether it be conflict or boredom – was movement.

On the drive home my eldest filled me in on the details of how life had been in my absence – 'Nan makes the best tuna toasties', 'Dad forgot my costume for swimming', 'Magdalena painted our nails'. This conversation went on until we arrived at the Big Red House, the name my daughters had given the home we bought soon after I'd joined New Namibia Books.

The rambling double-storey house was a ten-minute drive from my parents' home, where my children spent much of their time when I was absent. In the garden was a garage I converted into a room of my own. My desk was vast – there was enough space for my girls to 'work' while I did. They did so in silence, taking the books I was busy with and studying them before they made books of their own. These they titled, illustrated and wrote blurbs for, before adding them to the others at the bottom of my bookshelf. Behind this room was a gnarled old shepherd's tree, easily two hundred years old, which cast a generous circle of shade. I had run my hands over its rough bark, thinking, *Here under this sheltering tree I can learn how to be in one place.*

All the rooms of our home were jewel colours – the sitting room ruby, the dining room emerald, and the verandah, smothered by a hot-pink bougainvillea, a sapphire blue. Outside the butter-yellow kitchen, newly planted acacias were tipped with tender, furled leaves. *Duiweltjies* – little devils – pioneer plants buried for decades beneath the wilderness of cement we had crowbarred out, sent out runners covered with yellow flowers. Those flowers turned into barbed thorns that drew blood from a child's bare foot. I showed my girls how to spring from one protected patch to another to avoid the piercings.

'We need these devil thorns,' I told them when they cried and picked the barbs from their soles. 'They hurt our feet, but they catch the grass seeds when the wind blows. They cradle them until the rains come so they can germinate and make new veld for us.' This worked. They learned to spring from one thorn-free patch to another, and the *duiweltjies* caught the seeds that sprouted, shimmering their silver plumes when teased by a breeze.

After my first short, sharp training shock I travelled all over the country, trialling the materials New Namibia Books and other publishers had developed in schools. These books had been tailored for the new curriculum and were in English, the official language spoken by few people at the time. I worked in the arid south where the children spoke Nama and Afrikaans, in the war-scarred Oshiwambo-speaking north, and in Kaoko in the north-west.

Bordered by the Skeleton Coast to the west and the Kunene River to the north, this majestic part of the world is home to the nomadic OvaHimba, whose ancestral territory straddles south-western Angola and north-western Namibia. There, in Opuwo, the largest settlement and the capital of the region, I worked with teachers and children on the shiny new schoolbooks we had developed. These were jolly grade-one alphabet books, teaching 'O is for Orange', 'B is for Banana' and 'A is for Apple'.

All this fruit was a problem. Opuwo and its surrounds are desert. There are no crops because it never rains, and so the main diet of its people is meat and milk. The garish pictures of orange and green and yellow fruit I held up to the children were met with blank stares.

'These are fruit,' said their teacher. They shook their heads. They had never seen these kinds of fruit. The berries they ate were seasonal, harvested from riverine trees and desert bushes – these never found their way into schoolbooks. But the children were eager, and I was full of enthusiasm, and we soldiered on, finding ways, with English as a bridge, to a post-independence Namibia that required children to stay in one place to be educated.

This clash between settled and nomadic cultures burst into the grade-one classroom one hot morning when I was working with a teacher and her first graders, who sat quietly as I showed them pictures and trialled my lessons. A little boy who had been sitting right in front, paying rapt attention, went rigid when there was a tap on the classroom door.

Before anyone could get there, the door burst open and in rushed a herd of goats. They hopped onto the desks, knocking off the children's new alphabet books.

The boy in the front row leapt up and herded them expertly off the desks and out the classroom. A minute later I saw him driving the goats across the dusty playground outside the classroom building and into an enclosure. Once he had secured the gate, he turned around and raced back.

'Kazandu's mother,' the teacher explained with a shrug, 'she understands why he must come to school, but his father said he must take care of the livestock. So, he brings his goats to school.'

The boy reappeared in the doorway and, without saying a word, returned to his desk. He picked up his book and continued piecing together the English words as if nothing had happened. I would eventually turn that incident into a children's book called *Kazandu's Work*, one of many children's books I went on to write, but on that day, on the seven-hour drive back to Windhoek, Kazandu's impossible responsibilities occupied my thoughts. There was a gulf between how his parents understood him and what his future might be in this changed world.

History and its companion, violence, had shape-shifted Kazandu's mother's world as it had mine. In her own way, she had tried to find a way to help her son and herself carry the burden of change into an uncertain future; and I wanted to know more about how women navigated change – and power – in the intimate as well as the public realm.

twenty-two

Women from all over Namibia sent manuscripts to New Namibia Books, stories that broke the silence shrouding women's experience of war, displacement, exile and return. In 1995 we set about sifting through these texts for a collection we titled *Coming on Strong*, which also included oral testimonies. We received stories of interrogation, rape, assault and a mother-in-law shot by South African soldiers in a marketplace, as well as beatings and bombings. There were stories of love too: a reunion between a mother and a daughter separated by the migrant labour system, the erotic delights of a new lover, the gift of a child.

It was thrilling to see how much space this opened up for women writers: several authors included in the anthology would go on to publish collections of short stories, novels and memoirs. This was a vital form of public witnessing. Because there was no formal Truth and Reconciliation process, like the one that had started that year in South Africa, these women's words became an authoritative part of Namibia's historical record.

The war I'd known from a safe, white distance was made vivid by these eyewitness accounts. Ellen Ndeshi Namhila's tale of an injured toddler thrust into the arms of a teenage girl fleeing a bombing in southern Angola was one story I could not get out of my mind. There was an urgency to her writing, strengthened by its matter-of-factness. She described what happened with a journalistic precision, so the reader had all the facts. On 4 May 1978 the South African Air Force bombed Cassinga, a refugee camp. Over six hundred Namibians were massacred. But part of the story was missing.

Ellen, fifteen years old at the time, was a frontline nurse – the girl running through the bush with a wounded baby. She wrote that she did not know what became of the child after she handed him over to the people caring for the orphans and got on with nursing the many wounded. I wanted to know more about her war-scattered life. How she got to Cassinga, where she went afterwards. What happened to the baby. What she felt, how she thought, how she survived. How she had grown into the affectionate, sharply witty woman I knew.

'You need to write a book,' I said to her. 'Namibia needs your story. We need your story to make sense of the country.'

'You'd better come for tea, then,' said Ellen. 'We'll discuss this.'

Working together, we had become friends. The two of us had grown up on different sides of the war and she had questions for me: What was it like? What had I known? What had I seen?

I told her that for me, violence and war – muffled, ominous – was mainly off-stage. The dread of it had been inescapable, though. The bomb scares, curfews, roadblocks, the lines of armoured vehicles filled with soldiers driving north, where Ellen and her family lived. Where Ellen had been shot by South African soldiers as a little girl of ten – that war had been fought, according to apartheid propaganda, on behalf of white girls like me.

Ellen was my age-twin and, different as our origins were, Namibia's history and our mutual interest in writing had brought our stories together. We were also both pregnant with our third daughters. I had succumbed when Grace was three and the reckless mother in me craved the warm silkiness of a newborn's skin against mine. That craving drove me to have my contraceptive coil removed. I had fallen pregnant before I had a chance to think.

We agreed that the pull of motherhood was not a rational thing. Pregnancy did not take publishing schedules into account. Babies caused ghastly morning sickness – which was why, driving to Ellen's house to talk about her memoir, I'd had to leap out at a red light to throw up in the road. Proof to my two gleeful daughters that this new baby was a devil that made me sick.

When we arrived, our daughters eyed each other in that wordless way of children, and then they all went off to play in the garden.

'You said you might have written more,' I said.

'Look on the desk while I make tea.'

Little girls' voices were the background sound to my search. I picked up a manuscript and skimmed through it. Written in the matter-of-fact style of her story, the text pulsed with trauma and courage below its smooth surface.

Ellen was twelve in 1976 when she fled the terror of South African soldiers entering her village. She had crossed the border with another child, and they had found People's Liberation Army of Namibia fighters who took them deep into Angola. Two years later, Ellen trained to be a frontline nurse, moving from one refugee camp to another. The last was Cassinga, where the massacre happened. After that she went to The Gambia where she finished her high school education, and from there to freezing Finland. And then, in the happiness of 1989, her first husband – whom she had loved passionately – was killed in a car accident after his return from exile to work in Namibia's first elections. Her tale of courage and heartbreak was told with economy and humour, as if she were Everywoman and this was every life.

'You have to finish this,' I said when she returned with the tea tray and ginger biscuits for our nausea.

Ellen said nothing, but I saw the pain and patience in her warm, expressive eyes.

'We have to show how you carry the memories of the wounded and the dead,' I said. 'If I can understand your life, then I will understand mine.'

'Do you know what you are asking?' said Ellen.

'Yes,' I said, 'I do.'

But I did not. I knew nothing then about what it costs a woman to examine her life – what she has loved and what she has lost – and to write that down, but Ellen let me take the manuscript home with me.

I read it through, transfixed by the sparsely told tale of her life. When I returned it to her, she scanned my many questions and requests for detail, detail, detail.

She said she could not remember; I said she had to. It was what the story, painful as it was in places, demanded.

A few months later, Ellen returned the manuscript. She told me that she had gone back into places and experiences she had thought would be too painful to remember, but they had returned to her. She had shaken, she told me, and cried, as if she was leaving her family again, as if the bombs were still falling around her, but she had written it all down and the memories had released her, and now she felt something that might be called peace.

Printed copies of *The Price of Freedom* were delivered to the busy, ramshackle offices of New Namibia Books before I was due to go off on maternity leave. I took one and carried it over to my desk as carefully as I would a newborn. Setting it down, I ran my hand over the yellow-brown cover emblazoned with the image of a confident, smiling Ellen. We had chosen that photograph, taken in 1997, together. I turned the book over, and on the back was one of the few images that had survived her years of exile. It was a photograph taken for an identity card in The Gambia.

Ellen's account, bookended by those portraits, opened up a world I had been complicit in. A world I had no way of seeing until she told her story. Writing does not only illuminate; it can also heal writer and reader by connecting them. I hugged Ellen's memoir to my chest. She taught me that a woman publicly bearing witness to her own experience is a political act.

twenty-three

Two weeks past my due date in June 1996 the baby gave no sign of being willing to be born, but I was in no rush. The baby was not ready yet. I was also in no hurry because I was putting the last touches to my first book. The heroines of *Double Trouble* are twin girls who turn detective to save their father from being arrested for rhino poaching, for which corrupt police had framed him. These two young Namibian Nancy Drews were based on the twin daughters of my father's farm manager. He was a righteous and authoritarian man who ruled his wife and children by fear, but the family's survival was dependent on him and so, when he raised his stick-thin arm, they cowered and obeyed. Their fear of him and their loyalty – they had nowhere else to go – was palpable, as it usually is in dependent children and their mothers.

That was the true heartbeat of my story about brave girls and impossible odds, but I flipped their fear into devotion, and then wrote a proposal. A British publisher bought it. The thrill of that!

My editor phoned me from her home in rural England. She had a question about police corruption and whether I thought that was a suitable subject for a children's book.

'Yes,' I replied, surprised. How could it be unsuitable? It was an open secret in Namibia that both the police and the army were involved in poaching.

'But do you think it's a good idea for children to think that the police aren't there to protect them?' she asked.

'It's better for them to know the truth,' I said. And that's where we left things.

There were three of us around the kitchen table that cold June night, as a film-maker friend en route to the Kaokoveld was spending the night. Supper was simple. All I could manage was a dish of potatoes drenched in melted butter and Parmesan. We had started eating when the contractions started: machine-gun fire rat-tat-tatting against the walls of uterine muscle. My fork froze halfway between my plate and my mouth.

'Margie?' said my friend, looking at me intently.

I could not speak.

'The baby's coming,' she told Aidan. 'Go now!'

Aidan was not usually a man to be hurried, but he reacted to her urgency. They got me into the car, and he got the car onto the road.

I was on fire by the time he walked me through the doors of the maternity wing. A midwife took one look at me. 'O *fok*,' she exclaimed, feeling the bone-crushing grip of my hand, '*sy gaan druk* – fuck, she's going to push.'

Surges of pain, surges of power, cresting higher each time, battled with the impossible size of an infant bearing down, trying to escape the ocean of my body, in search of the dry land where I was beached, a whale on the hospital bed.

A doctor appeared and stood on one side of me. Holding my knee against his belly, he barked, 'Bear down, Margie, and push.'

Aidan stood on the other side, holding my hand, urging, 'Breathe, breathe.'

I knew how to breathe. I did not wish to be held. I wanted to be alone, to do this without instruction, without being observed, wild with power and love. I would have given anything to be a cat, not a woman. Cats slip away when it's their time. They hide under a bush and do this all on their own, sauntering out when they are ready, trailed by kittens.

The baby's head crowned, then she slipped out, waxen until she bellowed herself pink. The doctor's hands reached for the baby, but I was quicker. I snatched her first, pulling her up to my breast so that we could gaze at each other, new with love.

Three days later I returned home. I carried my new baby upstairs and the two of us curled up together on my bed. Her sisters – aged six-and-a-half and four – inspected her before returning to their games. When Jamie woke, she looked at me, and each time I was entranced by her smile of joyful recognition. I got to know her too – that mysterious new person who had lived inside me. I loved the wild-eyed look she got when she latched on to the breast and how she slipped off, asleep, when she was sated.

I gave in to that new baby without trepidation. I had learned that I would not lose myself in her. I knew it would be she who would, as her older sisters were already doing, lose herself in me – and then, some day when she was ready, she would move out into the world that awaited her. So, on Magdalena's advice, I stayed home for three months. I accepted all the help that was offered: meals, shopping, fetching my older children from school. When I needed more, I asked for it because I knew that time of blissful attunement, when all a baby wants is its mother, was so fleeting. I wanted to savour every second; by the time of my sister's wedding in October 1996, Jamie's toes had reached the tips of the stretchy zero-to-three-month suits, and I had hardly left the house.

'Why are you getting married?' I asked Melle one afternoon when she was at my house holding her sleeping baby niece in her arms.

'I've been on the shelf so long I'm dusty,' she replied.

'You are not!' I said, but her eyes flashed, so I dropped the subject.

Melle was marrying a man who had come to Namibia on a short-term architectural project. Theirs had been a whirlwind romance and I worried she had been mesmerised by this man, spoilt and clever, who had set his sights on her because she was rare, feral and beautiful.

Her wedding dress, made of ochre silk, had a quilted breastplate, and when she put it on, my golden-haired sister shone, a modern-day Joan of Arc. We argued about the shoes she would wear with her splendid dress. 'It's a waste to buy new shoes when the dress is long, no one will see them,' she said.

I suggested that she buy gold sandals, and she burst into tears, sobbing, 'I'm so hurt.'

'It's only shoes,' I said, putting my arms around her. 'You don't have to get them.'

'No, no, it's not the shoes. I'm hurt because you didn't invite me to your wedding.'

'You should've just come,' I said, crying too. If Melle had been there, if she had been my witness, she would have known that it was something I had simultaneously entered into and kept myself apart from. She would have seen there was something amiss, as I saw there was something amiss with this impulsive, extravagant wedding of hers. 'I didn't invite anyone. I didn't want to make a fuss.'

'But you're making a fuss now,' she wailed. 'About my wedding and the shoes.'

My sister and I did not discuss the shoes again, and on the day, I helped her dress. Melle stuck to her word and did not buy wedding sandals. She refused the shoes I offered her – too silly, too small – and so she was married in her heavy farm boots with a pair of Christmas socks. The wedding dress with its silk bell of a skirt hid her boots during the ceremony, but not when she danced, which she did with stomping abandon. It was her boots, covered in red dust, that were her centre of gravity.

My sister and her new husband were going to live in Italy for a year, but before they went, Melle took him camping in the desert for their honeymoon. It was a place she knew and loved, but when they returned, there was silence between them, which my loving, loyal sister did her best to ensure nobody else heard.

twenty-four

Not long after my sister and her husband left for Rome, my author's copies of *Double Trouble* were delivered to my house. The two older girls were eating their lunch when I took the box to the kitchen, cut it open with a carving knife, and took out the books. I was speechless with the wonder of seeing my name on the cover.

'What's that?' asked Grace.

'It's the book I wrote before Jamie was born,' I said. 'Look, here's my name.' I was lovingly tracing the 'Margie' and the 'Orford' when she snatched the book from me.

She sat down on top of it. 'You are *our* mum,' she said, her eyes ablaze.

'I am,' I replied.

'You belong to us,' said Grace. 'But if your name is on a book, then the whole world will see you and you won't belong to us any more. You'll belong to the world.'

I picked her up and put her on my lap.

'I'll always be yours,' I reassured her, 'No matter how many books I write.'

That was true, but what Grace said was also true. My work did take me away from her. Work took me away from all of them. The work I did carried me further and further into the world: I'd begun to research gender-based violence and HIV, as the disease was ripping through Namibia.

I did not belong to my children, but I was not sure I belonged to myself either. I had accepted an invitation from two renowned scholars of African literature to be one of the contributing editors to Women Writing Africa, a pan-African research project initiated by the Feminist Press at the City University of New York. The collection would be an archival retrieval project and it would do what second-wave feminist scholars have done since the 1970s – upend history by finding and republishing 'lost' women writers.

The opportunity was a dream come true. I knew the contemporary literary landscape, and so it was with excitement that I turned detective on Namibia's scattered archives. We drew together a group of scholars, writers and friends to search through papers stored in Windhoek, Germany, Finland and London, as well as in the whaling records of Nantucket.

White women appear occasionally in the colonial archive, but black women are almost always rendered invisible – a patriarchal sleight of hand. They were there and they had made their mark. We just needed to find out where to look for our foremothers. We found them hidden in footnotes, in court records, and in the appendices of colonial reports. Those testimonies, dating from the early seventeenth century, changed our understanding of what women are, of what history is, and of the struggles and creativity of the women who went before us. Women raised their voices in public to protest violation of themselves, their families, and their communities.

This is the writing that made its way into the archives, together with the records of colonial officials affronted by women who spoke with authority for themselves, their people and their country – a political realm assumed, by both colonialists and the male elders of those women's communities, to belong to men. These archival documents revealed the ongoing negotiation that lies at the heart of women's experience of family life – my own included. Women have always tacked between the demands of home – sex, food, babies, husbands, love – and the freedom (and the hostility) that being in the world and earning a living brings with it.

In 1998, the Women Writing Africa team of scholars, historians and writers met in the ancient university town of Fez in Morocco to decide which texts would make the southern region's final cut. We argued about the contextualising headnotes that would accompany each selection, and collectively drafted the introduction. It was exacting, exasperating, exhilarating original work done by a group of fierce, brilliant women who, during the years we worked together, became my friends and my mentors.

The work helped me to better understand the meaning of the experiences of the women whose writings and testimonies we had assembled, and the courage it took for women to bear witness, to claim authority and to change their worlds. I was beginning to interpret the patterns of violence and trauma I encountered in women's literature and orature. I wanted to see the anthology published – it was scheduled for 2004 – but I also wanted to dig deeper. I wanted to write about all of this. One morning in Fez, I asked the women I was working with what I should do.

'A Master's,' they said. 'Then a PhD.'

'How?' I asked.

'You will have to go away,' they said. 'You cannot do it in Namibia.'

Two of them were from Botswana and had left children with their mothers for years while they went overseas to do their doctorates.

'How else can it to be done?' one of them asked.

'You want to be a woman who can provide for her family,' said the other.

I did.

'Wasn't it your parents who brought you up? Made you the woman you are?' she went on to ask.

They did.

'Well,' she said, with a smile. 'They didn't do such a bad job on you. Trust them to do well with your daughters.'

Just then, the founder of the Feminist Press came over to our breakfast table. 'Margie,' she said in her New York growl, 'if you ever want to write, you're going to have to stop having babies.'

'Yes,' I replied. There wasn't anything else to say. It was the truth, and I took her advice for the warning that it was.

twenty-five

I had no time to weigh the merits of babies versus books because when I went up to my room soon afterwards, my father called me. He told me, his doctor's voice shaken by fear for his son, that my brother had been operated on in London for a non-metastasising cancer in the bone of his knee. My own knees went weak. John had survived a fast-metastasising soft-tissue sarcoma only five years earlier. Then the family had rallied around him in Johannesburg, and he had made it through. Non-metastising or not, we were taking no chances. I rerouted my return flight from Morocco through London.

My sister met me at Heathrow Airport. She had recently moved with her husband from Rome to Cambridge, but I was too distracted to wonder why she had two huge suitcases with her. We took the taxi to my brother's house in Whitechapel, a yet ungentrified part of East London. He was pleased to see me, and he was pleased to have Melle back.

'She saved me from the hospital,' he told me, hobbling to the kitchen on his crutches. 'Melle kept me alive.'

'How long are you staying?' I asked her as we took our suitcases inside.

'I'm not going back.' There was so much pain in those few words that the suitcases suddenly made sense. When I'd visited her in Rome the year before, a city she guided me through with love and expertise, her husband was impatient and capricious. She tried to cover for the ungraciousness of his behaviour, but the marriage was impossible. At my brother's, we could hold her while she cried. She told me, one fragmented story at a time, how her error of a husband made her suffer.

'It's the loneliest place, an unhappy marriage,' she said. 'I feel so ashamed. I failed at the most important thing.'

'There's nothing you could have done to make it work,' I said. 'You had to leave.'

The next morning, we got our brother out of bed, and helped him to dress and hobble down to the windowless kitchen. My sister tipped cornflakes into her bowl and poured red wine over them.

'No,' John and I said at the same time.

'Why not?' Melle wailed. 'It all gets dissolved in hydrochloric acid in your stomach anyway.'

'No,' my brother and I repeated in unison. 'You can't. You can have wine for breakfast, but you can't have it on cornflakes.'

I tipped out the bowl and refilled it with cereal and milk. John poured what was left of the red wine into a mug for her.

twenty-six

My sister returned to Namibia and retreated to the cottage with the creosote beams in my parents' garden. Her expansive hopes, her dreams of a family had been narrowed down to that hot rectangle of a room where a ceiling fan turned sluggishly in the heat. For weeks she lived in her dressing gown. She could not do anything or go anywhere. 'What for?' she asked when we made suggestions. The divorce was soon done – there were no children and no assets to delay the decree. But the heart struggles to take in what the mind knows and my sister was laid low by grief. Late one morning I had a call from my mother.

'It's twelve.' Her voice was tight with anxiety. An image of those thick beams above the bed flashed before me. 'And Melle's not up and all her windows and curtains are closed.'

I drove as fast as possible up the hill and tore down to the cottage and flung the door open. There were the beams. There was my sister in her bed, turning over to face me saying, 'What?'

I hugged her, overwhelmed with relief to find her alive and irritable that I had woken her up.

'What are you doing here?' she asked.

'Mum phoned me,' I said. 'She was worried.'

'About what?'

What to say? It was I who'd had the vision of those beams and the cord from her dressing gown. 'You've got to get up,' I said. 'You've got to wash your hair and get dressed.'

She turned her face into the pillow.

'No,' I said. 'Get up. Now. I need you.'

She let me walk her to the shower and then she put on the clothes I handed to her. There was a flash in her green eyes – the first I had seen for so long – and she smiled, 'You think that you can dress me up like your dolly because I am in a weakened state.'

'Any opportunity to make you look decent, I'll take it.'

I was so glad that she was teasing me about my lifelong attempts to make her dress up and wear make-up and do her hair and show off. She, unlike me, needed no embellishment; her beauty could silence a room full of people.

'Move out,' I said. 'Get your own place. Until you do that you won't be able to get yourself back together.'

'It's you who wants to be alone,' she said in a Marlene Dietrich voice, 'not me.' We both smiled.

Solitude was not my sister's way. She was able to turn to our parents in a way I could not. I carried within me the recalcitrant ghost of my fourteen-year-old self who, when she went to boarding school, swore on her life that she would never again ask for emotional support. Determined to do everything myself, I turned independence into a weapon. I thought of it as a strength, but it was a faultline along which I fractured.

I resisted taking other things too – love, advice, knowledge – even if it was good for me, even if I wanted it. Like my troubled relationship with food, which always felt like too little or too much, this refusal – a fear that merging with another would result in the loss of my hard-won self – was old and it ran deep. My mother has told me that as a baby, I guzzled fish and eggs, easy food to feed a baby, but when I turned two, I refused them. 'You clamped your mouth shut,' she'd say, shaking her head with the same frustration she felt at the time of my hunger strike. 'I didn't know what to feed you.'

My mother's food – always too much, seasoned with the love she expressed in heaped plates rather than words – made me mutinous. So did my charismatic father's words. The information he shared with us on subjects that fascinated him was freighted with his urgent love. Not to listen to him, not to share his interests meant not to love; he knew how to lasso me with his snippets of science, but when I found myself caught, I would rage inwardly. My father's interests were a wide, open territory, but it was his, and he did not care to travel through the mind-territories of others.

This had not troubled my sister because she'd absorbed his gift for and fascination with the natural world. And so, as we sisters sat together on the stoep of the hot cottage, she was lifted out of herself and her sadness by a bird call piercing the heat-thickened afternoon.

'There he is.' My sister pointed at the crimson-breasted bush shrike – called the *Reichsvogel* in Namibia because of its swastika-coloured feathers – scuffling in the dry leaves of the acacia before us.

Birds. My sister knew all their names. She had learned them, as my mother had, from my father, lining up her sight along his index finger as he pointed out a shaft-tailed whydah, glossy starling, chanting goshawk, Carol's penduline tit or masked weaver. The names, the beaks, birds yellow-clawed, red-clawed or black. Pinion feathers, a buff-coloured ruff, a flash of colour at the throat – a sunbird's necktie either green or red, and the indifferent drab females.

That feast of ornithological wonders had been set out for me by my father and his bird books, Roberts and Newman's, thumbed bibles of this precise world where beauty and camouflage are listed, calibrated and catalogued. That was the trail that might have led me away from my separate interests – literature, how and why people think, feel and act the way they do – deep into the forest of his love. Our hearts and minds could have been at one there, but I would have been lost. My sister went there and thrived.

That bush shrike, so distinct of call and plumage, made me think of the cisticola, a species of brown bird so tiny that they can only be distinguished by their calls, which fill the vast silence of Etosha National Park. That was where, from the late 1970s to the mid-1980s, my father's white bakkie with 'ETOSHA LION RESEARCH' stencilled on its doors would be parked, all of us wedged inside, noting when indolent lionesses my father had put on contraception slept, and when they disappeared into the tawny scrub.

My father was doing fieldwork for his MSc in Zoology, devising an alternative to a Parks Board culling programme that sought to protect prey species by controlling the number of predators: instead, he put three prides of lionesses onto the contraceptive Norplant. People have always justified killing in the name of science, but for my parents, massacring animals in one of the last remaining sanctuaries set aside for them was both unethical and scientifically wrong.

For this grand – and successful – experiment, my mother was my father's research assistant and his amanuensis. They would take us out of school for days on end to help them dart lions, insert a speculum into the lionesses' vaginas to do a pap smear, implant a slow-release contraceptive, brand each animal for identification purposes, revive them with an injected antidote, and then observe how this intervention affected the pride's behaviour. I can tell you it did not – no cubs were born, but the social relations between the animals, as with humans, appeared unchanged by contraception.

Hours of confinement passed in that bakkie, the heat building, my thighs sticking to the seat, the bleed of earth into sky complete, the only sound the call of the cisticola. No variation of either pitch or volume. Like a drill to the skull. In the front of the car, pages of bird books were flicked through by my father. So many tiny birds on the coloured plates in shades of brown and rust and cream with variously patterned feathers, their black eyes beads above tiny beaks, some able to crack grass seeds, some not. Their calls were the only thing that reliably distinguished them.

I did not want that knowledge, so I everted my eyes from those beautiful creatures. I put my bird's eye out so that my mind would not fill with ornithology. I wanted the territory of my mind kept pristine. I feared that if I gave up and took in all this fatherly information, the whole of the natural world that I, too, loved, it would weigh me down so much I would not be able to escape. I yearned to be sitting in a café at the edge of some esplanade where men and women strolled, and drinks were served, and the sun set over an ocean of water rather than sand.

I wanted to be elsewhere, but, trapped in the back of a hot truck, my only escape was to refuse to learn to identify the birds. I battened down the hatches of my mind and refused my father entry. Refused to know. Refused to catalogue those birds into categories of similarity and difference, to recall and compare, which gave my sister and my mother their bond with my father.

My mother had given up her tentative steps towards a return to her own career so as to assist my father with this research, which he fitted into the slivers of time left over from his busy medical practice. Trained as a nurse, she spoke with nostalgia and pleasure about her short working life on the wards. After I was born, she gave up working, and her qualifications and registration lapsed. The year after I went to boarding school, she had registered for distance learning: a nursing degree at the University of South Africa.

Unisa would post her readings and assignments. She would dive in, absorbed and focused, and write her essays. They would come back with top marks. She was so proud of herself; I was so proud of her. I admired the absorbed woman my mother became – waving me away without turning from her books if I wanted something while she was working. She was about to embark on the second year of her degree when my father decided to do his MSc.

The lion project required my father's frequent presence in Etosha, a four-hour drive north of Windhoek. When my father went north, my mother went too. If we children were home from boarding school, so did we. My mother gave up her nursing degree.

'Why did you stop?' I asked.

'I wanted to be with your father.'

'But you were doing so well.'

It seemed unfair that she should be eclipsed. I was as furious and as clear-eyed as only a fifteen-year-old can be.

'I'm going to help your dad with the lions.'

There was a smile on her lips when she said that, but in her green-and-hazel eyes there was a faraway look. As if she'd chosen between two precious things. It looked like loss to me, like surrrender. My father had appropriated my mother's time and attention, but rather than directing my fury at him, my mother became the target of my anger and disappointment: as I saw it, she'd capitulated, remaining dependent on his will, his approval – and his financial support.

Dependence. In my view, it diminished a woman not to have time – or money – of her own. Most white women I knew lived indolent lives, managing servants, their inborn talents channelled into fussing over husbands and children. The subsuming of the self and the thwarting of ambition drove many woman over the edge. My own aunt, a brilliant pianist, had tried to kill herself several times – her passion for music diverted into domesticity and childbearing, my mother once told me, her voice hushed and urgent, yet unreflective.

Dependent, I vowed, was something I would never allow myself to be.

My mother had courage; I had seen it. She was calm if there was blood or injury and a body needed assistance, but I did not forgive her for not standing up for herself, not finishing her degree, not flying solo as I thought she should. As I wanted her to do.

That anger, swallowed whole, was impossible to digest. It settled into something hard, sneering, which would later sneer at my own capabilities in the female realm of cooking and loving and homemaking. I did not yet understand the rules of love and family that can make a woman hide her true size and capacity to protect a man's love for her.

That was how I seethed in the back of that bakkie watching my mother open a thermos flask, pour a cup of her home-made lemon juice and hand it to my father. He would drink it, hand it back to her with a 'Thanks, Rosebud' and they would turn together to the bird books to work out which cisticola was calling.

I swallowed my inward rebellion and turned this enquiry outwards, staring at the vanishing point of the horizon, where the sky met the earth, knowing even as I sulked what a privilege it was to be there in one of the world's last pristine wildernesses. That stopping of my mind was a passive resistance, and it went unnoticed. It would cost me dearly, but I did not know how else to keep myself intact.

twenty-seven

In the summer of 1999, February, when it was at its hottest, I arrived at traffic lights in the centre of Windhoek at the same time as Aidan, but my husband did not see me even though the lights were red for both of us and we had stopped at right angles to each other. I would know him anywhere, the shape of his head, the set of his broad shoulders, but seeing him there in his orange Mercedes – apart from me and our children – I did not know him at all.

His window was rolled right down – it was as hot as it gets in Namibia, a soul-scorching heat that makes it hard to move, let alone think. But my husband seemed not to mind the sun at all. His suntanned right elbow rested on the car door and his fingers drummed the rhythm of the music playing in his car, which I could not hear.

I did not know where he had come from and I did not know where he was going, this man driving his car on some errand or to a rendezvous about which I knew nothing, where he would meet people unknown to me, and in which I played no part. But there he was, my unknown husband wearing the white linen shirt I had bought for him while making a short-cut through the men's department on the way to the cashier with a trolley load of groceries, thinking it would keep him cool, like the blue aviator shades he wore.

He was scanning the street, but still he did not see me. He did not know I was watching him and so I had a glimpse of him – as one rarely does with those with whom we are most intimate – as he was without me, contented, absorbed, complete. Simply as himself.

I watched, amazed in the way I might have been at a waterhole in a game reserve as a solitary animal, a kudu bull with an unwieldy rack of antlers, perhaps, or a rhino, had sauntered out of the bush to drink alone. It came as a shock to see him like this, to not know him at all. I saw that I had no claim on him. He was, in that suspended moment at a traffic intersection, a stranger to me.

It seemed impossible that I knew his name, let alone that we had made three children together and that we had just that morning been talking about repainting the walls of the bedroom we shared, which were an anaemic shade of peach. And so, instead of hooting to get his attention, I watched him, that stranger so happy, so at ease, so settled in his strong suntanned manly body that I touched daily, that I made love to often, which was now as remote as the moon. The lights changed to green, so I continued my journey. Where my husband went or what he did I cannot tell you.

When he got home that night, I ate supper as usual and we chatted about our days. I did not tell him I had seen him at the traffic light and that he had not seen me. I did not tell him I had seen him and not known him at all. In vast areas of our lives and days we were strangers to each other.

We discussed – as we often did those days – moving to Cape Town, but it was one of the half-hearted, circular conversations that we had been having for some years already. Nothing came of them because I was restless, but he, as far as I could tell, was content with where we were, with how we were, with who we were. I was the one pressed up against the limits of our life. At thirty-three, I wanted a more expansive horizon. There, elsewhere, I would do more, read more, write more, live more.

The fiery restlessness of my early twenties had returned, and it was a fire I could not put out by staying in Windhoek. I was giving up on the idea that I could or would settle. The constant physical movement I required – travelling up and down Namibia and in the region – no longer brought me peace. I called that restless urgency ambition because I did not have another word for the desire to become the author of books and of my own destiny. But there was something else at work, something malign nipping at my heels and making me pace back and forth in the cage of myself, looking for a way out.

twenty-eight

My way out came in the post. A letter from the American Embassy with 'URGENT' stamped on the narrow envelope hidden among the phone bills and bank statements I'd picked up on my way back from the school run. When we got home, my girls raced inside, wolfed down the macaroni cheese Magdalena had made for them. With a hurried 'May we be excused', they took their plates to the scullery, and bolted upstairs.

I took out the letter from America, but before I could open it, there was a helter-skelter of feet down the wooden stairs and three breathless little girls burst into the kitchen. 'Can you make us lions?' they asked.

'I can,' I said, taking my eyeliner out of my handbag. They held out their hands, fingers curled back, and I drew sharp claws on their knuckles, rounded ears on their foreheads, whiskers on their cheeks, then diamond shapes, making lion noses of their small human ones. They inspected themselves in the mirror I held up for them and they growled, then rubbed behind their ears and batted me with their lioness paws before dashing upstairs on all fours.

When all was quiet, I opened the envelope and held the single sheet of paper as gingerly as if it were a loaded gun.

At the top of the page was the date, March 1999; below that a formal address to 'Ms Orford'. Below that the words 'RE: SCHOLARSHIP'. Below that were three short, dense paragraphs that I could not read because the little black letters wobbled as if I was underwater.

Whatever was written on that thick imperial paper, it heralded my future. The future bearing down on me for the ten years since my body had bargained with my mind in that cold London bathroom. I had promised that if I could have my baby first, I would do 'everything' later. And 'later' had arrived, embossed with an American eagle. I knew I had to honour the pledge I had made.

From upstairs came the sounds of doors opening and closing, the setting out of toys, the intricate negotiations of the game plan. My girls were growling and roaring as they prowled – lion kings and queens of the savannah they conjured on the stairs. I couldn't think of them and the future at the same time. I had to think, not to feel, so I went into the garden and sat under the shepherd's tree with the letter clutched in my hand. This time I could read it.

The first sentence informed me without congratulation that their first choice of candidate had been forced to withdraw for family reasons and because I had been their second choice, my application for a Fulbright scholarship had been successful after all. The second stated that the Graduate Centre at the City University of New York had accepted me for a Master's degree in its Comparative Literature Program. The third informed me I would receive two years' tuition and living costs. No provisions would be made for accompanying dependents, although family members were eligible for visas. Then 'Yours truly', and a spiky signature in black ink.

My time in Windhoek was up. I did not know how I was going to do the impossible, but I would make it work. The future lay in wait for me. Even if I wanted to, I could not refuse. The letter I held in my hand, this scholarship to America, presented me with a variation of the dilemma I believed my mother, and almost all the women I knew, had faced.

Yet again, I thought of how my clever mother had channelled her considerable creative abilities into the smooth running of the home so that my father, the economic centrifuge of their household economy, could be launched without hindrance each day. My mother and her small army of servants made sure meals were on time, clothes were laundered, and the linen required for my father's consulting rooms was clean and ironed. Out he would go into the world, to doctor, to earn, to *be* in it. He returned for lunch and a siesta, and then went back to work. He played squash, tennis or golf before returning for drinks, dinner and the stories he would overhear my mother reading to us children at bedtime. My mother was the sun around which he orbited, but the sun, bright as it is, must stay in its place. She shoehorned her own world into the hours when he was out.

Their world of mutual dependence was divided into two spheres: the one public and masculine; the other private and feminine. These realms were separate but unequal in their division of labour. It was my father's labour that earned the money and the measurable public status. The private realm, the feeding, caring and reproduction – cyclical, repetitive – was necessarily rendered invisible. In my eyes, labour was bartered for the provision of food and shelter.

It was money that made the difference. Money was the measure of value. Even though I had a husband, I felt entirely responsible, in the way a patriarch surely is, for my children and for myself. I did not believe that love, apart from that between child and parent, was possible if either partner was dependent on the other. I wanted to be able to stay because I *wanted* to and not because I *had* to. I wanted freedom, but I also wanted it for my daughters. I did not want them burdened with their mother's disappointment, her self-sacrifice. Just then my lions came roaring through the garden. When they spotted me, they turned themselves into cubs. All three came to me, nuzzling my hands and batting me with the paws I had drawn on them.

'Why are you crying, Mum?' said Grace. She sensed feelings through her skin, as if the layer that protects one from the world was missing.

'Because I am so happy to see you.' That was the truth – not the whole truth, but true enough to satisfy her. She settled against me. Rose did the same. The youngest curled up on my lap. We sat so still that a mongoose crept from a tussock of grass and picked its wary way to the other side of the garden. Only when the slender creature disappeared through a hole in the wall did we go inside to drink the lemonade my mother had made and eat Zoo biscuits at the kitchen table.

I told Aidan the news after he got home that evening. He was happy for me. Excited for us. He loved New York and knew it well. Before I'd met him, he had worked in the city. It would be an adventure to be there with me. If I made the change, he was happy to follow.

We had earned differently but equally – I was working for myself, still editing for New Namibia Books, and also making documentaries, and researching HIV/Aids and gender-based violence for Unicef and UNAIDS; Aidan worked for an architectural firm. For this adventure, we struck a new deal: he would find a job in New York and earn enough so that we could live there. When we returned in 2001, I would support him and our children for two years so that he could start his own practice. We toasted our new future – oh, the fear and the stage fright! The following day, we told our children and my parents.

twenty-nine

My mother's eyes shone with the vicarious pleasure she gets from the travels of other people when I told her about the scholarship. 'You must go,' she said. She had travelled before she married my father in 1962, driving across Spain, skiing in Yugoslavia, sailing the fjords of Norway.

My father was less enthusiastic. He was not a man who liked change, nor did he approve of travel to places not connected to some or other Orford ancestor. America was such a place.

'You must go, and your father and I will help you,' my mother said, adding quietly, as if just for me, 'If you don't go, you will wonder, *What if?* And that is the worst thought a woman could have.'

My father said that if his granddaughters lived at their home, he would be able to give them a proper education – by which he meant he would continue teaching them about Darwin and evolution, all the names of all the birds of Namibia, and the trees' Latin names.

My daughters said they would miss us, but they often slept at their grandparents' house anyway, and Nan made the best school lunches. No stale sandwiches and raisins rattling around in the Tupperware. And besides, Magdalena would go with them.

The consensus was that this plan would be best for the children, who agreed – as much as nine-, six- and three-year-olds can agree. Aidan and I would go and find schools and somewhere to live, and in the meantime they would live with my parents, who would bring them over the following year. By 2000, I would surely have found my feet.

I was grateful. It would not have been possible without their generosity, but underneath it all I had a sense – which I tried to ignore – that I was leaving my girls in my place so that I could sneak away: my escape plan would not be noticed until it was too late. I knew if I left Namibia, I would never return there to live. This was a fork in my life's road from which there would be no return. I knew this would break my father's heart, and sure enough he arrived at my house unannounced in the middle of a weekday morning.

'You can't leave,' he said. 'You can't take my family away from me.'

His tears twisted my heart. It was hard to deny my father, a farm boy sent to boarding school at five; a man for whom the proximity of family – the whole tribe of us surrounding him – made his world secure. I had to steel myself when he called in the debt of his love and support. I could not give in to emotion, to patriarchal wiles, to my own impulse to placate and to please. If I was going to strike out on my own, if I was going to survive, I had to be ruthless.

'They are not yours, Dad,' I said. 'They're mine, and I will do this.'

'I had to say it,' he said.

'I know, Dad,' my own tears thickening my voice. 'But I can't do anything else.'

He left for his hospital rounds and I carried on packing up my house. With each object packed or given away I felt lighter, until it felt as if gravity was no longer doing the work of holding me to the ground. It might be unbearable, I thought for the first time, this lightness of being.

The house with its jewel-coloured rooms sold easily: a relief, as this meant we would have some money to cushion our gamble on New York. A friend adopted my girls' beloved dog. I took down the new lounge curtains and gave them to my mother. We hung them in her living room and the opulent red-and-gold Indian block print, not to my mother's usual taste, blended perfectly with her Persian carpets and oak furniture.

The children's sleepover rooms became their bedrooms. The two older girls were installed in my old bedroom, and the little one in what had been Melle's room. Their clothes, immaculately washed and ironed at my mother's house, were stacked in squared piles inside the cupboards. Their soft toys, books, toy horses and stables were arranged. Adjustments were made to my mother's orderly household, but my children, born into and raised by an extended family, were fully at home in their grandparents' house.

Before Aidan and I left for America, we all went off to my father's farm, a two-hour drive south-east of Windhoek. Omdraai Farm, with its ripple of red dunes the last outpost of the Kalahari Desert, was a place the children loved. My sister had been managing the land, the cattle, the staff and the game, still wearing the boots she had worn with her wedding dress.

My daughters loved being there with her, their other mother who did not fuss about face-washing, teeth-brushing or wearing clothes. When Grace went to Omdraai, she would call out to her aunt in the night – 'Dede, Dede, Dede' – in a voice as plaintive as the cry of a baby hyena. Melle would pick Grace up and take her into bed with her. Neither of them liked to be alone at night, and they would sleep, as I never could with my children or with anyone, for that matter, their limbs entwined until the sun rose and threw flame-coloured rays across the veld.

On that last visit, we stood in the sparse shade of a thorn tree and watched a Cheetah Conservation Fund vehicle bump across the veld. It was carrying three cheetahs that had been darted and captured. My father, who was on the board of the Cheetah Conservation Fund, had established a conservancy, persuading his neighbours to allow these exquisite predators to be relocated from land where they would otherwise have been hunted.

The air was motionless, and a plume of white dust drifted into the sky when the truck came to a halt. My daughters clustered closer to me, and we all took an eager step to look at the three wooden crates on the back. In each one was a cheetah. The game wardens accompanying the animals lifted the crates off the truck and placed them carefully on the ground.

The cheetahs hissed and circled as my three daughters, beside themselves with excitement, were picked up and placed on top of their cages. The cats went quiet and raised their heads. They sniffed, one eye then the other darting to the gaps between the planks where my daughters' feet were planted. For a moment they were one – three small girls on top of cages that contained coiled springs of muscle.

The fastest creatures on earth held their breath, and so did my children as they watched my father for the pre-arranged signal. I watched them crouched on their crates, waiting, as the veld orchestra of cicadas, bird calls and rustling wind seemed to have been suspended. The puffs of cloud on the horizon stopped their drift. My triptych of daughters, with their braced bodies and the firm grip of small hands that neither hesitated nor trembled at the power of the creatures they were about to set free, were motionless until the crack of my father's voice – 'Now!' – sprung each child into action and they released the mechanism on each crate. The doors shot open and the cheetahs – three streaks of brown-black-fawn – bolted.

Wild things. They were there and then they were gone. My heart went with them. A bid for freedom might not ensure lasting liberty, but it was worth the power, the speed, the joy of release.

thirty

We drove out to the airport, arms wrapped around our children, on the twenty-fourth of August 1999. It was the day before Grace's seventh birthday, and Aidan and I would not be at home to see her open her gifts or cut her cake. If I had not been on my way to New York City, she would be with me in the kitchen, sitting on the countertop. Her strong little hands would be clamped on the side of the bowl, holding it steady while I creamed the butter, added a cup of castor sugar, the three beaten eggs. She would sift the flour, cocoa, baking powder and a pinch of salt, alternating it with half a cup of milk until it was perfect. After that, she would lick the bowl while the cake baked.

She had done this at the end of January the year before, but that cake had been for her 'resurrection' rather than her birthday. I'd baked that three-egg cake because she survived being bitten by a snake on a sand dune outside Walvis Bay. Twice the fangs of that Namib sidewinder, *Bitis peringueyi*, sank into the pale inside of her wrist where the veins cluster.

The poison had shut down her central nervous system. I flew with her on a medical evacuation flight from Swakopmund to Windhoek. In intensive care, she lay strapped to machines that measured oxygen levels, temperature, pulse, as she hovered within whatever it is that lies between this world and the next. I did not leave her side. On the sixth day of this unbearable limbo, she opened her eyes, my little Lazarus, and said, 'I've got the spirit of the snake, Mum. You can call me Snakewoman.'

Her tenacious little body had broken down the poison. She had made it back. To mark her triumph over death, I baked her a cake, fashioning the batter into a taut zigzag. We iced it, mimicking the colours from the photograph of a Namib sidewinder that she found in *Snakes of Southern Africa*, which I had borrowed from my father.

She carried that snake cake to school, where she sliced it from its arrow-shaped head to the tip of its tail, then she handed a piece to every child in her class. They had eaten it in awe, as if it were consecrated.

Our luggage was wheeled from the car into the air-conditioned terminal. Last cups of coffee were drunk, final hugs exchanged. It was time. Rose was nine, and she put an arm around each of her sisters and drew them towards her.

My bewildered baby was only three, her infant's skin warm satin. She could not understand where I was going or why, but she held onto her big sister's hand and, although her bottom lip trembled, she did not cry.

I did not cry either. I was afraid that if I started, I would not stop. I promised them that we would find a house for us to live in and a school for them to go to, and that when we did, the five of us would be together.

'Daddy will be back in two weeks,' I said, holding them as close as was possible without squeezing them to death. 'I'll be back for Christmas.'

My three brave daughters, held tight by their grandparents, waved goodbye. I was afraid I would lose my nerve, so I took another Valium. With body and mind, feeling and thought severed, I boarded the plane. It was an amputation. My body felt crippled, aching for the absent weight of their bodies.

I curled my fingernails into my palms until there were four red crescents there. A scalpel would have been better. I could have cut right down to the bone. It would have been a better way of feeling the hurt of what I had done for the sake of my insistent mind that wanted too much.

NEW YORK

thirty-one

'Welcome to New York City,' said the pilot. I opened the blind and looked down at the city that stretched from the Atlantic in the east to the haze in the west where America rolled on towards the Pacific for an infinite number of dreams. Aidan took my hand, but touch was painful, so after a polite amount of time I took the hand back and placed it against the cool oval window. My children's vulnerability, though they were in my parents' loving, busy home, was too painful to think about, and anxiety knotted my stomach as we collected our hand luggage, disembarked, and went through customs.

'You like yoga?' asked the brawny border guard scrutinising my passport.

Was this a trick? I said yes, I did like yoga. The rule is to always answer a policeman truthfully if you can, and he grinned and stamped my passport.

'Corpse pose,' he said, handing it back to me. 'That's my favourite. Welcome to America.'

A hot wind was blowing when we left JFK, suitcases in hand, to stand in line for a taxi. I gripped the safety rail so my body did not turn me around and send me back into the airport, back home, away from this strange, loud place. I clung on until it was our turn to climb into a yellow cab. I showed the driver the scrap of paper with the address of the Greenpoint YMCA. This was where the university housing office had advised me to book a room.

'*Nyet*,' he shouted in Russian, shaking his bald head. He had no idea where it was.

'It's in Brooklyn,' I said, exhaustion sharpening my voice.

'Find!' He hurled his map book at me, and I flicked through it as he hurtled along the expressway.

'There!' I shouted as the Brooklyn exit flashed up overhead. 'Turn!'

The driver slammed on the brakes and, with the stench of burning rubber, we skidded off the highway and dropped down into Greenpoint.

I directed him in my most Russian-sounding English until we drew up in front of a squat block of a building. A banner fluttered over the entrance: 'The Greenpoint YMCA'. The lobby reeked of carbolic acid and boiled cabbages.

This was where fantasies of leading a bookish life lead a woman. This, said the punitive voice in my head, *is where women like me who leave their children end up.*

The receptionist handed me the keys to our room. 'Lock the bathroom,' he advised me. 'We've only been co-ed two months. They're not used to women yet.'

The 'Y' in the YMCA turned out to be a lie. There were no young men there. This place was one step away from homelessness. The other residents were army veterans and alcoholics who muttered to themselves as we dragged our suitcases up three floors.

The air in our room was hot and stale, so I opened the window the grudging three inches that was allowed. There was a police station across the traffic-choked street and I could hear cops talking to each other in loud American voices. It was like being inside a television set.

The bathroom, whose sign said 'WOMEN ONLY NO MEN', was at the far end of the dingy corridor. I was glad I had heeded the receptionist's advice and shot the bolt home because as soon as I had undressed, the door handle rattled. A male voice swore, but after a time he gave up and shuffled away. It felt good to wash away the grime from a long journey. I dashed, undetected, back to our stuffy room.

When Aidan had spruced himself up too, we took the subway from Brooklyn to Lower Manhattan and got out near Washington Square. Aidan went off to a job interview with his portfolio under his arm and I walked up Fifth Avenue towards 34th Street, part of this percussion of people, cars, subways, commerce and culture. I was an arrow. I had pierced the bull's-eye of the city which was the bull's-eye of the world. But I knew nothing about the discipline of Comparative Literature, which had been assigned to me by the Fulbright people for my Master's degree. I did not want to look as ignorant and out of my depth as I felt, so I did not ask. I reassured myself that I would, as I had done with motherhood, figure it out as I went along. Already seduced by New York's energy, full of its confidence and sense of limitless possibility, I entered the Graduate Centre of the City University of New York.

Charming professors in book-lined studies welcomed me when I arrived to register for the Master's programme. They were, they said, intrigued by my work on violence, women's histories, and the interplay between oral and written literatures. My proposed study of theories of trauma and the fragmentation of language by injustice and violence, as well as pain and shame, or a malignant mixture of these, would, they said, be a natural fit with southern African writing on resistance and loss; there, victims and writers often struggle to find the words to describe their sufferings, both personal and political.

I signed up for courses in feminism, narrative and violence, African cinema and literature, post-colonialism, and also psychoanalysis. I scanned the class times, all of them in the evenings, trying to imagine a life that did not involve fish fingers and bedtime stories. In the library, I ran the tips of my tingling fingers along the spines of the books on the stacks. Those volumes held the knowledge I craved. Touching them felt illicit. I had run away from home for these books, left my children for their knowledge, but I would have gone mad if I had turned that scholarship down, and what use is a mad mother?

I smiled for the photograph for my library card. With that and my schedule of classes starting on Monday evening, I rushed downtown to St Marks Place to meet Aidan and flung myself into his arms, my ear to his chest so that I could hear his heart. He had been offered a position with an architectural firm in Soho. They would sort out his visa. He would return to Namibia, tie up his projects there, and return to start work in New York in January 2000. Everything was going to work out.

In a bar in the East Village, we ordered fries and a jug of margaritas, and that was dinner. This dream would work out, we said, and clinked our glasses. We would find somewhere big enough for all of us to live together. When we found this mythical apartment, we would organise schools and our girls could join us for this great adventure. We toasted ourselves.

Limp with exhaustion, hope, and tequila, I pored over a map of the city, trying to work out how to get back to Brooklyn. A man sitting at the bar next to us leaned over. 'Lose the map,' he growled. 'You look like a fucking tourist.'

I left the map in the bar. I had come to live here, not to gawk at the lights on Times Square. My feet found their way along the late-night streets where steam and dragon smoke exhaled from the sidewalks, and we took the subway back to Brooklyn.

When we got back to the YMCA, I collapsed on the bed, listening to the cop cars' sirens. Their lights flashed red, white and blue on the ceiling I stared at while my husband caressed me. I so wanted to be able to respond, but my body was numb. I might as well have been a corpse. This must be the price I had to pay for abandoning my children, I reasoned. If that was the case, then I had no choice but to pay. It had been me who had exploded our well-regulated Windhoek lives to fly halfway across the world so that I could write and read books. I put my arms around Aidan and went outside of myself, watching the cop lights circle each other on the ceiling. Ten days later, he returned to Namibia.

thirty-two

I was desperate to escape the shuffling, muttering, leering men at the Greenpoint Y, but I could not do so. I took their presence as a kind of punishment for what I had done. I could not work out how to imagine a home, albeit a temporary one, that would be a shelter, a pleasure, for me only. When I tried, the coiled serpent of anxiety awoke and slithered out of the pit of my stomach, reached into my chest, and squeezed so hard that I could not breathe.

A South African friend, another Fulbright Scholar, took me in hand, introducing me to a friend who was subletting her apartment on Cornelia Street in the West Village. We met in a coffee shop the next day.

The woman had moved in with her new husband, but used her apartment to work on her PhD during the day. I'd have to be out from ten in the morning until six at night during the week.

'That's fine,' I replied. 'I'll be in the library when I'm not in class.'

'The weekends,' she said, as if giving me a gift, 'are yours to do with as you choose.'

'Fine by me,' I said on that balmy evening in early September when I had no idea yet how long a homeless day could be in the cold of a New York winter.

I was not to move one single thing, she said when she showed me around her cluttered apartment, not even a book. I said I would not – which was a lie – as I gave her a thousand dollars in exchange for the keys.

I was settled, I told my family on the phone that weekend, and I wasn't really on my own because my landlady had left her tortoise-shell cat behind as her husband had allergies.

The loneliness of those first desolate weeks almost killed me. I was free of the soul-crushing repetition of domesticity, but I was no longer contained by the needs of the people I loved. In that isolated autumn of 1999, I lived in a state of disembodied suspension. I had no one to cook for, so I did not eat. I had no one to read stories to and to settle into bed, so I did not sleep. My body, instead of troubling me with its yearnings and desires, shut down.

There were swathes of time when the only intimate contact I had in that city of strangers was when I phoned across five time zones to speak to my daughters. Through the transatlantic crackle and delay, they would tell me what they had been doing and my three-year-old would hold up the pictures she had made for me to the mouthpiece of the phone. It hurt her that I could not see them, and that broke my heart. We would send each other kisses with the sun. My kiss would wake her up in Namibia. Her kiss would wake me in New York. On the many autumn-into-winter days when there was no sun to bring my baby's morning kisses to me or mine to her, I was bereft.

Just go back, my mother-body pleaded. *Book a flight. Go home. No one will blame you. No one will even be surprised.*

But the cerebral part of my divided self would not capitulate. My clear-eyed mind overruled my soft, weak body, saying, *You'll be back for Christmas. That's less than four more months. If you go back now, if you give up, if you fail, you'll never get away again.*

I stayed put and lost myself in books. I had a decade of reading to catch up on and, because books were the place I had escaped to ever since I had learned to read, I went into a reading frenzy. I distilled what I read into sentences that occasionally had an elegance to them. I spent whole days in the library. Although ambition and work do not fill an empty Sunday-morning bed, and nothing substitutes for the joy of nuzzling the warm nape of a sleepy child's neck, I learned to live without this. No matter that it was hard, I was ecstatically absorbed.

I made friends with people in my seminars. Lilli, who took one look at me and saw me for who I was, would come for a drink with me after class. We walked to the KGB bar in the East Village and one drink would often turn into hours of argument about feminism and revolution over supper. Lilli gave me the footing I craved in the fiercely competitive city of New York; she showed me new ways to be a woman of the world.

The snow was thick on the New York sidewalks when I flew back to Namibia for Christmas. For six hot southern-summer weeks I threw myself back into the order of my mother's household, and disrupted things. At New Year, the start of a new millennium, we wore feathered Venetian masks as if it were a carnival. My three-year-old and I danced the twist in my parents' living room. At midnight we watched the fireworks on Independence Avenue, white-and-gold shimmers that were no match, though, for the dense, luminous carpet of the Milky Way. I had, I realised as I put my sleepy children to bed, seen no stars in New York, where the city lights eclipsed them.

Aidan returned with me to the brutal cold of New York in January, and we moved into the snug apartment that I, who knew how to make a home for other people, had in the meantime found in Brooklyn. We were a block from Prospect Park, the borough's great green lung. It was not the veld, but there were areas bushy enough for my feral daughters to be lions in.

My mother brought the girls over in May. On the day they flew from Windhoek to New York, I was demented with terror and excitement. I insisted on the subway rather than a cab in case the traffic seized up and blocked all the roads to JFK. I was worried, too, that an earthquake might derail our train, so we left with enough time to walk to the airport if it did.

Arrivals at JFK was the only place I wanted to be, watching the glass doors slide open and shut for hundreds of strangers until the miracle happened and they were there, three little blonde girls. My heart stopped for the time it took them to fly into our arms.

On the cab drive home from the airport, I held them as tight as possible without crushing them. The world felt right with our five bodies close together and the sun sparkling on the iridescent green of the spring trees. Aidan pointed out the sights everyone knows from the movies – the skyscrapers of Manhattan, the Statue of Liberty.

They told us about their schoolfriends, the antics of my mother's dogs, that they had been to the farm with Melle, and she was coming to New York to visit us. Then we ran out of things to say. The time of waiting was over, but where they were now was, as yet, uninhabited. Their day-to-day life, that of a child, was over seven thousand miles away, on the other side of the Atlantic Ocean.

I had a flash of memory of my father's long absence and his return when I was six. The time he went to London to write his exams to become a gynaecologist, and my mother stayed with me and my siblings at Bosworth, the Orford family farm near Klerksdorp in the then Transvaal. That farm and the grandmother I adored, whose name I had been given, were the still centre of my peripatetic childhood. Bosworth, with its immutable rhythms, is the only place I have ever thought of as 'home'.

When my father returned, it had seemed to me as if he had been gone forever. It was disorienting, that confusion of time. I remembered feeling shy when I saw him, absolutely the same and yet also a stranger, because I was different. While he was gone, I had done things and seen things he would never know about. When I opened the gift he had brought me, a smocked blue sundress from Liberty's, I thought it was babyish. He had not realised that I had grown up while he was away.

The yellow cab dropped us outside our building on 4th Street. The girls raced up to the top floor of our four-storey walk-up and burst into their new home. They went from room to room exploring their new territory, saying, 'I'll sleep here', 'You'll sleep there', 'Here we can play'.

thirty-three

They needed their own front-door keys, my brave daughters. They needed to be sharp, on time, and self-reliant. They needed to look out for each other, applying what they knew about the veld to this urban jungle. I was a full-time graduate student with a part-time job at the Feminist Press and a forty-five-minute commute each way from Brooklyn to 34th Street in Manhattan and back.

Childcare was a form of timetabling art. Aidan took off one afternoon a week. A friend in the neighbourhood, a broody human rights lawyer, had them for another afternoon. They were with me for the rest of the time, but nothing would have been possible if it had not been for school. Rose had a place in sixth grade at Middle School 51, complete with a concrete playground and metal detectors, six blocks from our apartment. Grace went to second grade at PS 321, a far less forbidding school around the corner.

Jamie, however, was a year too young for free public school. The gruff secretary at Grace's school, PS 321, had told me that I could bring my youngest for an interview.

'Mind you,' she said, 'There's only four places going on pre-K. The rest of the kids are allocated to us – crack kids, a lot of them that need a lot of attention. So they need kids that are real stable.' She looked me up and down, taking in my foreignness and the sheer lunacy of the number of children I had in this city of one-child families. 'You try this, honey, but it's a lottery.'

Private childcare was beyond our means, so my entire scheme for surviving the maelstrom of urban work and mothering depended on getting Jamie that one vanishingly rare free pre-kindergarten place. And so, on the day that my two older daughters walked straight-backed as warriors into their new classrooms, I took Jamie for her interview.

We were welcomed by two teachers and their classroom assistants. Jamie smiled angelically and sat, when invited, at the small table and conversed charmingly in her clear, piping voice. She did puzzles and drew pictures, as requested. She told them *The Velveteen Rabbit* was her favourite book and asked what theirs were. She told them we had eaten cucumber sandwiches for tea the day before. They said, 'How adorable.'

Jamie did not mention, and neither did I, that the reason she'd had cucumber sandwiches was that this was the only food in the house because I had not had time to shop, so I'd made the stale white bread edible with mayonnaise and sliced cucumber cut into tiny triangles.

The teachers thanked us and said they would be in touch.

Three days later, a call came from the school secretary. 'Ms Orford,' she said, 'I wanted to ask off the record, if you were to win the lottery place for your daughter, would you take it?'

'I would,' I said. 'Without a doubt.'

'Thank you.' She hung up.

A day later a letter came, telling me that Jamie had won a free place at pre-K. I cried with relief; it was all going to be possible. This hare-brained scheme of mine was going to work. On Monday I walked to school with Grace and Jamie and watched Grace dart across the worn Astroturf to her classroom where her teacher was waiting for her, the new girl who had arrived halfway through the semester.

Jamie started later, and so she and I would go across the road to a coffee shop called Connecticut Muffin. I would have coffee and she would have a muffin, and we would chat, the two of us, relishing the secret half-hour we had all to ourselves. A few weeks into this rhythm, Jamie said, as we sat in our usual place, 'You know, Mum, I speak two languages.'

'Really,' I said, 'and what are they?'

'I speak English,' she piped, 'and I speak Brooklyn,' she growled.

From then on, she would order for me, growling in a Brooklyn accent, 'My mum wants a coffee and a water,' she would say, dragging the vowels and dropping her voice deep inside her chest like a mini-mafioso, 'and I want a muffin.'

When our order was ready, she would hand it to me. 'Here you go, Mum,' she would say in English, 'your coffee and your water.'

We cleaned as a family collective on Saturday mornings to make the most of the time we had in New York. We would set a timer for one hour, put on the Ramones full blast, and all five of us would whirl around the apartment cleaning at top speed. The bath was Jamie's job. The yellow gloves came up to her armpits, but she would stand in the tub, her spindly legs planted wide, and scrub. When the alarm went and the hour was up, we stopped, put on whatever outdoor clothes the weather required, and went exploring.

In Central Park we visited the statue of Balto, the dog that saved the stricken city of Nome, Alaska. Afterwards we'd get hot dogs or pretzels from the vendors and drift with the torrents of people doing the same thing in the park. We went to the zoo, but the caged cheetahs made us sad, so we did not go back.

Once, at FAO Schwarz on Fifth Avenue, for reasons I never fathomed, a personal shopper attached herself to us. She led us through an ordinary-looking door and into a secret vault. This hidden shop within a shop was three storeys high, an Aladdin's cave of treasures. There was a miniature Ferrari, which, our guide told us, was wonderful for driving around the family estate. Barbie dolls had human hair and wore dresses sprinkled with Swarovski crystals, and the doll's houses made even Versailles look drab. On the subway back to Brooklyn, it was hard to believe it had all been real.

When I had no childcare, I took my daughters with me to work at the Feminist Press or to my seminars, where they would sit in the corridor for a full two hours, eating their snacks or drawing. Rose read her younger sisters the newly published Harry Potter, while, nearby, I discussed feminist philosophy, women's writing, the complexity of memory, and testimonies of personal trauma from South Africa's Truth and Reconciliation Commission. Now that I had the privilege of distance and the chance to draw breath, I saw things from a new perspective and began to puzzle over the ways in which many women's accounts were fractured, as if language itself broke down when they gave testimony.

At the end of class, I would put those thoughts aside, gather up my children, then run down the stairs of the Graduate Centre and onto Fifth Avenue. When their pent-up energy from being well-behaved and bored dissipated, we slowed down and wandered the bustling New York sidewalks, weaving our way between crowds of people. We marvelled at the extravagant window displays at Bloomingdale's, or took a shortcut through Macy's, trailing our fingers through racks of unaffordable clothes.

We took my sister there when she visited us, en route to a friend's wedding. It was wonderful to see Melle restored to herself. She had a new man who was smitten with my beautiful, funny sister, who had chosen him. 'I'm so happy for you,' I said.

'Ah, to have that rare thing,' she deadpanned, fixing her green eyes on me. 'A man.' We had armfuls of clothes for her to try on at Macy's and I headed for the changerooms. Melle took one look at the women standing in line. 'No way am I waiting in that queue,' she said as she stripped and, ignoring flustered shop assistants, chose a bridesmaid outfit.

How right it felt to have my sister with me, the shared mothering, the way she connected the divided worlds I inhabited. We talked and laughed the whole of that too-short week. Our conversation was lively in a way conversation no longer was with my husband. He and I discussed logistics, but aside from household mundanities, a silence was growing between us. I could not tell you how long it had been there, but in the cacophony of New York I heard it for the first time, and I felt so alone after my sister left.

thirty-four

It was on a midweek morning in March 2001, when I was rushing to get to the library early on a day my husband was looking after the girls, that I paused at our bedroom door to say goodbye. Aidan was lying on the bed reading to Grace and Jamie. He glanced at me standing there with my library books under my arm, but there was so much distance in his eyes, it was as if I was looking at a stranger. I saw in that seemingly inconsequential moment, one of millions in which marriages are made and unmade, that we were no longer travelling together. When I look back, I pinpoint that as the moment our separation began.

I could have put my books down and got into bed with him and my children, but I didn't. I did not want to. The terrain of my heart had shifted. As I stepped into the world, Aidan was stepping back. What I was doing had taken me away from him. My desire to merge into another person, so strong a decade before, had disappeared. I felt infinitely lonely standing there, holding my books to my chest as if they were a shield.

'Shall we go to Dizzy's Diner for supper?' I asked. I could not face the implications of my epiphany, and so I put it aside.

'Yes!' sang Jamie. 'It's my favourite.'

'Okay,' said Aidan, holding my gaze for a fleeting second.

Grace nudged her father. 'Carry on reading, Dad.'

Aidan turned back to the spell of the page, and I dashed downstairs.

When I stepped onto the pavement, I felt as Icarus surely did when he stepped off the cliff hoping that his improvised wings would fly him safely through the unknown element of the air. Be careful of wanting too much, I thought. Be careful of flying too close to the sun.

In the library I tried to lose myself in books, but concentration eluded me. My thoughts kept returning to the intimacy of that morning – a scene I had fled so that I could read and write. I had not known until that moment that a primitive and unreconstructed part of me *needed* my husband to be out in the world, shining, so that I could bask in his reflected glory. But Aidan avoided the limelight. He did not seem to want to be on stage. He avoided speaking in public, holding an audience's attention. But I did not. I felt stunned and ashamed of myself for not having seen this before. I was the restless one, the ambitious one.

If the ambition was mine, the desire to participate in public debate, like Mary Wollstonecraft and the women who came after her, then I had to own my desire and do what I wanted to do, be who I wanted to be. I could not live vicariously. My own mother-in-law, when it was time for seconds at dinner, would say sweetly yet firmly to her daughters-in-law, 'Leave the meat for the men.' And I always did, though resenting not having an equal share. I thought of how much my mother-in-law had given up – willingly, she averred – to make sure that the men were replete, seemingly unaware of the sacrifice involved. If I was to teach my daughters to say no to anything less than their full share, never to do with less so that men could have more, then I had to take full responsibility for myself.

I had brought with me to New York a photograph of my handsome Orford grandfather, a small but heroic piece of home. The picture was taken in 1945 in a street in Florence. It is of him and two other soldiers, all three in frayed khaki uniforms. My grandmother never said as much, but I suspected that during those difficult war years, she loved the independence. I imagined her running the farm, driving the truck, striding across the veld. I pictured her on horseback. I saw her alone with her children.

A brisk, well-dressed woman in charge of her herself and her domain, she had been my first ideal of female freedom. A woman free to ride out and look across the land, liberated from the tyranny of mealtimes and the domestic formality demanded by a husband.

This is, I came to realise, neither a mistaken nor an accurate image. My grandmother missed him when he was gone, but I think she was lonely in a different way when he returned. I wished I had known to ask what it was to wait for a man for five years, only to have him return with a head full of things he could not say. I wished I had asked how she had learned to play second fiddle.

I finished the article I was writing on Namibian literature, optimistically titled 'Transition, Trauma and Triumph', and sent it off before going to meet my family at Dizzy's Diner. It was a firm favourite, as the waiters gave the children balls of dough to make their own pizza shapes. They were watching them bake, standing as close to the oven as possible without catching alight, when I arrived. In the noisy harmony of the restaurant, my husband and I were reconnected by our hungry, happy children – but also by the practicalities of the fast-approaching end of our time in New York.

There were ways to change our visas so we could stay longer, and we considered this. The American dream is hard to resist, but we missed the veld, our families and being in a society we were part of. So, Aidan would take up the offer of contract work on a large public building in Cape Town after taking our daughters back to my parents in Namibia. It would do them good to return to their old school to tell their friends about their adventures, and to give them the presents they had chosen so carefully. He would go to Cape Town, where we would all move once I finished my degree. For now, we could all fling ourselves into the last wild rollercoaster of New York life, knowing it was for a finite amount of time.

That night I took off my jewellery. I wanted to feel at one with Aidan. The earrings clicked as I placed them on the bedside table next to my rings and bangles, stripping myself so that all that there was between us was skin. After we made love, I put the bracelets on, and they jingled as they met each other on my arm.

thirty-five

With the help of supportive professors I had converted my Master's degree into a PhD. This meant considerably more work – proving my competence in two modern languages in addition to English. The doctoral exams, set for April 2001, would test whether I had read every notable book from the Babylonian *Epic of Gilgamesh* to those of the twentieth century. There were too many books and too little time, but my brother came to my rescue by flying from London, where he worked in the City, to look after his nieces while I prepared for exams and completed the outline for my planned dissertation, 'Narratives of Violence'.

My girls had a great time with their uncle, and I passed the exams. In early June the girls had farewell parties. Before I knew it, they were packed and at the airport with Aidan. The security doors slid shut, they were gone, and I was alone, roaming New York, the noisy city I adored, for the hot months of June and July.

I had final meetings with my supervisor. Most of the literature review was done. I had presented my research at African literature conferences and published some of it in journals and books. I would write the dissertation in Cape Town, submit drafts by email, and he would respond. When it was ready, I would return to New York for my defence of the dissertation.

'It will make an excellent, if obscure, scholarly book,' said my professor, whose many obscure and scholarly books filled the shelves behind the leather armchair he was seated in. 'But I don't think the university is where you want to be.'

'Where do I want to be?' I asked. He had spent a lifetime of scholarship traversing the border between psychoanalysis, anthropology – including a study of white people under apartheid – and literature. He, of all people, should be able to tell me.

'You like to be in the world,' he said with a smile. 'You want to change things. Go back and do that.'

I put my papers back into my bag. He opened the door for me.

'Let me know how you get on,' he said. He shook my hand, though I wanted to hug him.

There was a lump in my throat when I walked out of that building on the corner of 34th Street for the last time. I was a different woman to the one who had first walked up Fifth Avenue, brimming with ideas, and overwhelmed – as all first-time arrivals are – by its grandeur, its tackiness, its noise, its infinite opportunity.

To escape the heat, I went to a diner on Bleecker Street. I was paying my respects, I suppose, to a city that did not look askance at a woman out and about alone. I sat down at a small table and ordered a glass of wine and a Caesar salad. I had grown to love the communal solitude of New York. I would miss this city where I learned to embrace ambition and to try things that felt beyond my reach, but much as I loved it, South Africa was the place where I felt there was unfinished business.

I opened my notebook where I had pasted newspaper clippings about the murder of a fourteen-year-old girl in 1999. Valencia Farmer was gang-raped and stabbed more than fifty times before her assailants slit her throat, leaving her for dead in a derelict house in Cape Town. Her mother, who had gone looking for her, had found her daughter. Valencia lived long enough to tell her mother the names of her assailants. Two years on, and the perpetrators, all members of Cape Town's notorious gangs, were on trial.

They would be convicted because of their victim's testimony – telling her mother who the men were that had tortured her.

How to account for men's brutality? I wrote in the margin.

How to account for the agony of a fourteen-year-old girl who, her mother said, had dreamed of becoming a doctor in a newly democratic South Africa?

How to account for the suffering of her mother, who fought for justice for her daughter? How to do justice to their courage?

An injury inflicted on one woman was a punishment delivered to all women – its effects restricting not only our physical freedom but our freedom to imagine, too. That call to solidarity and collective action resonated with my awareness that the power imbalance between men and women was political. It could, if properly understood, be changed.

Cape Town is a violent city where the currents of its brutal past – slavery, colonialism, apartheid – eddy below the surface. Valencia Farmer was just one amid hundreds of femicide victims whose punctured corpses haunted news reports and, whenever I visited the city, my dreams. If I was to live in Cape Town with my daughters, I would have to make sense of this violence as if it were a language that I could not yet understand.

I could not look away from the wounds men inflict on the bodies of women and children. I would try to map what it is that drives misogyny. To make visible how the unconscious, as unique to each person as fingerprints, absorbs the shocks of history and war, and repeats them. I saw violence, with its rhythm and repetition, as a symptom, a possible means to decipher a meaning from the rape, torture and murder of women. It would be from this material, these wounded bodies, that I would attempt to reconstruct an intimate history of a wounded country, as if I were a psychoanalyst and the patient on my couch was South Africa.

Fear makes women police what we say and where we go. I could not stand for that, so I would write. I would write myself free. But how? Raped women are silenced by shame, fear, disbelief and, all too often, by what is called love – of a husband, a father, a friend who harms them. The task I set myself as I finished my wine in that New York diner was to find a way to look, without flinching, at what is done to women by men, and to tell the truth about these unspeakable crimes.

I had started off my working life as a journalist because, at eighteen, I'd wanted to report on the violence of apartheid South Africa. The state had banned some newspapers for reporting the truth about the killings and disappearances, while others were severely restricted in what they were permitted to publish. Sexual violence created its own clandestine censorship, but sitting there in that diner on the eve of my return, I believed that if people knew the truth about bad things, they could be stopped, that the truth set people free.

When I get back, I wrote in my notebook, *I will arm myself with one question: why?* And yet, as I wrote those words, a familiar sense of doubt – a close cousin of futility – stopped my writing hand and I put down my pen. Words cannot undo what has been done. Words cannot repair torn skin. Even though they must be spoken, they do not right wrongs.

I learned this in 1973 at the age of eight, while on holiday with my grandparents on their farm. We had piled into the back of my parents' station wagon to visit a pig farmer and his wife. The drive was hot and took forever. When we reached the farm, the gate was closed, but as we slowed down, three skinny black boys about my age raced over to open it. My father passed me the coins to give them. One- and two-cent pieces, to buy sweets. I opened the window. A boy the same size as me held out his hand and, with mixed feelings of power and mortification, I placed the money in his open palm. It was hard to the touch.

My father drove towards the river, past the stables where a mare and her foal stood in the dappled light. I wanted to stop and give the horse an apple, but my father drove on towards the whitewashed farmhouse surrounded by oak trees. My mother said we had been here before, but I did not remember that. The farmer, his wife and their children greeted us as we got out of the car. We had drinks on the verandah, and went into the cool house for lunch. After that it was time for an afternoon nap.

I lay on my back, bored, watching the blades of a ceiling fan hack at the heat, and listened to the horse whinnying, summoning me. When the house was silent, I got up. My parents were asleep with my sister wedged between them on the bed. My brother slept on the floor, his thumb in his mouth.

I filched an apple from the fruit bowl in the dining room, slipped out of the house and ran across the lawn. A narrow path wound along the acacia scrub in the direction of the stables. The foal was testing its rickety legs. I extended my hand to the mare and she lipped the apple from my fingers, flattening her ears at the sound of a man's raised voice.

I crept along the wooden fence and, when I found a gap, looked through it. I saw a woman with her hands over her mouth. I saw the farmer tying a boy to the bench, his thin wrists to one end, ankles to the other. When the farmer picked up the sjambok, his eyes on the quivering back, the boy raised his head and looked straight at me.

I could not look away and he did not blink. I felt his palm on my fingertips. That morning, he had opened the gate for us.

The farmer ran the whip through his hands. Then he brought it down on the boy's back, ripping his white shirt open. His mother screamed, but the sound was trapped in her hands.

The boy looked at me, unblinking. I could not look away. The whip hissed again. The boy's eyes were stones. He would not make the sound that would stop the man. He would not cry. To make it stop, I stepped through the gap in the fence.

The farmer saw me, but, unashamed, he raised the whip above his head a fifth time, a sixth time, a seventh, the whip whistling through the air until silenced by the boy's wet skin. The boy's torn white shirt was red, and the man walked away.

The woman untied her son. When she cradled him, he lifted his arm as if to strike her, but she grabbed his hand and pressed it to her mouth.

I ran back to the silent farmhouse. I had to tell what I had seen their friend do to the boy. I had to tell them I tried to stop him, but I could not. I cried, 'Talk to the man; tell him it was wrong.' My mother hugged me, but it wasn't me who had been beaten, it was that boy.

My failure to help him crushed my words; words I did not have to make them hear a whip hiss through the air. To make them smell the tang of blood. To show them the man's face twisting as the boy's eyes, staring at me, accusing me, shaming me, turned into stone.

'Don't go off by yourself,' said my father, his shoulders hunched. I had hurt him by seeing what I had seen.

There was a braai that evening. There were chips for the children. 'Cokes for the good ones,' said the man. He gave me a bottle, but I did not drink it. There was wine for the adults, and they drank it. My father and the man stood by the fire talking, but the boy was not mentioned. The meat sizzled. The pork sausage done first. My father knew it was my favourite and he broke off a piece, blew on it and brought it to me. I did not want to eat, but I opened my mouth, chewed and swallowed.

When we left the next day, there were only two ragged boys playing at the farm gate. They stopped their game, but the gate was already open, so there was no need for coins to be dropped into palms. They watched us until a bend in the road shielded us from view. I felt sick, bile burning the back of my throat.

My mother laid her arm lay across the front seat and massaged the back of my father's neck. He loved that. I leaned against the closed window. Watched dust devils shimmy on the horizon. Saw the man's whip arm falling, falling, falling.

All writers have a primal scene and that one is mine. I do not know what became of the beaten boy, but his eyes still hold my gaze. I still hear his silence, denying the farmer the pleasure of hearing his victim beg. There is no such thing as an innocent bystander. I had seen what happened, which made me complicit. All I could do then was tell the tale; all I can do now is write.

I closed my notebook, paid my bill, and went back to my empty apartment. Later that humid July evening I took the train to JFK Airport. When the plane took off, I looked down at the glittering lights of that liberating city. I was already mourning New York, where the door to an alternative life, another self, had opened – but I had not stepped through it. Like a love affair not embarked on, it filled me with regret.

thirty-six

My girls ducked under the barrier when I came through the arrivals gate at Windhoek airport and ran towards me. They had shot up in the two months we were apart. Nine-year-old Grace sprang into my arms and wrapped her legs around me, but gravity got the better of her and she slid down to the ground. Spindly five-year-old Jamie could perch on the hip I jutted out for her, but there was no way I could pick up eye-level Rose.

'You've grown taller than me,' I exclaimed.

'That's hardly an achievement, Mum,' she said, picking up my hand luggage and sauntering off to the exit.

'Good to have you home, sis,' said Melle, linking her arm through mine as we wheeled my suitcases to the car.

The veld, bleached to winter shades of fawn and mauve, slid past on the other side of the window as we drove to my parents' house, which had once again been my girls's home.

Nan was taking them to horse riding, they told me, even though it made her so scared she couldn't look when they jumped, and yes, they were learning to jump, everyone loved the presents they'd bought from New York, they'd been to play with this friend and that one, and they missed America, but it was lovely to be back at their old school. They were finishing off the academic year at the school I'd attended for a year as a young girl, where I had participated in a programme designed for me and a couple of other children identified as 'gifted' by the new headmaster, who had come highly recommended by a private school in Johannesburg.

The three of them carried my bags down to the cottage where I would be staying alone. Aidan was already in Cape Town, working. The room was the same. The house was the same, except that there were more security bars. Nothing had changed, but I was a different person.

I did not know how to express that difference. There was no place for it and so, at dinner that night with all of us around the table – me like some kind of peculiar overgrown woman-child seated with my children – I folded that difference away and listened to my father's stories about farming and new archaeological discoveries relating to the spread of cattle in pre-colonial Africa.

I went to see Aidan, who had rented a large furnished house. He planned to start his own practice in 2002, so in six months I would have to restore order to our itinerant lives and fulfil my part of the bargain by being the breadwinner and giving him the two years of financial support he had given me.

I put out work feelers in Cape Town and looked for a home, a place where we'd live out the rest of our days. But my heart was not in it. I could not settle. I did not want to be domesticated again.

It was impossible to be in two places at once, and so I was in neither. Shuttling back and forth between Windhoek and Cape Town was familiar. A repeat of my school and university years. That oscillation, the limbo of the second half of 2001, meant that conflict did not have to be resolved, and difficult emotions were not faced because I would be gone again within a week. Why bring up sadness, anger, loss, loneliness when time together was so short?

Work had been easy to find in Namibia – writing textbooks, research into gender-based violence and HIV/Aids, workshops with trainee teachers, documentary films. The work I'd done before New York. I was adept at it, but it was not what I wanted to be doing. I had come back with the confidence and determination to write.

That needed to be put aside, though. I had bread to win and a family to support, so writing simmered on the backburner. I kept an eye on it as I worked late into the night at my mother's kitchen table, surrounded by documents and new school curricula. I cleared it all away for the girls to eat their breakfast before school. It was November by now, and hot, and so it seemed odd to see Rose wearing black cycling shorts under her red-and-white gingham school uniform.

'It's so hot,' I said. 'Why are you wearing those shorts?'
'All the girls do.' She looked embarrassed.
'Why?' I asked.
'When we're in the playground the boys try to look up our skirts,'

she told me, not quite looking me in the eye. 'And then,' she crossed her arms over her chest, 'when we leave the classroom the boys bump us and it hurts.'

I remembered the tender swelling of nipples. Stonies, we called them when I, too, was on the cusp of twelve, wearing the same school uniform. The memory was a short, sharp strike that precipitated a migraine. 'I'll speak to your teachers,' I said. 'It will stop.'

The next day I went to see the headmaster, a little man pumped full of evangelical religion and his own importance. When I told him what was happening to Rose and the other girls, that pillar of the community slapped his knees and laughed.

'Boys will be boys, hahaha! What can one do?'

'Stop them,' I said. 'Punish them. Monitor them when they leave the classroom. Make sure the girls are safe. Teach the boys that sexual assault is a crime. Expel them if they don't behave.'

'They're just boys having fun.'

'You condone this casual violence. You're schooling these boys in misogyny.' I sat on my hands so I did not hit this man. He did not care what the boys, little men in training, were subjecting the girls to.

'Come now,' he said, his voice hard-edged with disdain – for me, this mother complaining in his office. 'Let's be reasonable—'

'I am reasonable,' I cut him off. 'By doing nothing you're breaking the wings of those girls as they are getting ready to fly. You can stop the boys. You can teach them that assault, sexual assault, is a crime.'

'They're little boys,' he repeated, his eyes narrowing.

'What would you do, Headmaster, if a mother told you her son had been in tears because whenever he tried to leave the classroom the girls grabbed his penis, twisted his testicles, pulled open his shirt and elbowed his nipples? What would you say? Girls being girls?'

He was outraged. Appalled. He reminded me that he, a deeply religious man and a father, was shocked that I, a respectable woman from a good family, would say such things in his office.

'It's the same behaviour.' My voice was a blade. 'This is the outrage you should feel on behalf of the girls. Why do you allow this rape-training to happen here? This schooling in misogyny and impunity?

This annihilation of girls as they are getting ready to fly?' I softened my tone with difficulty. 'Talk to the boys. Let me talk to them if you don't know what to say. I'll make them understand.'

He stood up. 'Not permissible.' The meeting was over.

thirty-seven

I left his office and walked to my car, which was parked under the same trees that were there in 1977 when I, Lolita-aged as Rose was now, had been twelve and in my final year of primary school. I put the key into the ignition, but I did not start the car. I was burning, no longer with rage but with shame, that feeling that lives so deep inside the body it appears to exist prior to language. Oh, shame – the wound that must be healed before there can be reason and reciprocity in the polis – the word I'd learned from that other headmaster, who had been here for the single year, my twelfth, that I had spent at this school, who had taught me Latin, Greek, Logic and Rhetoric.

I had loved the magical strangeness of the ancient Greek, the rhythmic declensions of Latin verbs, the figures of speech – learning that ironic understatement has a name: litotes. I loved the formality of philosophy and how endless the reading was. Perhaps that's why I was at school later than usual that afternoon, standing in front of the noticeboard in the hall, when I heard the headmaster's familiar step behind me. I don't know why – because I cannot remember – or what happened because I was there late and alone; even now I can only recall fragments here, fragments there:

Before I could turn and say, 'Good afternoon, sir,' he pressed his body against my back and locked his arms around me so fast, so tight, so shocking. His heat through my school dress. His smell. His breath hot in my ear neck face. Steel-band arms around my chest. Hurting hands searching for my breasts. The beard and those lips. Spit on them. His knee pushing between mine, then the clang of metal on metal, heels clicking. His arms loosen. I snatch a breath. Kick him. Sprint out of the hall, down the stairs and out. I am at home, sitting at the kitchen table saying, 'School was fine'; I do not have words for the thing that happened so fast maybe it didn't happen at all. What kind of story would that be? I did not know what to say or how to say it so I said nothing and went back to school on the Monday and lessons carried on but the wonder at the new worlds he had opened my mind to was gone. I had turned to him, a sunflower to the sun, but it had all been a lie, a trick. He looked away from me in class. He made me invisible. I understood that he had never been interested in what I thought or said or wrote. Who knew if I was clever? Who cared? I had been wrong, all the time. I had been wrong about myself. I had been stupid; I had not understood.

A door had opened, and I had escaped, but I felt ashamed of what I had done and of what I had not done; of what I knew and what I did not know. None of which I knew how to tell anyone – not even my parents – because nothing of significance had happened to me. I was physically intact, unlike the ten-year-old boy who had been his favourite, a boy in my sister's class who found the courage to tell his tale when the headmaster turned his attentions to his younger brother: he spoke up for him. There was hushed talk and schoolboard meetings and, overnight, the headmaster, his nervy wife and three small children were gone. There was no trial, but there were rumours he was committed to an institution for the criminally insane.

I hope that's true.

I escaped my attacker because a door opened and my instinct to flee kicked in. But I did not feel heroic. I didn't even feel lucky. His assault – so fleeting, so frightening – filled me with shame because somewhere, somehow my conditioning into womanhood made me think it was my fault.

As I sat seething in the school car park, I recalled that white South Africans respond with the word 'shame' to the most inconsequential things – if you spill tea on your skirt, or lose your keys, or just seeing a baby, a kitten, a puppy. Here, 'shame' is an expression of helpless but transient sympathy or even pleasure. The repetition of that word has worn out its meaning. It has never been used for truly shameful things – like the tangled history of slavery, apartheid, white supremacy, sexual violence, and the 'dop system' used to pay farmworkers.

That sentimental 'oh, shame' bore no relation to the experiences of shame I'd had as a child. Those were moments when the shame of others was bequeathed to me. My inheritance was the doubled consciousness of the secondariness of my sex and the whiteness of my skin.

Shame, sex-shame, had been planted – as it is in the body of every little girl I have ever known – when I was about eight in the hot December holiday of 1972 when we went to Bosworth after my family's first year in Namibia, our new and still unfamiliar home.

When we reached my grandparents' house, I fell out of the hot car and dashed ahead of the others. My grandmother – we were each other's favourites, that had long been settled – opened her arms wide for me. When she let me go, I ran to the house, rushing through the little sitting room. A quick eye sweep: nothing had changed. I dashed down the dim passage to the nursery and stopped, scanning the toys – a carved elephant and tin soldiers that had been my father's – lined up on a shelf above the picture rail. I climbed onto the bed and stood on tiptoe, but still could not reach them. The relief. We had moved; I was at yet another new school, but here on the farm everything was the same.

I went outside to check on the dogs and found the gardener edging the lawn with a pair of shears. He looked up, smiled and said, 'Hello, Miss Margie.'

'Hello, Jackson,' I said , but I did not know what to say after that, so I just stood there. 'Your bike is in the garage,' he said, turning back to clip the grass.

'Thank you.' I didn't know what else to say, but I kept standing there, the sun burning my bare shoulders, watching him. His sleeves were rolled up, and each time he snipped, the tendons flexed. I knew those strong arms. I loved them. The year before, they had steadied me on my new bicycle. After everyone else lost patience with my clumsiness and tears, Jackson had taught me to ride, loping along beside me, one arm around my waist, the other along my side as he held the handlebars of my unruly bicycle, up and down the long driveway. When I finally found my balance, he cheered.

My grandmother called, and I darted to the front lawn. She turned on the tap, and the sprinkler rotated. Slowly at first, but when it speeded up the sun turned the spray into diamonds that scattered across the lawn. My mother undressed my brother, but my sister and I had already pulled off our sundresses and panties. We ran back and forth through the glistening spray. Those jets of icy water splashing legs, bellies, backs were heaven. We caught the water in our mouths and spat it out at each other. The grown-ups poured drinks and watched, smiling. A movement caught the corner of my eye. Jackson, a sack in one hand, clippers in the other, appeared round the corner of the farmhouse. I waved. He waved back before kneeling to cut the grass on the edge of the driveway.

'Margie,' I heard a voice say. My grandmother was stepping off the shaded verandah, striding towards us. Something was wrong. 'Put on your costume.'

'I don't want to.'

Her hands were on my wet shoulders. 'You can't be bare.'

'Why not?'

'You're a big girl now.'

Anger rose as hot and sudden as vomit. I'd seen girls only a few years older than me with their mothers on verandahs, just sitting there. I didn't want to be like them. 'I won't,' I said.

'Don't be silly.' She did not raise her voice, but everyone was watching. It was as if her hands on my shoulders were speaking to my skin on behalf of of them all. What had I done? What was it that I did not know? This separation – me from them – was frightening. It was exciting too, so I persisted. 'Why must I?'

'Because it's not fair on Jackson,' she said.

I turned to look at him kneeling in the dust, edging the lawn, the shears clicking.

'Jackson.' My grandmother's voice stopped the cutting. 'That's enough for today.'

He stood up and, shears in one hand, bag of cuttings in the other, disappeared around the side of the house. Bewildered, I searched my grandmother's face, but her eyes were hidden by her dark glasses, so all I found was myself reflected, tiny and naked. Nipples two bull's-eyes on the target of my chest, one hand creeping to cover them, the other to hide the cleft between my legs.

I put on my dress and slunk onto the verandah, sitting where no one could touch me. I was given a 'special-occasion' Coca-Cola, while my parents and grandparents sipped gin and tonic. I listened, my chest tight, to the ice cubes tinkle, shame burning me.

Shame has to find a home somewhere. And when the hot fire that scorches one's skin enters in childhood, it sends down parasitic roots, grows, becomes one's own flesh and blood.

A line of little girls in gingham and boys in khaki being shepherded across the car park to the hall jolted me back to the present. I drove out of the school grounds, cranking up the air conditioning to cool my fury. I had been unable to pierce the headmaster's smug armour when I spoke on behalf of my daughter and – as I then saw – myself. I'd lost that fight, but I had a clearer understanding of shame, how it paralysed girls in the way a wasp stings a spider, leaving it alive but unable to move, then laying eggs in its body. When those baby wasps hatch, they feed off the spider's living body. That is what swallowed shame does, feeding off paralysed girls as it had fed off me.

I had lost the battle with the misogynist headmaster, but I was determined to go on fighting the war. To be able to protect my daughters, I needed to understand the politics of violence, both intimate and public, in relation to women, trauma and shame. To understand, I had to write, but to write I needed my family to be together. Soon afterwards, I went to Cape Town to find us a house.

CAPE TOWN

thirty-eight

Our new home, high up on the slopes of Table Mountain, had terracotta roof tiles and bay windows with expansive views of Table Bay. We moved in once we had repainted the walls and lifted old carpets to reveal wooden floors that gleamed after being sanded. It was a sturdy, welcoming house, filled with gentle light that came in from every angle through mullioned windows. Twelve people, if they sat close to each other, could eat together at the kitchen table. It was a house with space for all of us and for the waifs and strays we took in over the years. There were many of all ages who stayed, some for one night, some for years.

My sister came down in January 2002 to help get us settled. It was blisteringly hot. The movers sweated and swore as they carried boxes and furniture up the stairs while Melle and I cleaned and unpacked, our energies matched, both of us skilled at rapidly setting up new homes. Our brother kept well clear of our frenzy, drinking beer on the lawn while keeping an eye on his nieces. They brought their toy horses and Barbie dolls into the garden, playing an elaborate game as Melle and I moved furniture and made beds.

The labour of homemaking is hard, but she and I admired tenacity and stamina. Up went the pictures, curtains and towel hooks. Out came pots, plates, cutlery and cups, with the wine glasses last. Those we filled and took out into the garden. The sky, which had been a relentless blue, was rippled with cirrus clouds. The southeaster was on its way. The wind barrelled down our street and into our house, where it slammed the doors shut. My sister, who, like me, hated loud sounds, pulled bricks out of the garden. That evening, after supper, she wrapped them in newspaper, transforming each old brick into an origami-perfect doorstop. A gift of quiet, they lasted all the years I lived there. It was only at the end that the wrappings frayed, and the jagged bricks inside began to scratch the wooden floors.

Table Mountain was wreathed in soft mist the morning Melle went back to Namibia. On the way to the airport we dropped the girls off at their new school. 'Hug Mum and Dad for me,' I said, and Melle promised that she would. My parents missed the grandchildren I had taken away. They visited us in Cape Town, but with us moving so far away from them, they were cut off from my daughters' daily rhythms. This pained me, but I had done it, I told myself, so that we could grow. There was no chance I'd have sent them to boarding school, and I wanted them to have a wider experience, one Cape Town could offer. If I was a success, which I defined then as providing for my family financially, as my father had done for his, then the pain I had caused my three-generational family by cutting and running would be worth it all.

With those guilt-demons nipping at my heels, I flung myself into work, taking on anything that came my way – reportage, educational films and textbooks, and editing, as well as various commissioned books on climate change, rural development and human rights. By some miracle, I earned enough to support my family. It was exhilarating to be the provider, in the way skydiving is – that lurch of the free fall before the parachute opens. Which it did, and there was enough left over to afford me the time to investigate the violence to which women are subjected.

The terrorisation of women seemed central to the construction of male identity. The attacks I knew about were so excessive it seemed the intent was not only to kill the woman but also to obliterate her body. As if the assailants were driven by an endless internal rage at women, which was – or so I speculated – a rage at the vulnerability women represent in patriarchal societies. Feelings, particularly those pertaining to loss, powerlessness and shame, are inexpressible in a macho world. I felt compelled to find out whether our collective failure to find a language for such emotions had turned South Africa itself into a serial killer, one that picked off the undefended to discharge some of its own fury, hatred and fear.

Journalism is one of the few legitimate ways of holding the pain of others in one's gaze, and I knew that not looking does not make injustice disappear. Writing would be a way of holding perpetrators to account, even if it did not ameliorate the victim's pain. Investigative journalism provided me with a persona that I could put on as if it were armour. As a journalist, I could legitimately go anywhere and ask any questions. People might not answer me, but no one ever questioned my professional right to be where I was.

I went where the stories took me; following one lead after another, I parsed the facts from the fictions that swirl around crimes against women and children. I investigated gang initiations like the one that had driven the murder of Valencia Farmer. I delved deeply into human trafficking, the trade in drugs and illegal abalone, rape, murder, the manufacture of child pornography and the sex industry, as well as organised crime links to many Cape Town clubs, especially strip clubs.

But I could not simply saunter in as a patron and watch. My presence – my ordinary, forty-year-old, clothed woman's body – would have interrupted the spectacle of young, pony-tailed girls performing in a display their male audience consumed. And so, I had to rely on other, indirect means. An art student's work gave me access to strippers in cramped dressing rooms in the city centre.

In one of these, a girl sat at her dressing table studying a Russian/English dictionary, the bulging bag of make-up pushed aside so that she could make space for the book. In another, a girl whose false eyelashes shadowed her cheek napped with her head on her folded arms. Stuck on the mirror next to her was a list of fines: R200 for 'chewing like a cow'; R500 for being late or 'fighting'. And R2 000 for the mystifyingly vague crime of 'not having a fantasy' – thereby forfeiting several nights' earnings.

I saw little of the supposedly liberatory aspects of stripping – or sex work. The women I interviewed worked within terms set by the male managers and pimps who run the business of satisfying other men's fantasies.

Men who hurt women – wives, girlfriends, daughters, mothers, colleagues, or strangers to whose bodies they feel entitled – believe that the woman herself is to blame. I knew this from my own intimate experience, and it was corroborated by interviews not only with survivors but also with perpetrators. To understand these complex crimes, the social and psychic systems that produce them, and why they are so difficult to prevent and to prosecute, I'd need to shadow the forensic experts who worked with rape and murder cases.

thirty-nine

The commanding officer of the medical forensic labs in Delft, outside Cape Town, took me through the laboratory. There, in the orderly medical hum of microscopes and Petri dishes, he introduced me to the sharp-eyed women bending over human tissue on glass slides. Then the contents of what to me looked like a deli fridge: panties, big, small, expensive, washed-out beige, one with a wisp of bloodied lace, and a red pair with the label 'Age 2–3'.

'What is this?' I asked the cop escorting me.

'The rape cases,' he said.

Forensics is where trauma is converted into evidence that can withstand the law's requirement that the guilt of the accused be proven beyond reasonable doubt. But there is more to these stories than that, I thought, as the officer led me through the complex. Justice, narrow and precise, tells only part of the story. Somehow, I needed to find a way of restoring those panties to their owners. I had to find the intimate pulse that preceded the assault, and I would do this by writing about them as women with lives, not mere metonymies of degradation and pain.

To do this, I delved deeper into crime investigation. Policing, like reporting, takes its toll on those who spend their days up close with the worst that men – and some women – do to those over whom they have power. I profiled specialist officers from Child Protection and the Psychological Crimes Unit dealing with serial rape and murder, as well as narcotics, weapons and gang specialists so as to decipher the patterns – the 'grammar', as I eventually termed it – of the violence I struggled to comprehend.

Through my connections with the specialist units, I met officers who did the day-to-day policing on the streets, a version of armed social work in many cases. Men who walked the fine line between poverty and criminality, daily. These detectives took me under their wing and out onto the streets. The police patrols I accompanied revealed a hidden circulatory system that ran below the public, legal one.

A detective from narcotics took me to the areas on the desolate urban periphery where bodies were dumped after being transported on back roads and unmapped tracks. I saw the dunes where executions took place, where bullet casings were picked up and sent to the ballistics unit on the other side of the highway. He showed me how the tik (crystal methamphetamine) pandemic had decimated the poorer areas of Cape Town, the routes the drugs travelled. I saw the human cost of this drug that infused the veins of poverty and hopelessness.

'There is the money,' he said, pointing to Table Mountain, which seemed as far away as the moon from where we were standing. 'Here,' he swept his arm to include the Cape Flats, 'is the pain.' Then he told me of his own addiction, about losing his family, his subsequent recovery, and how he had found God. As far as I could see, God, whose existence I do not believe in, had abandoned the Cape Flats.

An officer who had grown up in Mitchells Plain took me on patrol with him and we drove around the areas where he had grown up and which he now policed. He had known many of the local gangsters since he was a kid.

'We grew up in the same streets, went to the same schools. Same people,' he said as we stopped at a traffic light, 'different paths in life.'

A call came through on his radio, a woman's voice buried in static. The only words I made out were 'Honda' and 'hijacked'. The captain took off, speeding down the road, his radio spitting out locations. Then we spotted a white Honda ahead of us. He accelerated, weaving through the traffic, gaining on the vehicle, which veered onto a track leading to littered sand dunes. The wheels spun in the sand for a moment before we jerked across the dunes. The Honda slowed and the hijacker, in a red hoodie, leapt out of the vehicle.

'*Hardloop*,' the captain shouted. '*Vang hom!*'

I obeyed his command without a second thought, sprinting hell for leather, my eyes locked on the hoodie bobbing across the dune. I was closing in on him, and the scrawny teenager looked over his shoulder, seemingly horrified at being pursued by a middle-aged white woman.

We stared at each other for a moment, and, at precisely the same time, we turned and ran. Him deeper into the dunes, where he vanished, and me, now that the adrenaline had drained, back to the captain, who came running, his gun drawn. 'So sorry,' he wheezed, 'I forgot it was you. I thought you were my partner.'

That police captain introduced me to a gang leader who dealt mainly in drugs and guns. Violent, volatile men, affiliated with the deadly Number gangs that originated in the prisons, the gang leaders ruled the areas they lived in like warlords. The police were their adversaries, but there was a fraternal element to this dyad, twinned as they were in a dangerous and macabre dance. When power between the gangs and the police was balanced, there was less mayhem and collateral damage. There was carnage whenever a gang leader was released from prison. Then the hierarchies of power and the flows of money from drugs, gun-running and prostitution would be redirected by force as these men reclaimed lost territory.

When a truce was negotiated by the police or by the gang leaders, the streets were safer, and business, whether criminal or not, could be conducted more profitably. When the killings subsided, it meant an equilibrium had been restored and children could go to school without being killed in crossfire.

One of these armed truces was more or less holding when the captain took me to visit a gangster he knew. Outside the man's house were the remnants of an all-night vigil led by the women who lived in the neighbourhood. Inside the barricaded council house, about twenty young men hung about like courtiers around their king. The leader, shirtless, in crimson boxing shorts, sat in an armchair as a king would sit on a throne. There were several women present, but the only one to speak was the old woman cooking an aromatic curry in the open-plan kitchen. She told the captain to get rid of the neighbourhood women outside defaming her son.

The captain explained the harm her son was doing selling drugs, and advised another trade – selling tomatoes at the market, maybe? The gang leader listened but said nothing. All the while, a girl of about sixteen sat at his feet breaking off bits of a Sweetie Pie that she fed to him, as if he were a bird. The young men smiled and said there was no money in selling tomatoes, a point which the police captain conceded. It was surreal and calm as a vicar's visit until a little boy toddled in. He reached for the man, saying, 'Papa.'

The resemblance between man and boy was uncanny, but his father ignored him so completely it was as if the child did not exist and the child, sensing this, burst into tears.

'Think of the boy,' said the captain. 'Make him proud of you.'

The gang leader did not move a muscle. His eyes did not leave the policeman's face. The girl with the Sweetie Pie dropped her hand back into her lap with a piece of chocolate between her fingers. The old woman stopped stirring and, as I saw out of the corner of my eye, the young men closest to the doors melted away. I did not move, but my heart thudded. Then the child's mother darted in and snatched the boy. With her hand clamped over his mouth to muffle his sobs, she disappeared into the house.

The danger was that the police captain had appealed to this man's gentler side – which was not permitted to exist. He had drawn attention to the man's humanity, to the fact he had been a boy once, had a father, too, who neither held nor saw him. An admission of fellow feeling was not permissible.

The words '*Vrou is gif*' (Woman is poison) were tattooed on the gang leader's bare muscular chest. That there might be something feminine in him, something that might soften and give, was unthinkable.

The captain paled. He talked fast, walking this hair-trigger man back, telling him he would speak to the protestors outside the house, get them to give him a break. He was obsequious and deferential, and it worked. When the gangster's girlfriend lifted her hand and placed the piece of chocolate on his tongue, the cop caught my eye. We rose together, thanked them for their time, and got out of there.

forty

Dead women and children make headlines, but men dead from gunshot wounds, stabbings, drunk driving or suicide fill the Salt River Mortuary. I went there to learn the painstaking craft of autopsies from pathologists, who know how to translate injuries into information that might help convict the perpetrators of those wounds.

The bodies that mattered to me were female, most of them dead because of the carelessness or viciousness of the men close to them. One of the murdered girls who haunts me is an eleven-year-old, a skinny little thing, laid out on the mortuary slab. The pathologist recorded one hundred and three separate stab wounds on the figure drawings that form part of the autopsy report. It was impossible to say which had killed her.

She had been murdered in her bedroom by her stepfather. When the police searched the crime scene, they had found a diary she had kept. The pages of the school exercise book were crowded with her rounded handwriting, but instead of homework, she had detailed how her stepfather abused her after his release from prison.

Her writing did not save her life, but it left a record of her pain and outrage. Perhaps that is the case with all writing. It cannot stop or 'unhappen' violence – surely the wish of all victims. All a writer can hope to do, I thought when I read the murdered child's writing and heard her voice, is give an account, ensuring that what has happened is not erased from history.

I pictured her killer's arm rising and falling. Rising and falling as I had once seen a farmer's arm rise and fall, a whip clenched in his fist, flaying the back of the boy whose name I never knew. Neither my witnessing, nor my telling, had made the slightest difference at the time. This girl's fate was no different.

I drove to the sea to walk the horror of that impotence out of me before I went home and made supper for my children. Shocked as I was by what I had seen, I was not surprised. This violence, flowering like a malignant plant, is rooted in the past. It has a lineage. South Africa is a country that makes men by breaking them first. That is the masculinist ethos of the gangs, the police, the apartheid army, and of a wider culture slow to exchange words but lightning quick to trade blows.

I sat on a bench at Three Anchor Bay and watched black oystercatchers running along black rocks. I longed for a return of the numbness that pushed violence into places I could not access, like the time I was released from detention in 1985. Sitting beside that moody ocean I was flooded with the memory of a midnight interrogation by two security policemen. I realised that they, embodiments of the state, regarded me as they did all who challenged their humanity. It was in their eyes as they questioned me in that windowless cell: 'Who is behind this?' 'Give us their names.' 'Don't you know we do this to protect you?'

A theatre of cruelty: a young woman in a nightie locked in a room with hostile men, the barely concealed threat of rape. The shame when one of them stood so close to me my nipple became erect – from fury or fear I cannot say – but he saw it, and smiled. In that moment I saw myself through his eyes. I was expendable rubbish. I absorbed that; it lives in me as body-knowledge. Back in my cell, I curled up under a thin, grey blanket on the top bunk. The prisoner below me stretched her arm up, her hand finding mine.

'You're so cold,' she whispered. 'Are you okay?'

'I'm fine,' I said, but I wasn't. I took my hand back and tucked it with my other one between my legs, but I could not get warm. Every time I closed my eyes, I saw theirs. When I was in their presence, I had mustered enough anger to give me the backbone to refuse answers to their questions. When they put photographs on the table, I glanced at them – grainy surveillance stills of house parties I had forgotten about, clusters of beer drinkers and stoep smokers, pictures of rallies, public meetings – and then I looked away. I refused to pick them up, but that swagger leaked away, and shame, a primal response to vulnerability, flooded in.

Later, I awoke from a dream where twelve spectral men, gaunt as Giacometti figures, with burning coals in their eye sockets, were hunting me. Wherever I looked, wherever I hid, I would see first one, and then the others. I knew that when they caught me, they would shoot me as they would a stray dog. That nightmare continues to recur, enraging me that, by infecting my psyche, they have made me their creature.

I had talked to no one about my insomnia after my release. It would have been absurd when thousands of people were in detention. Movement, I knew already, always worked, at least for a while, and so in 1986 I had flown to Israel, where there were so many soldiers with automatic rifles slung across their bodies that it felt like home.

I had worked as a volunteer on a kibbutz near Natanya, where I assisted with the insemination of turkeys jammed into an enormous battery. The shift started at three in the morning, and it involved following Clayton, the man who did the actual insemination, with a tray of phials. He was also South African, an ex-soldier in his late twenties, and a former member of the Recces, the notorious South African Defence Force reconnaissance unit. The Recces had been responsible for killings inside the country and for horrific attacks in Mozambique, Angola and Namibia. Part of their training, reputedly, was to raise a golden retriever puppy and, when instructed, to kill it. I don't know if that was true – but if it was a lie, it told a truth about how it was imagined that boys are made into men.

I felt as if, instead of escaping, I had taken the country with me. Clayton had sinewy arms, sun-bleached hair, and blue eyes that never focused on my face when he looked at me. There was an adrenaline-tang to the smell of his sweat, and his contained, defensive movements spoke of a constant vigilance that I recognised.

It was cold that early, and dark except for the gleam of lights in the poultry battery. We went inside, stepping into the vast hangar that housed the birds. Our appearance made the turkeys restless. They stirred and shifted in their cages, calling through beaks that had been clipped so that they could not peck each other's eyes out. Feathers floated in the spectral light, and the restive birds, packed so closely that their wing feathers wore away, watched us through round, unblinking eyes.

The first night we did our jobs as we were meant to. Clayton would grab a bird and cross her legs, clamp her between his thighs, tip up her skirt of tail feathers, wipe her clean, and press her belly until her cloaca opened. Then he inserted a vent and injected semen into the protesting hen before tossing her back into the pen with her sisters. I moved alongside him with the tray of semen and instruments. We did not speak apart from the necessary 'Pass me that' and 'Do you need this?' The birds whirled feathers into air that was already thick with dust, but on we went. Bird, clamp, feathers up, cloaca, semen, next, until we heard the shouts signalling that the dawn shift had arrived to collect and polish the turkey eggs.

It was on the fourth night that things went wrong. Clayton was twitchier than usual, his rapid movements suggesting a building agitation. He had been drinking the night before; all of us volunteers had, passing around a bottle of vodka that cost a shekel. But he'd had his own bottle and kept it close.

He was still drunk, but with that focus that gave each of his movements a machine-like precision. As we stepped into the battery and closed the door behind us, he picked up a staple gun used to assemble boxes for transporting birds and eggs. I followed him to the first cage. He lifted a hen, but instead of flipping her over and jabbing her behind, he held the staple gun to her head and fired a bolt into it. He tossed her aside and grabbed another hen, shot her, and grabbed another, then another, the bolts from the staple gun penetrating skull after skull after skull. Blood and feathers whirled in the thick air as the birds grew frantic. Trying to escape him, they trampled the birds with staples in their heads. On he went. I found it hard to breathe. I called his name, but as I put my hand on his arm, he shook me off and carried on loading and shooting.

Then, as suddenly as he had started the massacre, he stopped, turning to face me, the staple gun in his hand. He pushed its cold nose into my belly. I held my breath. When he laughed, I laughed too, and he dropped the gun. It was as if an hallucination had ended.

Clayton's spree, I thought as I watched the sea churn around the rocks below the Sea Point Promenade, felt so normal at the time. Firing bolt after bolt into the brains of birds, my uselessness and horror and relief when he pointed the gun at my belly. I was sure he was going to shoot a staple into me, but I did not move or shout. I remember thinking, *If he shot a staple into my stomach, it would hurt, but he could do me no real damage.* I felt no fear, only a strange desertion of my body, and perhaps because I froze, he did not fire.

I don't know how long we stood there before the dawn shift arrived and there was pounding at the door. Only then was there the shock and shouting because of the blood and the feathers and the birds with bolts in their heads. They asked me what had happened, and I told them he had shot them with the staple gun. They took him away. When I went to his room in the volunteers' quarters later it was empty, and Clayton was gone. But that day in the mortuary, when I had imagined the stepfather raising his knife arm one hundred and three times to stab that girl, I felt that ex-soldier's ghost brush past me.

forty-one

In my early years in Cape Town, there were times when the dead and wounded women I was writing about inhabited my body. I heard their outraged voices in my head asking, 'Why me?' and their despairing imperative: 'Do something.' All I could do to quieten them was to write. Writing enabled me to escape my body, and to inhabit a cerebral, disembodied state where I could think and feel without being overwhelmed.

Writing, with the unflinching attention it requires, was where I waited until the possession was over. Eventually the voices, trapped in the bardo, would recede. When I could again hear the soft night sounds of my garden – an owl, a nightjar, the wind – I knew it was safe to return to myself, check on my sleeping children, go to bed and, in the morning, get up and work once more.

I reported accurately, but all a journalist can do is provide a never-ending list of facts, and those facts could not reach the complex, tangled truth. For that I needed the wider scope of fiction. The form it should take came to me while I was making a documentary in Walvis Bay in 2005. I was shooting inside an incinerator plant in that bleak Namibian port that stinks of fish and guano.

As trussed bags of rubbish were funnelled into the furnace, it occurred to me that this would be the perfect way to get rid of a body. And then, like some kind of annunciation, the outline of my lead character, my private investigator, my justice warrior, appeared to me. Clare Hart, part avenging goddess – a modern-day Fury – and part Tank-girl superhero came to me fully formed and flawed, armed with her PhD in rape and femicide. She would be an activist journalist who was also a profiler, determined to ensure that living women were protected and dead ones avenged.

I told my cameraman we would break early for lunch and dashed back to my hotel. There I rummaged around for some paper, and wrote: *Dr Clare Hart is a contemporary Demeter who avenges dead girls.*

She, like the goddess who rescues her daughter from the death god Hades, who abducted Persephone and took her to the underworld, rescues them.

The apparition of that character, who I imagined as a kind of eye through which I would see and say all the things I had not been able to say as a journalist, restored a sense of control to me. I would fashion the real crimes I knew about, with all their senseless loss, into something where there was meaning. With this fictional character, I would be able to write the endings I wanted – justice, revenge, survival. I mapped out a novel about girls going missing, weaving together elements of specific crimes, the survivors, and bereaved relatives I had met.

I felt a surge of excitement and joy, as if I was the first woman Dr Clare Hart rescued. I had already outlined a literary novel that purported to be a spare, restrained examination of South Africa. But it was derivative, sterile and insular. I was after a broad and cinematic sweep that would capture what I thought of then as history with a small 'h' – the experience of ordinary people – rather than the now-mythic capital-letter History of South Africa's transformation. I wanted to write about the complexity of what was actually happening, on the streets, the sand dunes of my surroundings.

Writing fiction about crime was the only way I could think of to capture South Africa's spectacular post-apartheid violence and its effects on ordinary people. I found a form that would allow me to examine the whole of the society that produced the crimes of violence. There was one problem – a feminist one. The 'pleasure' of crime fiction, like film noir, or any Hitchcock movie, is the spectacle of the femme fatale, the violated woman, the beautiful female corpse. But since this was the only literary frame I felt I could use to write about South Africa, I would bend the rules to make it work for me.

The second problem was financial. Several years had gone by, and my husband's one-man practice had yet to turn a profit, so I did not have much financial leeway. I did not know how to reconcile writing novels – a loss-making activity if ever there was one, as I did not have a publisher – with the necessity of feeding, clothing and educating our children.

I mulled this over, and by the time I got home, I had settled on making my fiction writing into a business. To pull that off, what I needed was a business card.

'I would like to get my card printed,' I told the graphic designer I met the next day. 'I prefer plain fonts without curls and flourishes. Arial or Helvetica. Something that does not draw attention to itself.'

'Okay,' she said. 'What is it you do?'

Too embarrassed to say I was going to write a novel, I gave her a long list of all the things I'd previously done. She look unhappy, so I said I created stories in different forms to help people make sense of difficult things.

Her face lit up. 'You're a writer,' she said, pleased that she had a simple word that would fit onto a small rectangle.

'Not really,' I said, uneasy with that claim. 'Not yet.'

'What else can I put on the card that will fit?' she asked me. 'You've got to start somewhere.' She had a point there, so I agreed.

A week later my cards were ready. They were in a plastic box, with a sample taped to the lid. In a bright and terrible orange, it shrieked 'WRITER'. The word was huge, taking up half the card.

'Why is that there?' I pointed at the offending word. The orange pulsed at me, and I felt the twinge of a migraine at the base of my skull pulse in response.

'It's what you are.'

A claw reached up through my skull, squeezing and twisting my right eye and shooting pain through my head.

'And here are your details.' Discreet silvery-grey letters and numerals that people who wanted a WRITER could use to contact me. Because of a special offer at the printer, there were five hundred cards; she thought I might as well have the extra cards so that five hundred people could contact me. There was nothing for it but to take them. The whole card and writing business felt like a scam, but that is how I became a writer.

forty-two

The pathologist who taught me what bullets do to the human body connected me with his hunting buddy and fellow gun enthusiast, the head of ballistics in the Western Cape. *Come visit*, the colonel emailed, *I will teach you everything you need to know about gangs, guns and ballistics*. On the appointed day, I drove along the windswept road that curves around False Bay until I reached the turnoff, barely signposted, to a weapons-testing military facility.

The guards at the gate already had my name and car registration. They gave me a visitor's pass and waved me through. I drove through dense scrub towards a cluster of prefab buildings. I parked, and a short, burly man in an immaculate uniform appeared.

I handed the colonel one of my orange WRITER cards, but instead of looking at it, he was peering over my shoulder. 'Where are your bodyguards?' he asked.

'I don't have any,' I replied.

'When Patricia Cornwall came here, she had two,' he said.

'I'm not famous.'

The colonel chuckled. 'Maybe you're just more used to South Africa than she is,' he said as he escorted me inside. 'The Doc – our mutual friend, the pathologist – tells me you're from Namibia.'

'I am,' I said.

'I love that country,' he sighed. 'I fought there in the Bush War. Me and my old army buddies still go hunting every year.'

We were walking down a dim corridor – the only light came from open doors through which I glimpsed women poring over papers on their desks. It struck me, as it had in the other forensic labs, that it was all women doing this work.

'Much better attention to detail than men,' said the Colonel. 'They stay calm and look for the evidence to convict in court.'

A policewoman who specialised in serial rape cases once told me that when she needed a break from her anger at the unrelenting trauma, she stayed home and drank for a week before returning to the work. 'Anger,' she told me, 'clouds your judgement.' I never took to binge drinking, but I also caged my anger. It took me years to connect the migraines crippling me several times a month with the fury I turned inwards: the conversion of righteous anger into pain.

'Men get angry,' said the colonel as we continued down the corridor, 'and they don't see what's in front of them, they just want to get out and *moer* the criminals.'

He opened the door to an office where a rosy-cheeked officer stood at a table covered with intricately marked sheets of paper. 'Sergeant Smith here is my secret weapon,' he said. 'I taught her, but she's the brains of this whole ballistics operation.'

'Stop it, Colonel,' she said in the half-amused, half-weary tone with which young women deflect older men who persist in claiming their work with avuncular charm.

The colonel stood proudly by as she explained how each bullet that's fired carries unique markings. When the police seized a gun, they fired it so that they could match the grooves to those on bullets extracted from a body or found at a crime scene. Smith used this information to track the weapons used in the sporadic taxi wars that kill scores of innocent Cape Town commuters.

'I match a hitman to his victim through these tracings left on the bullet as it's propelled out of the barrel of a gun.' She showed me the images. 'That's how we work out that the same guns are used in a number of hits.' Smith's mapping looked like a highly complex family tree, which Darwin himself might have admired. 'That,' she told me, 'guides us to the person who fired the gun. Once we have that, we can trace who it is that hires the killers. That's how we stop organised crime.'

Next, the colonel showed me an arsenal, enough for a small army, of semi-automatic weapons. 'These are the weapons from the taxi wars and cash-in-transit robberies,' he said. 'Over there,' he pointed to shelves of pistols and revolvers, 'the crimes against women you were asking me about.' The tags hanging from each weapon had a number, date and location. 'These were all used in armed robberies and domestics.'

'Do you shoot?' the colonel asked.

'No,' I replied.

'Then you must try it.'

Each of those guns had killed or maimed someone. I recoiled at the thought of touching any of them. I shook my head.

'How're you going to write about guns if you don't know what it feels like to fire one?'

'They've done so much harm,' I said.

'There's no such thing as bad guns,' he grinned. 'Just bad people. Come with me – you're going to love it.'

The colonel hurried me out to the shooting range, which had been made from a shipping container. Inside, it was padded with Kevlar to prevent a misfired bullet ricocheting off the metal walls and into anyone nearby.

'Pistols, revolvers, machine guns,' he told me, waving at various weapons. I was staring at the machine guns. They frightened me. 'Carry on,' said the colonel. 'You'll find your match.'

I ran my hands over several of the smaller guns, and then I saw a tiny Browning, picked it up and held it in my hand. It fitted perfectly. The charge it sent through my body was electric. The body does not lie – this was my match. I felt the power of that gun, so snug and small in my palm. The unnerving sensation that lethal object gave me was one of supreme power.

I took aim, following the colonel's instructions exactly, and fired the Browning at the cardboard cut-out of a running man on the far wall. Five out of six shots hit the target and brought it down.

The colonel was pleased with me. I was pleased with myself.

'You want to try an AK now?'

Full of adrenaline, I nodded.

'The automatic rifles are better suited to a man's longer arms,' said the colonel, handing me one. The AK-47 was heavy and awkward, and it threw me off balance.

'Hold it like you would a baby.' The colonel showed me how to balance the weapon by cocking my hip. 'If you're doing a bank robbery, you're inside,' he said. 'So, you must fire in short bursts otherwise the ricochets could hit you. But if you're doing a cash-in-transit robbery, you're outside, then you can just fire as if you were Rambo.'

'I'll bear that in mind,' I said, and I fired the first burst. The gun kicked against my shoulder, leaving a bruise that would last for weeks – but I obliterated the target that the colonel had set up. I had an inkling now of what it felt like to be a perpetrator. The sense of invincibility that comes from holding a lethal weapon is intoxicating. A gun gives you the power of life and death over another person. Momentarily, it turns you into a god. I'd not known that to write about violence, I needed to understand that thrill, that pleasure, that cruelty.

'You're a natural marksman,' said the colonel, taking the gun from me. 'You deserve a beer, but it's not Friday, so all I can offer is coffee.'

'I've got to pick up my kids from school,' I told him.

'No problem. Come back, and I'll teach you to throw grenades.'

I laughed and said, 'Just what I need to know.'

'What I've been showing you is the science,' he said as we walked back to my car. 'But in some cases it's just dumb luck. We had that now with a cold case. Arrested a man the other day for murdering a schoolgirl twenty-five years ago.'

'You had ballistics evidence to charge him?' I asked.

'No,' he said. 'The killer gave his new girlfriend a gold watch for her birthday. She saw a woman's name engraved on the back of it and she asked who it belonged to. He told her it belonged to a girl he'd killed and if she ever backchatted him, he'd do the same to her. So, she gave the watch to the police, telling the cops her new boyfriend had murdered the girl whose name was on the back of it. They checked. They found the name from twenty-five years ago. The case was still open, and so we got him. No science, just chance.'

To me, it sounded like a woman's courage, not chance, but I did not say so. Instead, I asked who she was. I went cold when I heard her name. Her murder had haunted me.

'She was from Namibia,' I said.

'That's right,' he said. 'Did you know her?'

'I knew of her,' I said. 'We were boarders in Cape Town at the same time. We never met, but our families knew each other.'

'Her killer will sit for life,' the cheerful colonel said. 'That's something for the parents, though it won't bring their daughter back.'

forty-three

I was oblivious to the traffic roaring past me as I drove home that afternoon. My thoughts were with that murdered Namibian girl, whom I will call Constance. You could say I wrote my novels for her. But saying I wrote my novels because of her would be right too. I somehow absorbed her when she was murdered. No matter how much I tried to forget her, bury her settle her ghost, she fought on. Though she could not speak, she would not be silenced. Her ghost – her shock, her fear, her rage at being murdered – had taken possession of me, set up house, and stayed, despite my attempts at eviction.

My boarding school was close to hers. Like me, she had been sent south to be educated, and was walking back to school the night she was killed. Namibia, referred to as 'the Border' in those apartheid days, had no social currency in Cape Town's insular adolescent universe. Maybe she, too, had sensed the exclusion I'd felt, driving her to walk home. Or maybe all she wanted was the cool, dark freedom offered by the night.

But this is what I do know: Constance was invited to a party on a Saturday evening. She went, but at some stage in the evening she'd had enough, and decided to walk home, except it was not home. Perhaps there were attempts to stop her, perhaps not, but no one arranged a lift, so Constance walked alone down the quiet, tree-lined streets of moneyed Rondebosch, and she was attacked.

She fought back – that much was evident from the autopsy report. But to no avail. She was bludgeoned and stabbed to death, her battered body left in a littered patch of shrubs alongside a busy road, cars passing by while she'd defended herself and then died of head injuries and stab wounds.

All culpability lay with the perpetrator; the violence was his pleasure. His hands first maimed, then killed. No sense can be made of any of this unless one starts right there, with him. But that is not how the world thinks, and so Constance's death became a cautionary tale.

That a girl could be blamed for her own death because she decided to walk home, maddened me as much then as it does now.

If I could have spoken to her, I would have asked: *What drove you to walk alone at night? What happened at that party? Was it courage or shame that made you take your life in your hands? Were you possessed by a wish not to be alive? If so, then who or what caused that death wish? Isn't it better to give in than to be dead?*

Back home in Oranjezicht, I looked for the collage my sister had made from my school photos. There, in the bottom right-hand corner, was the black-and-white photograph taken at my Standard Eight dance. I am smiling like a girl at a dance should smile. Except, if one looks closer, there is nothing in the eyes but a manic glitter. I lifted the sticker I had placed over the face of the boy-man on whose lap I was sitting.

The sight of him, obscured for years, was a shock. Mine being an all-girls school, and me not having been in Cape Town long enough to know anyone to invite to a dance meant that the older sister of a classmate had to arrange a partner for me.

My blind date was exactly as I remembered him: black hair, a moustache, and high cheekbones that made his face look like stubbled granite. He had been twenty to my fifteen, a gulf of years as he was already halfway through his university degree. I knew he'd had to be persuaded, and I recoiled from his cursory perusal, but I smiled and tried to be entertaining to make up for my disappointing appearance. He hardly bothered to reply, and did not ask who I was, where I was from or what I was interested in. I wanted to run, but instead I climbed into the crowded, drunken car that picked us all up.

We arrived at a palatial house with a marquee near a swimming pool, and a lawn that disappeared into shadowy trees. There was a big bowl of punch, and smuggled-in vodka and gin. I didn't notice much food, but I wouldn't have eaten much anyway. I had starved myself the previous week, and I remember the pleasurable feeling of my hipbones against my sage-green skirt. I had made myself as thin as possible. I wanted him to think I was pretty, to approve of me, though there was nothing about him that I liked. I did not know what to do except pretend that his resentment didn't exist. So, I tried to smile and make conversation, but eventually I stopped talking and just sipped my drink. When he said, 'Come outside with me,' I went, though I did not want to.

I did not know the etiquette of refusal, and so I let him lead me into the darkness. As soon as we were beyond the light from the marquee, with its dancing people and the thump of the music, he pulled me down onto the wet grass. Without any warning, his uninvited hands were under my shirt. He tried to kiss me, and the inside of my lip split where he jammed my closed lips into my teeth. He forced my mouth open so that I had to take in his tongue. I did not move or resist; I wasn't able to say no – it was difficult to breathe – so I vanished into myself. From there, I could see what was happening, but it did not reach me.

When someone called his name, he discarded me and went back inside. My thighs hurt. So did my ribs and breasts. All of me hurt because, to him, all of me had been there for the taking. I followed behind him because there was nowhere else to go.

Later, when photographs were being taken, he pulled me onto his lap and laughed. How *easy* I was. That is what he whispered. There was nothing I could do or say right then, but it made me understand why a girl would choose to leave a party and walk into the night.

forty-four

I put the collage back into the kist jammed with photographs, but that memory would not go back into its box. Instead, the reliving of that experience brought into focus how, even though I had split it off, I had not freed myself. Three-and-a-half years after that scuffle on the lawn, I set out to master my feelings about men and sex. At the time, I mistook the ambivalent mix of fascination and fear for desire, which perhaps it was.

I was eighteen, and having just finished with school, I was determined to divest myself of my virginity, which, I felt, carried the embarrassing stain of innocence. I was determined to get this over and done with during the summer between leaving school and starting university. Sex would release me from the prison of childhood. Sex, on my terms, would be my secret but unilateral declaration of independence, as long as it did not involve love.

Love had derailed girls I knew at school, sex being the high price they paid for being in love, a state I had secretly yearned for but which seemed to short-circuit the capacity to think rationally. It was this fear of the stupefying effect of love, or so I told myself, not the fear of vulnerability, that had stopped me from sleeping with the boyfriend I sneaked out to see in my last year of school. I was sure that if *I* chose the person, place and time, I'd avoid losing control by falling in love. I approached this mission as if it were a military campaign. I wanted someone who knew what he was doing. He had to be older. He had to have had sex, which meant he had to have had a girlfriend.

I met a suitable candidate at a party in Windhoek. He was a South African army medic, doing his two-year military conscription in Namibia. He was twenty-seven, and had lived with a girlfriend. He wasn't bad-looking – eyes a soft brown in his tanned face. I didn't get too irritated with his conversation, but most importantly he lived alone – there'd be no witnesses. And so, after we had been seeing each other for about a week, he picked me up one hot Saturday afternoon and drove me to his flat.

It was not much cooler inside, though the light was less blinding. In the kitchen he poured me a glass of water because my mouth was dry; there was some food on the counter, and beers in the fridge. He opened one for himself and gave me a sip.

The bathroom, which I needed as urgently as I had needed the water, was dirty. It smelled of man. It smelled of him. There was a splash of urine on the floor, which turned my stomach, but I was determined.

There was the bedroom, and there he was, in it, waiting for me. I went in and put my bag down. I had to keep the momentum going, so I lay down on the bed. I looked up at the stained ceiling, wondering how the roof could have leaked, as there were four or five levels above us. Then the mushroom-coloured stain undulated as he began to move on top of me. After the first sharp stab I got used to it. Then he stopped. The sound he was making also stopped, which was a relief because it sounded too raw. As if he had forgotten himself.

I was elated I had passed this milestone to womanhood, but I wanted him to get off me. I wanted to get up. I didn't know how to tell him that without seeming rude. I wanted to go home. I wanted to be alone.

He propped himself up on his elbows and smiled down at me. There was sweat on his forehead. When I sat up I saw the streaks of blood on the sheet. His eyes filled with tender amazement. 'Why didn't you tell me?' he asked.

'Tell you what?'

'That you were a virgin.'

'It wasn't important,' I said. What I actually meant was that it was none of his business, but I could see that he thought it was. He put his arms around me and cradled me, murmuring my name into my sweaty hair. He was claiming me. I seethed with rage. I had done this to claim myself. I had ceded *nothing* of myself to him.

I carried on seeing him. There'd otherwise have been questions I wouldn't have known how to answer, but at the end of January 1983, I left for the University of Cape Town. There, he said, I would become a woman's libber and stop shaving. I laughed and said I wouldn't. When I returned to Windhoek at the end of my first term, the first thing he did was check under my arms. He tweaked the hairs. It was true, I had stopped shaving. He said he'd known this would happen because of my attitude.

The woman's movement, I told him, had opened my eyes to things. I didn't understand how he could serve in the apartheid army. He said that hadn't bothered me at Christmastime, when he was my boyfriend. When I said he wasn't my boyfriend, I felt like crying. Even though I didn't like him, I'd really have liked to have a boyfriend, but it could never be him. I had used him, and now we both knew it, so that was the end of that.

forty-five

The murdered girl from Walvis Bay, whom I called Constance, haunted me because her murder had pierced a protective illusion of mine – and that of many other women too, I think. She was my doppelganger. She was beaten to death, but it could just as easily have been me, which is one step away from thinking that if it had been me, then she might still be alive.

I was burdened with the feeling that she had gone in my place, a form of survivor's guilt. We had done the same things, after all, gone to the same places, walked the same streets. There is no reason why one girl is murdered, and another is not. It's a matter of wrong place, wrong time, and the bad luck of running into a bad man.

I entwined Constance into my fiction to honour her ghost and manage my fear, my misplaced guilt. Fiction gave me an imaginative power over the lives and deaths of women that journalism did not. I dealt with the haunting effect of Constance's murder (and my not-murder) by changing the ending of her life. To do this, I made Constance the twin sister of my heroine, Clare Hart. Though neither sophisticated nor original, this literary gambit gave me a way to examine how violence divides women from themselves.

My cerebral and impenetrable heroine, Clare Hart, could walk by herself at night with impunity, and as a schoolgirl she does this. But her twin, Constance, cannot. Clare, who, one evening, was returning to boarding school from an illicit tryst, comes across her battered, left-for-dead twin, who had tried to follow her, and she ends up saving her sister's life. Constance is her other self, or her body-self. Clare's determination to bring male perpetrators to justice determines her career as a journalist and profiler. My fictional character's resolve reflected my own.

But fiction only goes so far. I could bring Constance back to life, but only as a reclusive Lady Lazarus. The damage and the scars women carry cannot be erased, but they can be understood and avenged. And so, the resolution of my first novel, a serial rape-femicide thriller, is achieved through the actions of a character who survives a brutal assault and seeks redress at Rape Crisis – a Cape Town organisation to which I personally had referred several women and girls.

I knew the centre well. It was in Observatory, round the corner from where I'd lived as an undergraduate; in my student days, I had done fund- and awareness-raising for it. I met with the director, who had been a fellow student. She was as thoughtful and steadfast as I remembered her to be. I found her informed belief that a woman's life, if interrupted by an assault, could and would go on, restorative. She and the women working with her did their best for the rape survivors who came for counselling and then, with varying degrees of success, pieced their lives together again.

This talking cure, this reshaping of an obliterating experience by means of a story that could be told – certain elements foregrounded, others left out – seemed to me to return a sense of agency and control over an experience that had stolen a woman from herself. Was it this telling and reshaping, I wondered, that helped alleviate the sense of shame that took up residence in the victim, seemingly at a cellular level? As if shame was somehow a psychic virus transmitted by the perpetrator. I came to know the divide, experienced as a rupture in time, between a woman's sense of who she is prior to the attack and afterwards: the shattering of that self.

That break in time is at the heart of the traumatic experience, as is the compulsive return to the experience. The psyche tries to stitch together the tear in linear time and to restore the woman to herself, intact. But this is not possible. We cannot go back, we cannot make things unhappen. But we can go on, and that is what we, as women, try to do.

Male violence makes women police what we say and where we go, but to reclaim our streets, homes and bodies, we must break the silence. Speaking out is one aspect of this, legal redress another. Rape Crisis volunteers are available to accompany survivors to court, and I once accompanied a woman and sat beside her as the rapist's lawyer shredded her account, her integrity and her reputation. The director was a proponent of pressing charges, even if the justice system – cops, prosecutors and judges – rarely believes women, and frequently blames them for the crimes committed against them.

Rape Crisis, with its solidarity, kindness and belief in women, finds ways of converting hopelessness into resilience, and anger into action.

And I was angry. To survive as a woman in South Africa, I had to be angry; just being a woman means you're afraid a lot of the time. Most of all, though, I needed to be a feminist to channel my fury and fear into a transformative politics.

I held poetry workshops with rape survivors, which helped me understand ways in which women are able to reject the shame of rape, returning it to its rightful place: the perpetrator. With the women's permission, I wove much of this into my fiction, transforming their stories into a broad canvas of crime committed against girls and women in my country.

Two things struck me about rapists I'd encountered in my research – their ordinariness and their shamelessness, minimising their own crimes. One man rattled off a list of things he had done on the day of a rape: woke up, had cornflakes for breakfast, spoke to a friend on the phone, watched TV, 'had sex with' a girl, hung out with friends, watched more TV, went to bed. The rape – which he did not name as such – was no more or less consequential than anything else he had done that day. And so his sentence, several years in prison, seemed to him totally out of proportion to something that was, to him, as inconsequential as eating breakfast or having a beer. For the victim, however, it had been a day of trauma, forcing her, like so many others, to spend months or years or forever dealing with the fallout of a catastrophic event.

The shamelessness and the solipsism of that rapist transfixed me. It was as if, through the malignantly transfiguring power of his act, he was able to rid himself of his own shame and vulnerability – which, unable to integrate, he projected onto his victim. She, vulnerable at home and also outside of it, then absorbed and carried the perpetrator's shame as if it were her own.

forty-six

Questions of power lie at the heart of my novels. Each one has started with a vision that comes to me in the form of a single close-up of two people caught, as if by a flashbulb, in a situation of dominance and submission. These mental snapshots have been the kernel of all the stories I have told. There is nothing mystical about these images – they come to me in the everyday course of my life when, out of the corner of my eye, I glimpse an interaction, often quick or quickly hidden, that reveals a more complex, frightening, malignant connection between the pair. That is what intrigues me. To unspool the narrative I sense behind the still, I begin a storyboard with that single image. As a film director might, I map out the scene in a sequence of frames so that I can see what things look and feel like from the point of view of both characters.

Once I had written the first few chapters of my first novel, I sent them, together with a proposal, to several publishers. My anxious waiting was met with several agonising weeks of silence. I thought that was bad, but then the rejections came, thick and fast. Some were curt, some not, but they all said no. It was crushing, but I wasn't giving up.

I signed up to do another writing workshop with the late Anne Schuster, a gifted poet and teacher who showed me how to write from the margins, to find my voice, to say what I wanted to say, and to say it true.

Anne's intensive writing course stretched over five days in a café overlooking Kalk Bay harbour, and it was during a mid-morning coffee break on the last morning, a Friday, that I received a phone call from the publisher of a tiny new women's fiction imprint, Oshun.

'I love the proposal and your first chapters,' Michelle Matthews said. 'I love your lead character, Clare Hart. We want to publish.'

I was speechless.

'Are you there?' she said into the silence.

'I'm here, I'm here,' I squeaked. 'You can publish it.'

'Can we meet on Monday?' she asked. 'We can talk about when you can deliver the manuscript. Does that work for you?'

That worked very well for me.

I sat down. My legs seemed to have stopped working. I had a publishing deal; now all I had to do was finish the book.

I went back into the workshop. Everyone was writing. I picked up the prompt: 'Standing at the garden gate … ' I was meant to freewrite for twenty minutes, but my writing hand was frozen by the enormity of the new task I now faced.

Anne, sensing my agitation, came over and asked what was wrong. I told her what had happened, the euphoria of my success already being washed away by the terror of not being able to follow through, of not being able to live up to the expectations of others. She put a hand on my arm. She was a warm woman, but she had never touched me before, and the feel of her cool palm on my skin was a comfort. I composed myself.

'What is this?' she asked me, picking up the storyboard I had brought with me. It depicted the stick figure of a girl crouched in a corner, her arms over her head, the threatening figure of a man looming over her.

'It's for the prologue of the book I have to finish,' I told her. 'This is to be its heart. I am trying to understand what happened to the girl.'

There was more I wanted to say – things about plot and how thrillers are all about the second act, so they needed action – but my throat closed, and I couldn't speak.

Anne picked up the poster-sized sheet of paper and put it aside. 'For now,' she said gently, handing me my pen, 'write what you know.'

She intuited rape was something I knew; she gave me the permission I did not know I needed to set it down. I ask you to bear with me, reader, while I tell you about the rupture I circle in my writing about women. This is what I wrote down:

On a weekday evening in 1984 when I was twenty, I visited a rundown student house a few blocks away from mine. Someone from that other house must have invited me to come by, I can't remember why. The façade of the house was painted with patchy whitewash. Dry leaves skittered on the oxblood-red stoep. I knocked on the panelled front door. The door opened. The passageway was crowded with magazines, book bags and a bicycle. The kitchen was at the end. There were four plates streaked with spaghetti and tomato sauce on the table. I was not offered anything to eat.

They were older than me, the people in that house. They did real politics and they called each other 'comrade', or 'com' for short. They talked about the class struggle and the military industrial complex. They debated tactics for dealing with the apartheid state. They had many facts. They had few doubts. It was apparent, to my shame, that I did not think the right things, say the right words, dress correctly. I wiped off my lipstick when no one was looking. I was handed a glass of wine.

Maybe by him, this man with his eyes fixed on me standing in the middle of his bedroom. His hair lay flat on his head, leaving his skull exposed but not vulnerable. I turned to the piles of books and papers on his desk. Notes for essays. Thick textbooks – thicker than mine.

'My subjects have thinner books,' I said.

'Yes,' he said, with crushing certainty. I laughed, not because he was funny, but because I was ill at ease. When he shut the door, I dropped a book.

'Butterfingers,' I said as I picked it up and put it back.

I don't know why I was in his room. I can't remember how I got from the table with the others to this room where there was only him and me. I don't know why I sat on his bed when he told me to. I don't know why I could not move when his lean arms went around me. I don't know why it made me laugh when he kissed me, but his cold, fat tongue bottled the sound in my throat. I don't know why I did not bite.

He let me go and my shirt was off, and on the floor.

The door was closed. It was not locked, but I did not know how to get to it because my legs had stopped working. I told them to walk, but they ignored my instructions and betrayed me. My grubby beige bra was there on the floor too.

'On your knees,' he said.

I obeyed.

'Your hands and knees.' His hand was on my back. Between the shoulder blades. My skin twitched, but it could not dislodge him. He pushed me down and there I was, like he had told me to be, on my hands and knees. Like a dog.

Stupid to have worn a skirt. My panties went. There they were on the floor too. I tried to crawl forward, but he had my hair, which was dirty, in one hand and my waistband in the other. He was in. It hurt. I turned my head. His lips were a thin crimson slash in his face. He went faster. Something tore. The shame of the noises he made.

He was done.

He freed himself of me.

I dressed. Said goodbye because I did not know how else to make this thing-that-happened unhappen, to make it be another thing. I don't remember how I got from his house back to mine. I do remember that I lay on my bed and stared at the ceiling and waited for the night to pass.

forty-seven

It had not occurred to me that I was finding ways to look at myself, but indirectly, so that I could examine experiences I was unable to integrate in my own psyche, but that I could tell as someone else's story.

It had not occurred to me that I was trying to heal my own wounds.

It had not occurred to me I was writing to be free.

It had not occurred to me that I was using the investigative eye I had constructed in my fiction as a reflective shield, so that I could regard Medusa, herself a raped and wounded woman who turned any man who looked at her into stone, and that I could do this without turning into stone myself.

It had not occurred to me that what happened in that room was connected to how confused my eating habits became. All I knew was I did not want to take anything in. And if I did, I threw up.

Now I can look at my twenty-year-old self and see that in that room I had not been able to disappear or control my own body – but beyond that, I could control food. To ease the anxiety, bondage-tight around my chest, I starved myself, as if making myself disappear might be a solution. For surely it had been my fault? I had gone into his room, but what had I done to make him do what he did to me? A misunderstanding, perhaps. If there was a way to view myself with less dishonour, I could not find it.

I was a fighter. I have come to think that my angry not-eating was a riot of sorts: a protest in a language I did not yet know how to interpret.

And I had insomnia.

A few weeks later I made an appointment with Student Health, which offered a free service for students who had, in its words, 'trouble coping'. I arrived at two-thirty, but the nurse who checked my name said I wouldn't be talking to her, that I must go into the consulting room to see the psychologist.

The man sitting at the desk had naked, hairy thighs protruding from blue rugby shorts, but it was too late to back out. 'So, Miss Orford,' he said. 'What's the matter, then?'

'I can't sleep,' I said. 'I can't concentrate. I have headaches. My heart races.'

He noted these down. 'Anything else?'

I felt around for the words to tell him about the feeling I had of futility and despair, but those were words I could not find, so I said, 'It's difficult to eat. I—'.

He cast an eye over me, interrupting, 'You don't need to lose weight.'

'I'm not dieting,' I said sharply, angry at him for talking about food when I was trying to tell him something about sex. 'It's just, I don't want to take anything in.'

The man smiled. It was funny, I supposed, me scrabbling for the words I did not have for what had happened – which was not, as a friend had suggested, just bad sex. I knew what bad sex was. I'd had plenty of it. Bad sex was sad, funny, disappointing or just silly. It had never left me feeling exiled from myself. I could not tell the doctor any of that.

'Well then,' he said, 'the best thing to do is to go to bed early, to eat regularly, to take plenty of exercise, and to do your work.'

'I *do* do my work,' I was not yet ready to give in to him. To give up. 'I go to bed, but I don't sleep.'

'Early nights.' The counsellor snapped my file shut. 'Try that for a few weeks. It usually does the trick. If it doesn't, come back and see me.'

It had been a mistake to ask for help for something I could not name. *Fuck you*, I wanted to say, but I did not.

The unspoken fury burned as I walked out, burned as I drove home. Burned until I got home and stripped and stood naked in front of the mirror. Then the rage, with nowhere else to go except inwards, flipped and turned to self-loathing.

How disgusting you are, mocked the metronymic inner voice, a shark that had scented blood. *Fat. Useless. Ludicrous that you are even alive.*

The glare I had internalised, the gaze of patriarchy, had its sights on me. It would have destroyed me, but that day my anger at the psychologist, his patronising dismissal, his grotesque sexism, gave *me* the power. Then it came, my lifesaving 'No!'

A new voice, distinct and clear, authoritative yet kind, had intercepted my familiar mad spiral.

'No,' it said to my reflection in the mirror. 'You can starve yourself for the rest of your life,' said that steady, no-nonsense woman's voice. 'Or you can do other things.'

Other things, I knew, meant reading, writing, becoming a useful person. So, I turned my back on the reflection of my body in the mirror, a body that got itself into bad situations and did not defend itself. I did not want that recalcitrant body to drag me down. To save myself I had to ignore its wilful refusals. I was not hungry, but I felt faint. And so, resolute as a warrior, I put my clothes on, went into the kitchen, got out the bread, cut two slices, and put them into the toaster.

Pop. Out they shot. Something wrong with the mechanism. I picked up the pieces and put them on a plate. Spread butter. Grated some cheese and sliced a tomato. Sprinkled salt. Crackled pepper. And was at a loss.

'Bite, chew, swallow,' I told myself. 'That is how to eat. Bite and chew.'

The crusts sliced the roof of my mouth, but I didn't stop. I didn't spit it out. Even though masticated food would stick in my throat, I swallowed. I got it down.

My stomach turned at the arrival of the intruding bread, but I would not give in. I would not be sick. I would not lean over the toilet and vomit. I would not let my rebellious body turn on me. The sandwich went down, and with it I swallowed everything I could not name.

I left the kitchen and opened my books. My second-year exams were coming up soon. My intellect would save me. All I needed was to hold it together and get a sprinkling of firsts, the results I needed to get into Honours, do a Master's and, one day – the yet unforeseen Covid lockdown of 2021 – the PhD that would make me, like my father, a Dr Orford.

forty-eight

The publication of my first novel, *Like Clockwork,* in 2006 was a joy. I kissed my author's copies when they arrived at my house and signed many copies for friends and relations. Soon after publication, I found a literary agent in London. She auctioned the rights to that book as well as my second novel, *Blood Rose,* published the next year, which was set in Namibia. The auction was as thrilling to me as a prize fight would be to a boxer.

Both novels were translated into German, French, Spanish and several other languages. I went on book tours and did press interviews. I had become, to my astonishment, a professional writer. The Clare Hart series freed me from my other work. The deadlines felt like a heart attack, but putting words on the page was how I sustained my family. There was nothing for it but to put my impostor syndrome aside and write the next book in the series.

That is what I was doing when I received this lovely Facebook message from Georg, a man I had loved and travelled with twenty years earlier. It gave me much pleasure to see his name, although I had not seen him since I was twenty-two, at the end of 1986, my travelling year. We had parted in Morocco, with him going back to Italy. I had lost my nerve, and instead of travelling on with him, I went back to South Africa. Seeing his name again conjured that parallel life, one I didn't lead, as I opened the message.

> *Margie,*
> *It is you! This is us! Writer. Photographer. Our dreams came true.*
> *Love Georg*

He had attached a photograph of two books displayed in a shop in the Italian Alps. Our names, side by side – the German translation of my novel, *Blood Rose*, and his magnificent portraits of the Dolomites.

I felt such a rush of affection for him and for my young self, finding each other at that terminus in Lisbon. We had missed the bus south because neither of us understood Portuguese, which was how we came to strike up a conversation of mutual commiseration. I spoke English and the rudimentary German I had learned doing horse riding in Namibia. Georg spoke Italian and German. And so, when we found another bus, we spoke German all the way to Faro.

When we arrived, we hadn't said all we wanted to say, and so on we went, falling in love, both frustrated and exhilarated by the limits of language. We were still talking when we reached Gibraltar, so on we travelled, to Tangiers, Fes and Meknes. In Marrakesh we slept on a rooftop, lying side by side looking up the stars.

'What do you want to be?' asked Georg, resting his warm hand on my belly.

'A writer. And you?'

'A photographer,' he replied, 'of mountains.'

Later, I had startled awake from a dream. I could not recall the details, but I had dreamed in German, the language Georg and I shared. Until then I had not realised that one dreamed in a language, or that the unconscious had a mother tongue. In the German dream, I had been as foreign to myself as I'd felt when confessing to Georg my deepest wish, which was to write.

He must have sensed something because, in his sleep, he reached for me and pulled me close. In his arms, and for as long as night lasted, I felt safe with the stranger I had become. After we parted ways in Casablanca, I cried all the way back to Tangiers. But now he had written to me, I saw that Georg, who had loved me with such tenderness, had kept my younger self safe until it was time to return her to me intact. We had fulfilled the delicate magic, the hopefulness of our time in Morocco. A quarter of a century later, our books had reconnected us. The serendipity of it all restored to me a forgotten sense of dreaming and roaming: *Blood Rose* had travelled all the way to Georg's alpine village.

forty-nine

The work I was doing was starting to take its toll on me, and Georg's delighted note of a dream come true was a lifeline, so I grabbed it. I was, I realised after I wrote back to thank him, losing faith in writing, which was the same as losing faith in myself. What good, in the face of all this violence, did writing do? I did not have an answer, so I put the question aside and went back to work on my third novel, a kind of prequel in which I would explore the erotic backstory to the professional partnership between Clare Hart and Riedwaan Faizal.

In May 2007, a literary festival in Franschhoek held a prize-giving ceremony for poetry written by inmates of the maximum-security prison on its outskirts. The competition had been part of the festival's community outreach. I was pleased to join other writers invited to attend the ceremony at the prison. On arrival, we were each assigned a group of prisoners who had submitted their poems.

The minute we went through the gates, I was assailed by memories I'd thought had lost their potency years earlier. I had, after all, turned my prison sojourn into a party anecdote. But driving through the huge gates looking up at the inhumanly high razor-wire fences, the guard turrets, the dogs knotted my stomach. By the time I'd got out of the van my body was as numb as it had been in 1985 when, as a student, I stepped out of the armoured vehicle.

Our group of chattering writers filled out forms and had bags searched but, for me, the forgotten sounds of prison intruded. By the time my turn came, I had lost sight of the woman sitting behind a desk welcoming me and asking simple questions requiring simple answers – name, sex, place and date of birth, age, address, occupation. Instead of her, I saw the put-upon clerk who had booked me that first night in Pollsmoor. Then, there had been a tray between us. I put all my things in it, my movements robotic. Right arm emptied pocket of purse and keys. Left arm stripped of its jingling gold bangles. Body searched.

'This way, please, writers,' said our literary festival minders, and I took a deep breath and followed along a walkway. We went past clipped lawns and beds of red roses. The public face of the prison was some distance from the cell blocks, so we could not see the prisoners, but I could hear them calling, hissing, clanging spoons against bars.

That prison din had assailed me when, in Pollsmoor, the guards escorted us through a labyrinth of corridors. 'Stop,' they commanded. 'Stand here. Don't move. Walk.' It was many hours past lockup, and the crowded cells were full of prisoners I could not see except for the flash of an eye, cupped hands reaching through the bars in hope of a cigarette, nostrils, lips pressed between the bars, a fish-eyed leer and a cacophony of industrial clanging, disembodied shouts, sirens, baying dogs, jangling keys, until my body, no longer mine, was propelled through a doorway, alone. The steel door slammed shut. Silence, lying in wait in the corners of the cell, had uncoiled and slithered over my feet, up my legs, wrapping itself around my hips, chest, neck, finding its way in through my ears and my nostrils until it reached into my belly and brought up bile.

'This way, if you don't mind.' The courteous prison official's voice brought me back to where I was. The other writers had gone ahead. He was waiting for me to come and meet my group. Two hours, I reassured myself, and I would be back in the sunshine.

I followed him into the classroom and then invited the prisoners to write about their five senses. We sat in a circle, me and the twenty men assigned to me, and they wrote. As in any writing workshop anywhere in the world, they then read out their words about touch, smell, taste – all written in the past tense, telling of lost scents and mothers' food some had not tasted for decades.

I was sorry for the inadvertent cruelty of my assignment, but I also found it hard to focus on what they had written because I could not tell them apart. The older men wore bright-orange boiler suits stamped all over with the word 'PRISONER'. Those between eighteen and twenty-five were dressed in dark denim. The uniforms stripped the men of their specificity, reducing all of them to the same man, the same story. I could not remember their names until I noticed their shoes, which were not prison issue. There was an unbelievable array – snow-white Pumas, Nikes, polished black school shoes – everything individual distilled into the one thing they could choose for themselves.

At the end of that prison experience, a shy young murderer caught my arm as I was leaving and asked, 'Will you come back?'

'I will,' I said in response to the smile in his eyes.

fifty

Three weeks later, on a crisp Friday afternoon in July, I drove out to the prison for the first creative writing workshop. I was afraid of what it would mean to work with the men who filled my books and the newspapers with broken bodies. I drove past the prison, which was fronted with steel mesh, a giant aviary, three floors suspended between metal poles. There was bedding hanging from the bars. Thin brown hands extended through the bars, rattling spoons against the mesh. I parked as directed. The pastor, a kindly man, was there to welcome me.

'A riot,' he said of the din coming from the prison. 'It was subdued last night. Your men will be a little late, but they're on their way,' said the pastor as we walked. 'I have a favour to ask. Could you take on one more man, a young man? I know you said you couldn't work with more than fifteen, but he's young. Eighteen. First-time offender.'

Unusually for me, I hesitated. All the men I would be teaching had been screened. They were meant to have served a good part of their time, long enough to have acknowledged that they had committed the crimes they had been convicted of, so I was cautious. 'Why this one?' I asked. 'What did he do?'

'He's the youngest of the four men who killed that baby,' said the pastor. 'He was sixteen at the time.'

His words were a blow to the back of my head. I knew the case. A young woman had approached four men, all strangers, at a taxi rank in Cape Town and had hired them to kill a baby, the six-month-old daughter of her fiancé's ex-girlfriend.

'There's a chance for him,' pleaded the pastor. 'His whole life is ahead of him. He could be saved.'

'No, I'm sorry,' I said. 'I can't take him.'

That boy and three accomplices had sharpened a knife and slit a baby's throat for money. I could not teach him because I knew what he had done. I could not teach a man to write using the same hands that had killed a baby.

'That's okay. I had to try, but I understand.' A gate opened and a group of men in orange surged towards us through a tunnel of razor wire. The pastor said, 'There are your guys from maximum.'

They were tattooed and hard-bodied, bigger and tougher than the denim-clad juveniles coming towards us from the opposite direction.

I followed the men into the gym. There were weights at one end, basketball hoops at the other. I had been allocated a corner, and fifteen men were clustered in desks around mine. Other men – fifty or more, all in orange – filed in after me. They picked up weights, watched me, asked the men with me what we were doing, only drifting off when the wardens insisted.

We skirted the subject of who we were, our pasts, and talked instead about what we wished to do. The talk was tentative; the men were from different sections of the prison, different cells. Not yet acquainted, wary of each other, of me, of the process. Prisons are not places that foster intimacy and trust. Despite, or perhaps because of, the extreme overcrowding, they are also intensely lonely places in which a man's sense of self – already fragile for many, as I was to discover – is constantly eroded. The sameness of the routine; the uniforms that were too tight for the big men, too loose for the smaller ones; the undifferentiated tracts of time through which these men trudged towards the decades-distant ends of their sentences – this smothered the human spirit.

Where to find the threads that would bind those men and me together? Childhood seemed like the place to start. That first day, they worked in groups of four, telling stories, drawing pictures that they annotated. These provided glimpses of the boys they had once been, simple anecdotes of casual deprivation. A beating with a belt; a fishing trip on a boat with a father briefly sober; angry mothers with blackened eyes and too many children; school attempted and abandoned. For one man there had been a blue-and-yellow bike for his ninth birthday.

It was hard not to touch an arm here, a hand there. Touch is a language that comes easily to me, but how does one speak it in a men's prison? I decided then that the only way I could share a creative space with them was if I did not know the specifics of the crimes they had committed, although I had an inkling – rape, murder, armed robbery – as they told me how long their sentences were. Decades, some of them. Others would never be released.

We took a break halfway through the three hours. There was a dull menstrual ache low in my belly and I needed the bathroom, but there were no facilities for women, so an armed warder led me to the facilities at the end of the gym. He told me to wait and, hand on his weapon, he checked each stall. There was nobody there, but the door did not lock, so he stood guard outside. In that moment, silence fell in the gym. I blushed at the echoing cascade of my urine in the bowl. When I returned, not one of them looked me in the eye.

After that first session in the gym, the workshop took place in a classroom. For the next year, I drove an hour there and back every Friday, time that provided a buffer between my two worlds. I never once considered giving up on my commitment, but working with those fifteen troubled men, flesh-and-blood versions of the spectres who filled our newspapers and our nightmares, burdened me heavily.

They were impeccably behaved, but I felt the spirits of their victims crowded into the classroom with them, and it took a great deal of psychic effort to get those angry ghosts settled enough for the men to do the work I prescribed – from which, I assured them, a book would be produced. They were disbelieving. I couldn't blame them; a finished book was the maddest thing to imagine, but over time – the one thing they had in abundance, many of them being lifers – they created one.

I was not their first reader. The workshop was the frame I provided, but they wrote for themselves and each other. They could choose whether or not to read each other's writings. I guided them, using what I had learned from my own writing teacher, encouraging fruitful ways of responding to the thoughts, feelings and imagination of others.

They learned to listen to each other. I listened to them, but I did not have a way to reconcile their humanity, which manifested itself through their shared writing, with the evils they had done, the acts that had brought them to that prison and the space I shared with them for three hours each week.

Their last activity was to return the library books they had borrowed and take out new ones. A young murderer oversaw the box of donated books. He kept a close eye on who read what, and not a single book went missing. After that we would say goodbye, and the men would linger for a last rollie before filing back to their cells.

After each class, I would drive back to Cape Town and, invariably, a migraine, which the teaching kept in abeyance, would spring into action, contorting the muscles on my scalp, knotting my shoulders, blurring my vision. It would last four days. By Wednesday it began to lift; Thursdays it was a ghostly imprint in my skull; Fridays, when I went back to the prison, it was gone.

No medication could take away the pain of those headaches, and so I went to see a psychoanalyst I had interviewed for an article about women who tended to the spirit as well as the mind.

'It's as if the angry spirits of the victims of the men I teach each week clamour around them,' I told her at my first session. 'I need help. These headaches I get, I'm sure they're a response to that cacophony of suffering.'

I talked to her about the necessity of bearing witness to the pain of others, something she did in private that I felt compelled to do in public, through my writing. The conversations with my therapist made those headaches bearable, even though the pain never diminished. So I came to accept them, as I accepted that it was impossible to reconcile the harm done by the men I taught with that done to them as children by the violent country I loved and lived in. I settled into the rhythm of the workshops, the migraines, and the writing of my third novel. I drove out to the prison every Friday, and we talked, and the men wrote.

We read together, too. One poem that caught their attention was a clean-lined beauty about fatherhood, love, fear and yearning. Here, for the first time, was an umbilical connection with the subject of the poem. Their lives as sons had been scarred by absent or violent fathers. The men shared their poems about feared and longed-for fathers. One Friday a twenty-two-year-old gangster stood up and read aloud for the first time. It was a poem he had written for his son, saying he was sorry for his violence and his absence, saying 'I love you'.

I pictured that little boy reading a poem from his father telling him how he had wanted to be a father to him, even though he'd failed; telling him that he loved him even if he did not know how. It was more than many boys had. It was more than the grown men had expressed. I suggested that he send his poem home.

That was just before the Christmas break, and on my return in mid-January, he told me that his ex-girlfriend had brought their six-year-old son to visit. 'I held him,' he said. 'I could feel him in my heart. It hurt when he left.' The loneliness in his eyes was unbearable.

How could I have forgotten that the spirit of a prisoner follows the person who came to visit, even as they themselves are led back to their cell? I had felt this myself, walking back to my own maximum-security prison cell twenty years earlier. That experience had catapulted me into what I thought of as adulthood. It imprinted in me the unshakeable belief that, to survive, I had to cope on my own because, in extremis, there was no one else there. How could I have forgotten how alone you feel when you watch someone you love leave, knowing they are returning to the light and the life of the world, and you are not?

'Let's break early today,' I said to the men, and when they went out to have their mid-morning smoke, I walked to the toilets, which, as the only woman there, I knew I'd have to myself. I went into one of the cubicles, locked the door and attended to my own prison memory that had arisen in response to the gangster's words.

I had been in prison for more than a week – I can't be sure, as I could no longer distinguish one day from another – when a face appeared at the metal grille of my cell and said, 'You have a visitor. Brush your hair and come with me.'

I did as I was told and followed the guard to Pollsmoor's visitors' section, where she ushered me into a windowless room. It was empty apart from a chair facing the perspex window. Next to the window was a silver button and a small metal box attached to the wall.

'Sit,' instructed my escort.

I sat. She stood behind me, out of my line of sight. I looked at the empty room on the other side of the scratched window, with its fluorescent light, dingy walls and the chair.

The door opened and there was my mother. She was so much smaller than I remembered. She spoke, but I couldn't hear her. Her escort pointed towards the window. When she saw me, her mouth formed a silent 'oh', and she sat on the chair opposite me. Her escort stepped back. My mother put her palms to the glass, as I did on my side.

Her mouth moved, but I heard nothing.

We spoke, but neither of us could hear and we laughed, though tears rolled down my mother's cheeks. Down mine, too.

'Press the button,' said my guard. 'Hold it down when you speak.'

My mother and I held the buttons down. We pressed and spoke. My father sent his love, she told me. He was worried, but was in Windhoek because of his patients. Such short notice.

Yes, I said, that made sense. No need for him to be here. How were the dogs?

She said they were fine. She told me where she was staying, but my mind did not retain that information. She had been to a meeting with other parents whose children had been imprisoned. She was speaking to lawyers.

The intercom attenuated my mother's voice, made it strange.

She said they were doing everything they could. She was crying, but I could not comfort her. I took my finger off the button because it was no longer possible for me to hold up the weight of my arm. Although I no longer heard her, I watched her anxious face. How her mouth moved as she talked, until the warden behind my mother leaned forward and tapped her shoulder at the instant I felt the tap on mine. Our hands with their mirrored palms touched the glass, and my mother was gone.

We were approaching the end of our writing year together, and the prisoners had produced piles of handwritten stories and poetry. When they handed me their long-list, the paper carried with it the smell of prison: a dusty grey hopelessness of lives turned to ash. It turned my stomach because I had absorbed it too. My body and their bodies had that much in common: a knowledge of what it feels like to be locked away.

I took their tales home and read them at my writing desk. Their stories illuminated the legacies of racism, poverty and emotional deprivation as well as the brutal, brittle masculinities that had derailed their lives. Their book, *Fifteen Men: Words and Images from Behind Bars*, was published in 2008.

The oldest man in the class, incarcerated before the end of apartheid, but who would, because of the severity of his crimes, never be released, wrote:

I am
A book with a damaged cover, but what is
Written between the lines could save a country
From a disaster.

His words brought home to me that the men we shun out of fear and revulsion were once children in need of hope, love and community.

I had my work cut out trying to finish my third novel. *Daddy's Girl* was a child abduction story with a seventy-two-hour timeline: the amount of time the police presume a missing child might still be alive.

For a while, I had been clipping stories from the Cape dailies. In one shocking two-week period, nine girls under twelve were murdered. I investigated those cases, but there was no serial killer at work. Some were killed by family members, some by opportunistic strangers, some in the crossfire of the gang wars raging in Cape Town.

It is a perverse comfort to believe that if one evil man – a serial killer or a paedophile, those staple scapegoats of crime fiction – is caught, then social order will be restored and civilised life will continue. That is not true in South Arica. The country has had its share of serial killers, but the mundane murders, so chillingly common, prompted me to think of South Africa itself as the serial killer. A society preying on the most vulnerable citizens, young girls, with impunity. That was the context. The plot hinged around the abduction of the seven-year-old daughter of Captain Riedwaan Faizal and his desperate search for her.

The fear of a snatched child, the panicked heartbeat of that novel, is a universal one, but I wanted to examine how a man might become the killer of a child. The answers did not lie with the victims; they lay with the perpetrators. It was their hearts that had been stripped of compassion; their hands that killed and maimed. So, during the year of my prison writing workshops, and for a few months afterwards, I wrote about that heart of darkness.

Daddy's Girl, published in 2009, is as much a book about crimes against women and children as it is about the relationship between Clare Hart and Riedwaan Faizal, her partner in work and in bed. The spark between them, which I had loved writing, had given me – and, hopefully, the reader – emotional respite from the apocalyptic social landscape that the two characters navigate.

I needed a love story that offered an affirming alternative to the sexual violence I was writing about. In the character of Riedwaan, a composite of the good men I knew, I created a man who celebrated a woman's 'no'. A man who wants a woman because she gives herself freely, out of desire for him, rather than to satisfy his own desire, or to placate him. Ultimately, though, I could not keep the characters together. Clare's capacity to relate to the man she loves, and who loves her, falters.

The series of crime novels turned out to be an oblique self-portrait of what happens to a woman working closely with the victims and perpetrators of violence. It would be no plot spoiler to say that her work wore Clare Hart down, and it wore me out.

fifty-one

For my husband's fiftieth birthday in August 2010, I organised a wildly extravagant party. It was not what he wanted; he said he didn't have much to celebrate, what with his work being the way it was – or wasn't. I felt compelled to gather everyone together to shore us up, so I disregarded his quiet protest and invited everyone I could think of: our extended families; the decade's worth of friends made since our return to Cape Town – dinner-party couples with children the same age and at the same school as ours; all the book people I knew; old lovers, both mine and his, to conjure the ghosts of prior lives and alternate futures; university friends from whose orbit I had drifted.

The house was already full just after nine on the night of the party when I slipped out of the front gate and walked up the steep road, lined with cars, leading to Table Mountain, and into the quiet embrace of the night. I stopped where the road ended and the fynbos started. It was a warm evening for so early in spring. There was no wind, and I could hear the hum of the city in my right ear, while in my left the mountain's silence was punctuated by the call of a nightjar. I lit a cigarette and looked down at the solid, four-bedroom family house. The place where I had written so many novels.

It looked like something out of a children's book: the pitched red roof, ochre-yellow walls, mullioned windows framed in ruddy Javanese teak. The house, filled with yellow light, was surrounded by a dense, rustling forest of indigenous Cape trees I had planted – wild peach, yellowwoods, and the keurbooms that reached through the gaps in the blade-tipped steel fence and scattered pink blossoms on the pavement, where I watched a four-by-four pull up and a couple getting out with gifts in their hands.

Time to return.

On the front verandah my cousin shucked oysters he'd brought from his oyster farm up the West Coast. Hundreds of them packed on platters lined with crushed ice. The guests crowded around as he cupped oyster after oyster in his palm, inserted a dagger into each sealed shell, prised it open and placed it into an outstretched palm. That live salty shudder went into mouth after eager mouth. He held one out to me, but the glistening creature with its delicate folds exposed spasmed in its pearly shell and I could not.

In the jammed hallway the barman poured champagne. I reached through the crowd and snatched a glass. With this as my shield I navigated knots of talking-laughing-drinking people – kissing cheeks with a 'hello I'm fine thanks for coming lovely dress' – before I reached the sanctuary of the kitchen, where the caterer was slicing seared fillet, the blood pooling on the chopping board and dripping onto the floor where the dog lapped it up.

I moved into the dining room, where my daughters had cleared the furniture away. The wooden floors gleamed, as did the DJ's serious young face, illuminated by the glow of his laptop as he played hits from the 1980s. The Clash's 'London Calling' was drawing people away from huddled conversations about schools (the best) and murders (the worst), and onto the dance floor. This interrupted my hostess whirl, and when a glass fell to the floor there were bare feet to think of, so I picked up the pieces and escaped to the sitting room with them. There, Aidan's parents and mine were standing by the fireplace with champagne flutes in their hands. I placed the broken bits in the empty grate and was about to go back when my father placed a broad, freckled hand on my arm.

'It's quite a party, this,' he said. 'Like something out of *The Great Gatsby*.'

'It is,' I said, with a tinkling Daisy Buchanan laugh, stepping away from him into the bay window.

I opened one of the leaded windows, resting my hot face against the cool burglar bars. Cape Town was a glittering carpet spread out below me. On Table Bay, the lights edging the water gleamed like a pearl necklace, a ship trailing silver in its dark wake as it passed the end of the dock where a light blinked green.

Like that suggestive green traffic light just four months before this mad party, which had beckoned from the cobbled street six floors below the Lyon hotel room where I'd perched, watching a flock of starlings swoop through the April morning. I had longed to join them.

To fly. To remove myself. To absent myself from *being*, that perfect spring morning in France during my book tour. So glamorous to be in France – Paris first and then Lyon – my novels translated into French; a big deal, though I felt no elation, no pleasure at all, no sense of ambition fulfilled.

That was the first and last time my husband accompanied me on a book tour. I had gone alone before, putting meticulous plans in place for the women I employed to mother in my absence. I would return exhilarated, exhausted, and laden with gifts – only to find that I did not know how to fit how expansive I felt out in the world into the wife-size I thought I should be at home.

I had invited Aidan, hoping I would find a way back to him, that we would talk to each other – something that we'd been doing less and less ever since our return from America nine years earlier, maybe even before that. I was possessed by a growing sense of despair that I could confess to no one, certainly not to my husband, who lay on the Lyon bed I had just left.

Jump, that alluring green light tempted me. *Jump*.

Why had escape not occurred to me before? Leave everything behind. That it could be so simple was a revelation. The relief I'd felt, the clarity, as I opened the window and in rushed the buoyant morning sounds. The light was green. I should jump.

'Margie.' Aidan's voice brought me up short.

I closed the window on that promise of escape and turned to face him. He held his hand out to me, but I could not take it. It was so long since we had spoken to each other of the affairs of our hearts. I could not bear to be pulled back into the lonely silence of his touch.

'Coffee?' I offered instead.

'I thought we'd have more sex.' He dropped his hand. 'Here. Away from everything.'

I had thought we would talk more, but our conversation had been stilted and sparse.

I phoned room service and ordered coffee. Then I went back to the window and looking out at the sky, blank and blue.

The contrails normally crisscrossing the sky were gone. An Icelandic volcano with an unpronounceable name had erupted, and the airborne particles threatened aeroplane engines, so it was said, resulting in flight cancellations. It was, the television vulcanologists had said, a reasonable precaution in the face of a great if invisible danger. We could be stuck forever in this flightless limbo, I feared.

There was a knock on the door, and a waiter came in and set a tray down on the table. I poured two cups of coffee and gave Aidan his. I took mine and balanced on the sun-warmed windowsill to drink it. The traffic had stopped on the cobbled street on the other side of the glass. No one was going anywhere. The lights were red.

In Cape Town, the harbour light was still flashing green when I turned from the bay window in my living room and looked back at the way I had come. People were eating the bloody steak. The dance floor heaved. The barman was handing out drinks. It was time for the speeches and cake. The DJ faded the music when I held up my hand to stop the chatter. I herded the guests into a celebratory circle and stood in the centre with my husband and our three daughters. The quiet turned to silence. There were one hundred and fifty pairs of eyes on us.

'Speech,' chanted the guests, champagne flutes at the ready.

Aidan looked at me expectantly, but speech was impossible for me. I placed my hands on my daughters' backs and propelled them into the open space between us and the guests. They looked up at their tall father with love and said how gentle he was, how patient, how good he had been at playing Barbies and horses with them when they were small, how beautiful his drawings were, that they were so proud of him, how they loved him. Then they flung their arms around him. There were tears in his eyes when he looked over their heads at me.

'Speech, Margie,' insisted the restive guests, but I dared not open my mouth. The words shuttered behind my teeth – I no longer believe in you, I want to die, I can't breathe in this house, this marriage, this life – were bullets and, if I opened my mouth, those bullet-words would tear through everyone I loved and kill them. I kept my teeth clamped shut, caged them, and raised my glass.

A toast was drunk.

The candles on the cake were lit. 'Happy Birthday' was sung. After the obligatory three cheers the candles were blown out and not that long afterwards the guests went home. The party was over, and my marriage and I were in trouble.

fifty-two

Work was the redoubt into which I retreated. Writing was where I hid when I needed solitude, but as my marriage, so long my shelter, fractured, solitude turned to loneliness. My only solution was more work, so when then President Zuma introduced legislation that would severely curtail writers' freedom to report on corruption – an attempt that ultimately failed – I joined PEN South Africa, the local chapter of the international writers' organisation that campaigned on behalf of imprisoned writers and for free expression. Shortly afterwards, I became president, but I would also be elected to the international board, which advocates for persecuted writers all over the world. This meant more travelling.

This dispersed my anxiety, as moving always did; and paradoxically, being away obscured the growing distance between me and Aidan. When I was at home, I retreated to my writing hut at the top end of the garden, and the following year, 2011, I published *Gallows Hill* – my flawed favourite of the series.

Set in a forgotten informal slave burial ground unearthed during construction work in central Cape Town, the plot involved a cold case investigation into the disappearance of an artist murdered in the 1980s. Pushing as hard as I could against the tight-laced conventions of procedural crime fiction, I examined how the legacy of slavery shapes the violence plaguing present-day Cape Town. When that book was done, I had another book to deliver as per my publisher's contract, but I was exhausted.

I told Aidan I was not coping, that I needed him to share the burden of making money, to take its full weight off my shoulders so I could rest a little. The helpless look in his eyes, as if he were the proverbial rabbit trapped in the twinned headlights of my need and exhaustion, made me understand he could not, or perhaps would not, help me.

I gave up on talking; it was as if the words I spoke, the help I asked for, hit a pane of glass that had formed between us while I had been so busy. For a few moments we could see the words, as if they were tiny, stunned insects on a windscreen, before they slid away, unheard. And so, unable to draw breath, I got going on my fifth novel. There, I turned my gaze towards the family, which can be a haven or a prison, and is sometimes both at the same time.

Water Music was a vivisection of the role of the head of the household and the patriarchal family, where a man presumes to have the power of life and death over his wife and children. Disturbed by the frequency of family murders perpetrated by angry and despairing husbands and fathers, and the chilling cases of men who impregnated kidnapped girls or their own daughters, I took on the nuclear family.

This intimate territory lies on the borderland of crime fiction, but I drilled down into the silence, power and coercive control that is the bedrock of patriarchy. The traditional family, a site of unquestioned power if ever there was one, is the formative site of the self and of unequal gender relations. I had been putting Clare Hart, the repository of traumas I myself could not look in the eye, into increasingly dangerous situations. In this novel, Clare, ambivalent about whether to see her just-discovered pregnancy to term, is abducted by a man she suspects of holding another woman captive. He immures Clare in a lightless basement beneath his house. To survive, and to ensure the survival of the other women she finds imprisoned there, she will have to rescue herself. As I would have to. As all women must.

The psychic wear and tear on Clare Hart, her proximity to the trauma of violence against women, the inevitable numbing this causes, had altered her as it had me. It was magical thinking to believe I was protected by the distance I imagined fiction writing would afford me. My heroine's physical imprisonment, as I see only too clearly as I write this now, paralleled my own sense of psychological entrapment. It was there in the novels, in plain sight, but I could not see it at the time, just as I could not see how bad my mental state was.

The state of the nation was not much better. Several crime investigators I knew had been deployed to the riot squad, which was tasked with crushing township protests against abject poverty, the state's failure to deliver basic services, and widespread government corruption.

I was halfway through *Water Music* when, on 10 August 2012, thirty-four striking mineworkers were massacred by the police on a desolate koppie near Marikana in North West province. In horror, I watched footage of miners carrying kieries and pangas being mown down by cops. It was obvious that the police, as a commission of enquiry would find, had fired with deadly intent. The reputation of the South African Police Service had suffered an irredeemable blow.

That stopped me in my crime-fiction tracks. The genre is premised on a concept of justice: an evil event occurs; the wrongdoers are brought to book; the status quo is restored. If the state turns on its own citizens and devours them, if the police turn on the citizens they are meant to protect, then the moral frame of the crime fiction I had been writing collapsed. Also, character is plot. What we do in life and in fiction is determined by who we are. That is the basis upon which I had crafted my books – by setting the scene and then observing what my characters did, and writing that down. That is how my novels had come to life. It was impossible for Captain Riedwaan Faizal – an imperfect but instinctively ethical Everyman, someone who sensed the distinction between what was legal and what was just – to stay in the police. He gave me no choice but to let him resign because of the massacre of the miners at Marikana.

So, there I was, with Clare Hart in a dungeon, and a book to finish. Freed from procedural crime fiction with all its rules and the forensic tests that cops must do, I was now in the terrain of the psychological novel, towards which I had, without being fully aware of it, been moving. That took me away from crime and justice and towards notions of sin and vengeance. It was wilder and freer to write about a woman, turned feral by male violence, coming into her own power, and exacting her own retribution.

Water Music, eventually published in 2013, had disturbed me from the start. It had always felt too familiar, too close to home. I liked the rage I found in Clare, and her capacity to fight to the death to protect her baby, but I was unsure about what to do about my loss of faith in what the law and the justice system could do for women. All I couldn't say, and all I failed to capture, plagued me. I wrote the last words, printed the manuscript, and then carried it everywhere with me.

'My dead baby,' I joked to anyone who asked. 'I'm like one of those mad women who carry the corpse of their baby everywhere with them because relinquishing its body would mean it's finally over.' I got some odd looks, but to me the comparison seemed perfectly sane.

I said none of this to my therapist, that my work defines what I am and all I am – when I say 'I am a writer' that is what I mean: it is not a cloak I sometimes don. And I did not want the banalities of bank balances and money difficulties cluttering her dimly lit, soporific consulting room. So, I went on at her about my eccentric but good-enough childhood and my well-intentioned parents, doing my best to keep from her everything that really troubled me.

The experiences I could neither name nor claim, I had channelled into my writing. I saw no reason to repeat them, but I suspect I knew even then that if I did, she would be onto me – and there would be nowhere left for me to hide.

fifty-three

At the last possible minute, I handed the manuscript for *Water Music* to the editor for its dissection and reassembly into something that resembled a saleable book. Once it was with her, it was no longer my responsibility. I responded to queries obediently, relieved that other, more competent people had taken charge of my unsettling creation. They would organise it, package it, make it a book. When I received my author's copies, I looked at them with astonishment. I had no recollection of what I had written or why.

I went on a book tour and told tales that conjured women's corpses, mortuaries – and the criminals who were responsible for filling them. I hid what writing that book had cost me, but reading from my work in public made me ill. It never occurred to me that I had burned out and was breaking down.

At the end of that 2013 book tour, at a literary festival in Franschhoek where I had done three consecutive events, I had a publisher's dinner to attend. My nerves were raw. I did not want to speak to anybody. More than that, I wanted nobody to speak to me, but I put on a cobalt-blue dress and red combat lipstick. When it was time to leave I put on my coat, but when I got to the door I could not leave my room. The thought of going outside made my chest tighten up.

You must breathe, I reasoned with myself. *If you can breathe, you can get out of the door. If you get into the car, you can carry on being yourself.*

By sheer force of will, I returned to myself, left the room, and walked to the restaurant where the authors' dinner was being hosted. I smiled at anyone who looked at me, sipped champagne and drifted to the edge of the crowd, where I smoked cigarettes until a publicist called me back. The publisher called for a toast and then we took our seats at the long table. A plate with a tiny starter in the centre, like the bull's-eye of a target, was placed in front of me. I got it down. The charming crime writer next to me asked why I was so pale.

'Exhaustion,' I said. 'Too many events.'

'They work us like dogs,' he joked. 'But it pays.'

I drank more wine. I was fine until the main course arrived, a lump of rare fillet oozing blood over the plate. Panic returned, gripping me in its steel talons. I stood up. My dinner companion had turned to the person on his other side, so there was no need to make my excuses before leaving the restaurant.

It was May, and the night was cold. I walked fast, my mind churning with the unease I had felt at my events and the evening's failed conversations. I was too serious, that was it. I did not understand the game, mainly played by male writers, of arranging dead female bodies in a tableau, as a spectacle, as a fictional puzzle to be solved. The violence was too visceral, too real. It was written onto women's bodies, a runic language, often indecipherable, a lethal form of communication which, to survive, we needed to be able to read.

Writing had been a barrier that I could hide behind, but it made me afraid, too, because the places I went to were so violent, so dark, seemingly unrelated to me and my own experiences. When I started writing it had been a way of keeping the darkness outside of myself. I had written to keep the brutality, broken limbs, broken hearts at bay.

But no matter the amount of research and thinking, no matter how much I tried to pull the wool over my eyes, what one writes comes out of the self, I now knew. I named things on the page that I did not fully know until they were written down, creating a navigable archipelago in the sea of the unknown and the unsaid. Those words came from and through me; I could no longer deny their origin.

The novels I had written, born out of fury, were not a liberation. They were transcriptions of fear, abandonment, betrayal, and up-close misogyny. My approach had been medical, legal, literary, but it was ultimately women and their bodies I was concerned about. Our bodies, in their muteness, suffering, rebellion and pleasure, are the origin of all we know. A body of knowledge. A body of work – a writer's cumulative effort remains a body.

Psychoanalysis, which holds both the body and language close to its heart, had given me a path from body to language, then back to the body. As I approached the street where my guesthouse was, I remembered something D.W. Winnicott had written. I loved him, as all negligent mothers do, for his idea of 'the good-enough mother', but I was not thinking of that as I slid the key into the lock; I was thinking of his assertion that 'what matters to the patient is the willingness of the analyst to help'.

To help, I thought, as I got my door open. That is what I'd wanted to do, but I had not been able to help anyone. I saw it clearly. My hubris. The deeply embodied writing I had worked hard to create, writing that would make me and my readers *feel*, writing that came from me and through me, had merely made me ashamed. It brought nobody back from the dead.

I collapsed on the bed, allowing my mind to storm, unable to stop the swirling vortex of fragments, broken women and their incoherent voices crying out in a language I did not understand. Who I was slipped from my grasp. Why was I in that luxurious hotel room? I got up and paced around. There were books on the table with my name embossed on the covers. These were the books I had written to get the living and the dead into some semblance of order.

Writing was my vocation, but it had broken me. The writing that had once given me solace now felt like a compulsion akin to madness. The temptation of disappearing, of escaping, which had first appeared in Lyon as I had sat at my hotel window, stepped seductively out of the shadows and beckoned. I felt for my phone and scrolled through my photos. The pictures of my children steadied me. I studied their faces. They were real. If they were real, then I had to be real too.

But the thud of my heart said otherwise. And there was no one to call.

I recalled the shock, quickly set aside, that had coursed through me when I wrote the last lines of *Water Music*: 'Marriage. Being two, becoming one. That's a step too far.'

It had taken me five novels, all of five hundred thousand words, to comprehend Clare Hart's terse response to the tender marriage proposal of Riedwaan, the father of her unplanned, unborn baby. That merger, the loss of self that wifehood required, was unthinkable. Was this the truth I had kept hidden from myself? Had I written half a million words just to arrive at that? It was as if my writing self, separate from the rest – what I thought of as *myself* – had addressed the last line of that novel to me, calling the foundation of my life into question.

I did not know where to turn to for help to bridge the gulf between me and my husband of twenty-five years. Maybe I was too proud, too ashamed to admit failure, but I also knew that there is something cultish about the institution of marriage, a secret society of two, a kind of mafia, seemingly inescapable, and governed by omertà. That is the way I understood it then, which made it impossible for me to tell of my awful, secret disillusion, not to anyone, not even my sister, the person who knew me better than I knew myself.

When the sun came up, I drove home.

I tried to get myself in hand by writing: there were bills to pay. I was fortunate enough to be contracted to write the sixth and final novel in my series. I had outlined what abuse does to children. I wished to illuminate the darkness we all know is there – no one can miss the stats – and from which we avert our eyes. This I knew from a senior investigator in the Child Protection Unit who had a mountain of dockets – two hundred or more ongoing investigations into child abuse – on his desk.

'Read those,' he said when I asked him if what the papers said about child abuse was true. I read through them in an afternoon, examining illustrations of the children's injuries, even pleas to go back to the homes they had been removed from. To find some way of managing this devastating flood I had outlined a plot in which Clare Hart, now a mother, would investigate accusations that her partner and the father of her newborn son had been party to the sexual exploitation of children.

How I was going to pull off a high-stakes investigation with my lead character breast-feeding a newborn, I could not have told you. How I would be able to do this, considering how my mind was unravelling, I cannot tell you either. I could not imagine what else to do, which is not a good state for either a wife or a writer to be in. But like always when things were tough, I thought by holding an imaginary gun to my head and working, I could fix myself, my life, my marriage.

fifty-four

On an unseasonably warm winter's evening, Aidan and I were sitting on the stoep with sundowners in our hands. The lights of Cape Town were twinkling around the dark ocean rippling at the edge of Table Bay and we were filling the distance between us by talking about our children and their plans. Rose working in Istanbul, Grace at university and living in a communal house, Jamie with eighteen months of school left and talking of a gap year.

We said nothing about ourselves on the other side of the empty nest. So questions about what we would do, where we would go, what we wanted lay between us, unasked. I did not, I realised, want to ask them any more. I had lost the capacity to imagine the future with Aidan, the man I'd loved and lost faith in.

'I can't go on,' I blurted, setting down the marriage as if it were a lead-heavy trunk I could no longer carry. 'I can't go on as we are.'

I glimpsed a flash of relief, quick as a fish in Aidan's eyes, then it was gone, and in its place was hurt, disbelief, and rage.

But I could not take my words back. Not even for our children, whose lives would be altered forever because I no longer had the strength to continue as we were in a joyless marital vacuum.

I said I was sorry his practice had not worked out, but hard as it was to admit that there was something I couldn't do, I was desperate. There is kudos for a man who supports his family, but if a woman does so, she must hide it from him and from the world. Mostly, however, she must hide it from herself so that she does not feel abandoned.

I was no longer able to hold up the shipping container that was our family's needs on the beanshoot that was my creativity, I said. Not because I didn't want to, but because I couldn't. I could no longer work. I had burned out. If I could no longer write and he had no work, then how would we eat?

'You leave as things get difficult.' Aidan's words were daggers and they struck home.

But things were not difficult. They were impossible. There was no way I could retract. By then, the way he and I inhabited time was different. For him the time had not been enough, but I had no time left.

'I need a break,' I said. 'To find a way out of this impasse, this talking around and around in the same circle. We've talked about it before, but nothing changes and it has driven me mad. I've been too alone in things for too long. Alone and afraid.'

He was silent.

Aidan was quiet for so long I wondered if he had heard me. Then he suggested we try couples counselling.

'No. It's too late for that,' I said. We would take a break and see what, if anything, could be salvaged.

Neither of us knew how to bring the fear or the loneliness into the light to examine.

The truth was I was afraid of my bullet-words, the ones I had kept prisoner at his birthday party. I was afraid of what they would do – the fear of a writer, perhaps, who must believe that words have the power to change worlds. But that refusal meant that the sinkhole I called migraine opened its maw.

You did this, it hissed. *You laid this mine. Detonated it. You must pick up the pieces and reassemble.* Then it swallowed me whole.

We finished our drinks and went in. I made dinner and we ate as usual, but family life as it had once been was over, though we pretended that night that no landmine had gone off and that the bleeding people at the table were eating with real and not phantom limbs.

We did not shout, though. We did not fight.

'We never fight,' we'd said, as if this was a thing to pride ourselves on.

But silence can be lethal. Neither of us came from families in which conflicts between husbands and wives, or with parents, or their children, could be aired and resolved. I don't think either of us knew what to do. There had been too many years of repression and evasion for it to be cured. Like the house of a hoarder, ours was cluttered not with objects but with arguments and differences that had long passed their sell-by date, but that we had never been able to dispose of because we had only known how to pretend they weren't there.

By August Aidan had found work in Windhoek, and he left. I watched him drive down the road, away from the house. When the car turned the corner and he was gone from view, a weight lifted. The lightness of being there alone would, I thought, be bearable. Not long after he arrived in Namibia, he met someone. The thought of his warm hands on her young body made me savage and I could not bear the thought of him ever touching me again.

'A soluble problem,' my soon-to-be ex-sister-in-law observed during the last lunch she had in my kitchen, 'has been replaced with an insoluble problem.'

She was right. The idea of a salvaged marriage filled with savagery but without touch was intolerable.

In Iceland, where I went for a literary festival in September that year, I visited a freezing plain where the Viking settlers had their medieval parliaments. That plain has a deep gash running through it because that is the place where the Eurasian and the American plates are moving away from each other. You can see the gash in the earth where the tectonic plates are separating the landmass into two continents. It is a wound, as what is one becomes two. That awful inevitable process of individuation.

fifty-five

'Can you walk okay in those?' asked my lawyer, all perky curls and encouraging chatter about getting divorces settled quickly and cleanly as we walked down the cobbled street to the Cape Town High Court.

'Yes,' I said, but that was a lie. I was wearing a jaunty red wrap dress and a new pair of suede kitten heels, which had given me blisters.

She suggested we stop for a coffee. 'You look like you need some fortification.' She placed her order at the kiosk. I was looking at the tray of doughnuts. They reminded me of Aidan's sugary fingers brushing mine in the student canteen the first time I met him. 'Will you eat something?' she asked.

'No,' I said. He would be my husband for one more hour. 'I won't. I can't.'

'You're going to feel so much better when this is done,' said the lawyer, striding along, double espresso in hand.

She, like everybody else, inhabited linear time, which I seemed to have been cast out of since I'd stunned myself and Aidan by saying that I could not go on.

What had I meant? I no longer knew the answer to that question as I hobbled towards the High Court with its Doric columns, heavy teak doors and marble floors.

My lawyer clamped her thin fingers onto my elbow, as if she sensed I wanted to cut and run. She marched me up a flight of stairs and down a crowded corridor.

She was right. I did want to escape. I pulled my dress tighter around my body, wishing it was body armour that could deflect the blows that were to come.

There were so many rooms in the courthouse and staircases – seeming like an Escher artwork to lead back onto themselves – and a flurry of people. As the lawyer donned her black robe I somehow got separated from her, caught in the slipstream of the crowd flowing towards Courtroom A.

'Wrong door.' My lawyer caught my arm again. 'That woman had her husband murdered. We want Courtroom B.'

I glimpsed the wife – now widow – who had organised the hit on her husband. She was elegantly dressed, her face regal and blank. I had read news reports about her. She had paid for her unfaithful husband, a judge, to be trussed up in clingfilm and suffocated. There were allegedly no extenuating circumstances. What, I wondered, had tipped the judge's wife towards Courtroom A, and murder, rather than Courtroom B, and divorce.

It was a relief to sit down in that room filled with a sense of efficient and courteous sadness. The judge, a small, neat woman, looked out at the marital refugees gathered before her, all of us fleeing a failure to uphold the vows we had made, with varying degrees of carelessness or hope, to men or women we could no longer tolerate. We, unlike the woman in the court next door, had not killed. Instead, we had asked lawyers to list assets and enumerate amounts to be paid towards the upkeep of the children we had made together with the men we had married. We wished to be freed of the bonds of family that had either choked us or not held us close enough.

The judge called one case after the other. I was astonished at how many people got divorced in a single morning. The judge paid careful attention to the cases before mine where there were minor children. She adjudicated the settlements with hawk-eyed clarity. She checked the maintenance to be paid to the soon-to-be ex-wives who would – whether willingly or not – be bearing most of the care and the cost. She did right by them; I liked that about her.

My name was called, and it was my turn to stand before her. The judge's eyes were on me. I felt, for a moment, that I was in the dock, but no crime had been committed. She said my name and I felt her kindness and was glad of it. As she glanced through my case, a bald summary of assets, property, financial obligations, I wondered if she was married. Or divorced.

How did it feel to enter this room every day to face this sea of disillusion and sorrow? To declare with a stroke of the pen, a strike of the gavel, that a marriage was now null and void?

My marriage, the frame of my life for twenty-five years, was over.

On the first of April 2015 I was publicly stripped of the title 'wife'; without it to hide behind, I was undefended.

The word 'undefended' reverberated in my head. What to do, how to be, now that I was so publicly alone? Without the sheltering institution of marriage, I would be open to all kinds of scrutiny.

Undefended: the word was so surprising. I had not seen it waiting there in the wings, limbering up to elbow me out of the way and take centre stage. But there it was, cocksure and looking at me with mocking blackbird eyes.

Undefended. I tried to shut the word out, but it kept pecking at me with its crow beak.

My lawyer hugged me. Her work was done. She said we should go for lunch sometime soon, but she had to dash now. 'Are you meeting someone?' she asked. 'You know, to celebrate.'

'Oh yes,' I lied.

'Wonderful,' she said. 'Go somewhere nice.'

I could not lie down there on the marble floor and watch all the brown and black court shoes go by, so I didn't. The pain felt like too much to bear, but there was nowhere to put it, so I walked out of the courthouse and carried it through the Company Gardens.

The air had a champagne sparkle. The summer had turned towards autumn, but the trees were not losing their leaves yet. They leaned over and embraced each other in the air so that the broad path looked like the nave of a cathedral.

As I looked up at those tenderly touching branches, it came to me that the love there had once been between Aidan and me was surely as great as the pain I was feeling. I had loved him. I had loved us: the two of us, then three, four and five, a family completed. I saw this only now, when things were irrevocably over. I cradled that agony as if it were a stillborn child. The slither of a migraine, that familiar serpent uncoiling in the base of my skull. I welcomed its strike. Physical pain I could bear.

fifty-six

Somehow, I got home and up the stairs and into the hallway where sunlight slanted through the mullioned windows as I stood there, surveying the museum of my daughters' childhood where the air had turned into a suffocating substance I could no longer breathe. When it had been me, Jamie and their classmate who lived with us, the house had been a haven. The Home for Lost Girls, as the two of them called it. And it was just that: a refuge for women seeking sanctuary – but now the house was a shell, and it had divested itself of me.

Jamie, who had matriculated the year before, in 2014, had set out on the gap year they needed after all the chaos and heartbreak. Our gap years, we had joked, when we planned to meet up in England. We would see Rose, who was doing her Master's at Oxford. Grace, finishing her degree in Cape Town, was staying. It was 2015; student protests were gaining momentum, and university campuses were not only turbulent but also increasingly incendiary. I swallowed my anxiety about leaving her.

Grace was twenty-two. She would be fine without me, I reassured my sister when I phoned to tell her the deed was done and I was now a divorcee, that ambiguous entity some married women hesitate to invite to dinner parties, fearing they might run off with husbands they had only half-liked all the while they'd been friends.

'Rubbish, you just feel conspicuous now, that's all,' said Melle, who had known the pain of divorce, its shame, the sense of loss and failure.

She had wailed, 'No one in our family gets divorced,' when I'd tried to comfort her in 1998 when her two-year marriage ended. But I only knew now how she had felt then; in my imagination, the bombproof marriages of my parents, grandparents, uncles and aunts were arrayed accusingly before me.

Melle had told me that the worst thing about her divorce was the death of her dreams. She hadn't known she'd had this idealised picture of house, husband, children, she said, until it dissolved like a mirage the instant it came into focus. She knew a dream wasn't real, she said, but that did not make losing it any less painful.

She was right about that. I felt acutely that loss of a hazy future time with someone who could remember how I had been when I was young. That the misty outlines of imagined grandchildren and daisy-filled fields were clearly plucked from advertisements for retirement homes made no difference to the way I felt. It was a future I would not have, and it had unleashed in me an intense nostalgia.

Melle said divorce was much more painful than the death of the man she later met and loved. 'We were happy when Louis was killed,' she told me a few weeks after the accident. 'The cut was so clean. We were talking on the phone, and he said *"Ek het jou lief, Engelsman"* as he was about to go out of range near Solitaire in the desert.' Half an hour later the truck he'd gone to fix crushed him and he was dead. 'He was there, then he wasn't,' she had said. 'But we knew we loved each other.'

I could see the advantage of that, but I also remembered how she had been when we arranged to bury Louis – choosing coffins and flowers, neither of us with any experience in funerals. How stunned she had been when we packed her boxes, as I was packing mine now, and moved the belongings she had once moved into his house out again. Back to our parents' house.

'Just decide what you want, sis,' she said to me as I sat with my phone pressed to my ear on my unmade bed, strewn with that divorce morning's rejected outfits. 'Then do that.'

'I don't know what I want,' I said. That was half the truth. The full truth was that I did not want anything at all. 'I feel like a captain who has abandoned her ship,' I told her, 'I failed my marriage and now I'm running away.'

'Utter rubbish,' Melle said again. 'You made your career. You've been given these residencies because you worked. It wasn't luck. You aren't running away. You're going towards yourself.'

I could not see this, but I did not argue with her. I had, after all, given her the same pep talk when she left her husband. 'It was good you left him,' I'd told her then. 'Perseverance is the most overrated of virtues. Knowing that something is not working and giving it up is admirable,' I, complacently married at the time, had said as she had sobbed. But I had chivvied her up and out of bed and on with her life, overruling her when she begged to be left alone, and now she was doing the same for me.

'You've got to be tough for this life,' my sister reminded me.

There was no disputing that. Her belief, and my own, in keeping on when you can't was the only thing that would get my packing done, so I put down the phone, took all my clothes out of the cupboard and dumped them on the bed, trying to imagine what I would need for the nine months I would be in Europe.

I had no idea what to take with me. I did not know who I was any more or where I was going, so I folded a mishmash of things and put them into the new red suitcase I had bought. Twenty-three kilograms of luggage was all I could take with me. The same amount of luggage I had taken to join Aidan in London twenty-seven years earlier. When I could fit nothing more into the suitcase, I snapped it shut. It was done. The relief. The knowledge that departure was imminent was a familiar comfort.

I had spent the last ten years travelling. When I was in motion the pain lessened. I knew what to do. One foot in front of the other until I reached the new place on the other side of the horizon, where things would be different.

I crossed Aidan's name out and wrote my sister's name and phone number in the next-of-kin slot in my passport. Melle, who had come to hate travelling, would get the call if I was injured – or dead. She'd be the one to come to wherever I was to pick up whatever pieces were left.

I looked around the room. Everything was gone apart from a framed photograph on my dressing table. I picked it up and wiped the dust off the glass. Me and all three children piling onto Aidan's lap. I thought about packing it, but there was no space, so it went in a box destined for the garage. My tenants, due in an hour, would not want my detritus lying about. When they arrived, a couple and two little girls, I gave them the keys to my house, as well as Molly, the silky-soft mongrel my daughters smuggled into their beds when they thought I was not watching.

I knew I would not live there again. The pang was knife sharp.

I had time to kill at the airport, so I wandered through the duty-free shop. I tried perfume after perfume until a pretty, plump-cheeked girl called me over to her stall. 'I can give you a makeover,' she said, 'if there's time before your flight.'

I put down my bags and perched on the stool. There were lipsticks in every shade of pink and red, smoky eyeshadows, and concealers to hide the shadows under my eyes. I shut my eyes and offered up my face to her. When she massaged cream onto my face, the gentleness of her touch made me cry. Suggesting a waterproof mascara, she wiped away my tears.

IN TRANSIT

fifty-seven

Dawn rays flashing on the wings of planes circling Heathrow Airport, metal vultures waiting their turn to glide down to the rain-washed city of London, where I would be staying until I took up the first of my writer's residences. I had been awarded three, one in England, one in Scotland, and one in Italy, but the bounty my writing had brought gave me no joy. I had lost my surefooted confidence – on the page, as I had in life.

I collected my luggage and made my way to a friend who had offered me a bed for a couple of months. Once there, I hauled my red suitcase up to the top of her narrow house and unpacked in the first of the innumerable rooms I would stay in over the coming years.

Three weeks later, at the beginning of May, I took a train to York, where I was to be the John Tilney Writer in Residence at the university. This public honour, and others that followed, had no connection to my growing sense that it had all come at the cost of my marriage, my home life, my private life as a woman. It seemed an incalculably high price to pay. But I partitioned those feelings of loss and failure, dressed smartly, put on my red lipstick, and immersed myself in teaching my students what I had discovered about the ethics and aesthetics of writing about violence. The requirement to be both authoritative and outward facing steadied me. I felt assured that I had something to give back to the world – to repay the good fortune I'd had as a writer.

In July I went to Cove Park, an artists' retreat on a rocky spit of land between Loch Long and Gare Loch. There, I lived in a converted shipping container for three months. In the mornings there was mist suspended between the mountains on the opposite side of the loch. If there was wind, the water was opaque, and when it was still it was a mirror, boats moving silently, trailing wakes that were like arms reaching toward the shore. At midday, four Highland cows would make their way down to my little cottage and graze companionably for an hour or so. The daily fellowship was a delight. The quiet rural rhythms of western Scotland gave me the respite I needed to return to the book that the turbulence in my life had interrupted, and I wrote like a woman possessed.

That book, publicised as the sixth in my Clare Hart series, though never published, told of the sexual abuse of children and its lucrative by-product, the child pornography proliferating on the internet. The subject had been on the periphery of my research since a detective who had taken me on patrol had told me about the gangsters who would pick up young girls, get them high on tik, and then film them having sex. Once they'd made a blue movie of the girls, the detective told me, those gangsters had them. Cost them nothing, but made them a lot of money.

'Big men,' he told me, 'with children. Girls of twelve, thirteen, fourteen, who want love and attention. Just like the boys those same gangsters already had running for them when they were seven or eight. They're given drugs. They're disposable. There are always more of them.'

Trawling through this horror, I felt sullied, depressed, and silenced by the subject matter. The gnawing feeling in my gut told me what I was doing, the way I was writing it, was wrong. The problem was the point of view. No matter how virtuous the observing eye – whether my own or that of my feminist warrior, Clare Hart – what I was writing was a replica of the pornographer's gaze: a sadistic, scopic power that pierced its victim's body and pinned it like a captured butterfly to a collector's board. I could not find the right way to look at this subject, but I could not give up on those girls, so on I went, knowing that if I stopped, I would lie down, and if I did that, I would not get up again.

I took my manuscript with me when, in the autumn, I went to Civitella Ranieri, a castle in Umbria given over to artists, musicians and writers. Twelve of us arrived for our two-month sojourn; each of us had a private suite of rooms and a studio. It was heaven. Lunch was brought to us, but each evening we gathered, like apostles, to have dinner together. It was boar-hunting season and, as I continued to write in the wrong direction, I'd hear the pop of rifle fire and men shouting to each other as they stalked their prey through mist-swathed fields.

It was the end of the year and I had written hundreds of pages of a novel that made as little sense to me as my uprooted life did. Throughout that strange lacuna of a year, I spoke at arts festivals about books and jailed writers. I did okay, as far as I know, but I don't remember much. I was stunned, as if by a bomb only I knew had exploded.

fifty-eight

In December I went back and joined my family in Namibia. It was Christmas and Aidan came to Swakopmund too, as if nothing had changed. It was surreal, all being together, though we were not. Navigating it all felt like walking barefoot on broken glass; to escape, I arranged an endurance ride for me and my daughters – eight hours through the Namib Desert.

The sea mist thinned as we drove away from the chilly little holiday town huddled on the windswept beach. We turned off the tarred road onto a track that bumped down to the Swakop River, which winds its waterless way from the Namibian escarpment to the Atlantic. At the stables, quick-stepping desert horses and a guide welcomed us for our endurance ride. We set off across the riverbed, making our way through copses of tamarisk trees and onto auburn dunes undulating south as far as the eye could see. The only sounds were the shush of hooves in the desert sand and any words we cared to say to each other, which were not many, enveloped as we were in the silence. Grace and Jamie – Rose was in Istanbul that summer – were loose-limbed and free as we rode. We picnicked looking over the ocean before heading back.

Eight hours later and the strength in my legs was gone, my jeans wet from a pelvic floor weakened after bearing three children. The wind scudded over the sand as the horses started to surge towards their stables in the Swakop River. A plastic bag, perished by the sun, writhed on the freshly graded surface of the road. A flicker of tension across my horse's skin – but I was too tired to notice, absorbed with stopping my involuntary flow of urine, frozen by a humiliating image of old age coming at me over the horizon.

But still that bag up ahead, whipping this way and that, and my knees, my thighs no longer able to steer my horse, my eyes lifted to the dunes rather than the litter in the riverbed.

That bag, enraged to be trapped by a heap of sand, whipped this way and that. The horse, tired of me on its back, veered left sharply. I corrected my weight to go with him, but he swerved right.

I fell, hitting the ground with a force that knocked the breath out of my body and that turned the bright-blue sky black.

When the light returned – the sun drilling through my closed eyelids – my legs were numb. I could not move. I am not dead, I thought, but I am broken, and if I am broken, I will be admitted to a hospital. Part of me longed for that hospital. To be admitted. To have sedatives administered to me. Painkillers. To give up the burden of living. I had dreamed of a sanatorium in the Alps where the air is pure and so good for the mad women sent up there to recuperate on the edge of a lake, the only sound the lap of water on the shore.

I had fantasised about a hospital where there was a routine of walks and sleep and activities set out by benign but rigid authorities. In that dream place I would do nothing in between the allotted times for meals and medical interactions, just flip through the pages of old magazines, look at the knitting in my lap, listen to the silence that filled a valley, eternally green like the one in *Heidi*, which I had read over and over as a child. I dreamed of sitting there uninterrupted for eternity.

'Mummy,' sobbed Jamie, flinging themself off their horse and onto me. A grown child – an adult – needing my body. Hugging me, hurting me, needing me to be alive, but I could do nothing but lie there on the hard desert. Grace had shock and fear in her eyes that were so like my sister's. I had to move. My arms first. Fingers then wrists so that I could lift my arms and put them around one daughter then the other. A mother's reassurance that this was not it. My life was not over. It was because of my daughters that I had to go on. It was for them that I could not drift like a jellyfish in the ocean of my life. I understood then the Faustian pact I'd entered into when I conceived them. I was not allowed to break – not if I could help it. That is what I had not understood about mothers.

The air returned to my lungs in gasps. I moved my feet. I bent my knees, ashamed of the urine, hoping no one could smell it as I waited for the pain to recede. My children got me back on my feet.

'You've to get up on the horse,' they said. 'You have to break the fear.'

That's what I myself had learned from horse riding. That's what I and their riding teachers had taught them.

I mounted my horse. It hurt, but the three of us rode side by side back to the stables.

fifty-nine

A week after New Year, bruises purpling my back, I returned to Cape Town. I had intended to pick up the dropped stitches of my life and knit myself together again. I could not do it. Too much had come undone. I had unravelled during the slow-motion psychic spiral that had ripped apart my marriage and brought my writing, which had earned me both a living and my public place in the world, to a halt. This breakdown – a nervous breakdown, though I did not use this old-fashioned term – had gained frightening momentum.

I called the therapist I'd consulted during the period of excruciating headaches while teaching prisoners to write. It felt like a miracle that she was not on holiday. That she had time for me. It was a homecoming to sit with her in her familiar room, which had been the repository of so many conversations about men and violence and how to live with witnessing it all, with writing it down, with trying to understand and heal and love.

'I don't want to go on,' I told her. For a fraction of a second her face lost its usual expression of dispassionate compassion, and in that moment I could see myself mirrored in her distress. She believed me, which made me believe that what I had said to her without meaning to say it at all – I was going to say something else, about how hard I found making a home only for me – was really true.

'Phone your GP,' she said, her gentle voice firm. 'Phone her now and make an appointment.' I did as she said, glad that someone was taking charge, making decisions that I could not.

My doctor asked me what was wrong, and out of despair, I made a list, and she wrote it all down on my card. I left with a prescription for pills that would, she said, help with the depression. I took them religiously, but if I was going to recover, I had to leave Cape Town. I had lost my place in that world, and I did not know how to remake myself. I had been gone nine months, but still, I could not bear telling the divorce tale and I did not have a new story yet. A cover story. Now, no matter how many clothes I put on, I always felt naked.

Until my marriage was over, I'd had no idea how integral the institution, that imaginary place, was to my sense of personhood in the world. I felt publicly stripped, and my feminist mind could not persuade that abjectly female part of me that felt ashamed and exposed. I had been barely out of childhood when I'd stepped into marriage and I remembered thinking how, by being married, I would not have to think about how to navigate the world as a woman alone. For it is true that marriage gives a young woman all sorts of defences from a predatory patriarchal world. I'd always experienced romance as disruptive, while marriage had given me a place to settle myself and think.

When I'd been in Windhoek that December, after my fall from the horse, the loneliness, the brokenness of me, of our family, had driven me to park outside the garden flat Aidan was renting at the time. Unlike my horse-riding injuries, the pain of a broken marriage could not be soothed. And so, there I'd sat on that Windhoek street, where a hot, dry wind drove dust across the tar; I did not know how to endure my feeling of evisceration, which I imagined I'd seen mirrored in his eyes.

I opened the car door. But I could not get out. *If you go in*, admonished the voice of fairness – or possibly vanity and pride – *you can never leave again. You cannot do this to him or to your children: go in and then leave again. Because you will. You know you will. You did not leave on a whim*, counselled a calm voice, *it took you years to face the death of that love. You cannot go in and settle there – a dog in a manger you do not want.*

I did not go in; instead, I sat in the car. I would have to be my own knight in shining armour. I would have to defend myself. Instead of being 'spoken for', I had to speak for myself. I was astonished at how powerful and how enduring my sense of shame was after the divorce; how much I desired a relationship, not for connection and closeness to another person, but to provide me with the social fig leaf of belonging to someone.

Aidan did not come out. He did not know I was there. After half an hour or so, I drove back to my parents' house.

I told my sister I would be leaving again. First for America, where I had been invited to give a lecture on African literature and crime fiction at Yale University, then England – I had a fellowship at the Oxford Research Centre in the Humanities. I also had a home at St Antony's College, headed then by an eminent historian. Noticing that I needed the rhythm and order that the colleges of Oxford had, for centuries, given to men, she arranged for me to have dining rights. Because of my role with the international free expression organisation, PEN, I was among those who consulted on ways to resolve the increasingly contested issue of free speech and the structural inequalities of the post-colonial world.

I believed that in Oxford I could refashion myself, as if the past had never happened. There, among strangers, I would pass for normal. There, in the magical land of elsewhere, I would be able to write again, to live. I would take Grace with me – she'd had a tough time the year I had been away. I could mother her. That would be useful, surely?

'You're a like a wild animal that's been let out of its cage,' Melle said, 'bolting about in different directions, not knowing what to do or where to go.' I didn't mind her saying that. It was true.

'I'm too mad to stay,' I said. 'Everywhere I go, every person I speak to reminds me of what I lost, what I broke.'

'Ag, *my sussie*,' she said, the compassion in her voice making me cry. 'I know it doesn't help, but I love you.'

At the end of January 2016, I was back at the airport with Grace, who needed to get away from Cape Town too. She was in a wheelchair, having done a cartwheel on the verandah and slicing her foot open on the security gate – just two hours before we were meant to leave. After a display of unmaternal fury and a visit to the emergency room, there we were, on a plane to the United States. I felt that familiar anticipatory tingle of pleasure – a feeling I kept secret and to myself – at the thought of presenting my own work together with that of other African women writers, all part of the African Studies Seminar Series at Yale University.

We stopped off in New York – Grace's first time back since she was a seven-year-old – where she'd be staying for as long as her visa allowed. I had arranged to visit an artist I had got to know in the castle in Italy, and so we went downtown, where Serkan Özkaya showed me the new piece he was working on. He had installed video surveillance cameras on the outside walls of a gallery which projected images of the streets onto the walls inside, thus dissolving the barrier – the wall, the skin – between inside and outside.

'It's like the start of every crime novel or movie where a woman will be mutilated and murdered,' I said, watching the spooky, silent images. 'This electronic eye we've all become so used to, and internalised – it makes everything look suspicious. But there's another gaze' – I had not thought about any of this, but it came to me as I watched – 'there's the human eye. It can't take everything in at once, as the camera can – information, but without meaning.'

Then I said to Serkan, 'I'd like to come and sit in the gallery and write down what I see, to record as much as I can of the world as it goes by – my eyes alongside the eye of electronic surveillance.'

I wanted to know how I, a woman, might see things; the female gaze, and what happened when a woman looked at things rather than when she herself was looked at. I had been thinking of two women artists in particular, Sophie Calle's work on surveillance and Marina Abramović's experiments with radical presence, since I was interested in endurance, especially physical endurance. Serkan, taken with the idea, told me about Georges Perec's book *An Attempt at Exhausting a Place in Paris* – an in-situ writing experiment similar to the performance art I was proposing. Our attempt to 'exhaust' a place in New York was arranged for the summer. For three days I would sit in the gallery in Tribeca for the entire time it was open and write down everything I saw. At the end of the three days, I would do a public reading from those notes, with simultaneous camera footage playing.

There is a hum to the body when a new idea is conceived, when the tight defensive bud of the self opens. There is no feeling quite like it. I'd thought that life-force joy, the imagination, was lost to me – but without warning, it had returned. I held in my hands a grappling hook that would swing me over the abyss of the present and land me safely in the future.

sixty

Hedgehogs rustled in the grass outside the ground-floor flat I rented in Oxford. Rose had lived in it when she had done her Master's degree the year before, and it was a comfort to feel her presence in the neat, square rooms where I unpacked my possessions. Jamie had decided to go to university in England. After a couple of months Grace, who was applying to art schools, returned from New York and came to live with me. I would provide them the home they needed in a new land. 'That's a worthwhile job,' my sister said to me. 'Honourable.'

Motherhood can be a useful disguise for grief, existential drift, and loss.

During that period, I started drafting a Women's Manifesto together with the first woman president of the writer's organisation, PEN International. I had been haunted, ever since working with women writers in Namibia, by the complex ways in which women are silenced, censored and made prisoner, not only in jails but also in their own homes, and by the carapace of gendered convention.

For many women in the world – and for almost all women until relatively recently – the first, and the last and perhaps the most powerful frontier was the door of the house she lived in: her parents' or her husband's home.

These opening lines have great personal significance for what it means to be a writer and a woman. The collectively written manifesto articulated the layered complexity of being a woman who writes, which means a woman who does not stay home.

For women to have free speech, the right to read, the right to write, they need to have the right to roam physically, socially and intellectually. There are few social systems that do not regard with hostility a woman who walks by herself.

This manifesto, adopted by PEN in Lviv, Ukraine in 2017, has since been used to defend persecuted women writers the world over. It was also, however, an affirmation of years of advocacy work, which I could only glimpse through the cage of what the doctor had called depression.

This was the wholly inadequate word for the demon that had me in his grip and which, with the tenacity of a stalker, punished me for any time I spent away from him. The little pills my clumsy morning hands let drop sometimes, making me scrabble on the bathroom floor to retrieve them, dulled the impulse I had to check out of life. While those tablets suppressed my troublesome spirit, they left behind the husk of a body that did not know what it was searching for, or how to fill itself. I bought food, but I could not eat. I was starving, but I had no appetite, and, when the food went off, I threw it out.

A bit of romance, people told me, would fix things.

Find a new man, they said. But I was woefully out of practice – I'd been twenty-two the last time I had done any of this.

'Who?' I'd say to my sister when we spoke on the phone. I could practically hear her rolling her eyes. Then I'd ask, 'How?'

'God, Margie. You know that all you need to do to get a man is make eye contact.'

I laughed – that's what I'd told Melle when she had been heartbroken, and it had worked. She had made eye contact with Volker, the kindest of men, and the two of them were now making a desert garden in the house they shared.

I felt lopsided; twenty-five years is a long time to pattern yourself around a man and a house. Coupledom, even if brief, is an art, and I had lost the knack. Much as I wished to be taken in, the relationships I attempted were a disaster. Though pleased to be touched, I felt nothing – not on my skin, and certainly not in my heart. Whatever might once have been alive and responsive in me was dead. The love affairs I attempted were unendurable because I could not bear to see my loneliness reflected in their eyes.

Being alone, being silent, I could tolerate. Being with any other person – apart from my children, with whom I could easily be silent – for more than an hour, attending to them, talking to them, or worse, being talked to, attended to, knocked me out.

I could not write. It was as if I had somehow been disappeared by those life-saving yellow tablets, which I had taken religiously since leaving South Africa. Being alive felt like a mere technicality. The dullness, the lack of intensity, the flatlining of emotion and sensation was a kind of chemical neutering of the self. The anguish that had made me want to kill myself was blunted, but so was any responsiveness or joy. To achieve this supposedly life-saving inertia, the fiery mustang that was my life force had to be converted into a pliant, plodding carthorse that never lifted its head to see what was on the horizon.

In that state I could not write, despite writing being the only way out of the darkness in which I was lost. It not only made me a living; it was when writing that I felt alive. And so, without consulting a doctor – as I knew I should, as I would have advised anyone else to do – I threw away the pills that made me feel as if I'd had a lobotomy of the soul.

sixty-one

I returned to the novel I had so far tried and failed to write. I had done all my usual research – reading, talking with victims, listening to the silences between their halting words. I had interviewed perpetrators, too. One, a man convicted for possession of pornographic images of children, told me, 'It's only pictures.'

He had been in my professional orbit for several years and I was shocked when this behaviour came to light, but I found it impossible to assimilate his dismissal of the severity of his crime. When pressed, the urbane charm vanished, exposing the aggression and narcissistic entitlement that lay beneath. He, like many sex offenders I have met, believed something terrible had been done to him. It was the actions of the police – not his own – that had resulted in his wife leaving him, the ruin of a stellar career, and a criminal conviction. He was utterly divorced from the reality that living, defenceless children are used in those two-dimensional images.

It was the same with other men I interviewed. The arousal stimulated by the cruelty on display cancels out the humanity of the child.

For some time, I pretended to myself I'd make this novel work too, as a crime to be investigated. But I could not. How to look at these images? How to regard the pain of other women, of girls? How to write about a lucrative business where the criminality of the image has been elided? The images were themselves crime scenes. The act of looking, of observation, of seeing was itself criminal.

The crime novel – the model of the procedural where I, a woman, was looking at criminal images – seemed to be a reproduction of that prurient gaze. It was fundamentally unethical, and I could no longer bear to look. It was immoral to reproduce in a novel the gaze which causes so much harm to children, especially girl children. So, even though the rights had been sold and a 2016 deadline agreed upon, I cancelled the contracts. I could not bring myself to publish that book. After that, I started cancelling my public events, practically destroying the professional writer's life I had built over the previous decade.

It felt momentarily like liberation, but in truth the carapace I had formed around myself to write 'objectively' about violence against women had cracked. The barrier between me and my chosen subject matter had collapsed. But that very porousness was what I needed to understand, to utilise, if I was to write anything. If I was to survive, I had to write a book about what it feels like to be looked at in ways that strip a girl, a woman, of her humanity.

I needed to distil, to somehow shift the incoherence of experience into the ordered dimension of the novel. I wanted to reveal what lies unnoticed below the surface. But I felt unable to build the word-bridge between my heart and my voice, so essential to telling the tale I wanted to tell.

Telling tales breaks the strictest of childhood taboos, so that shame is carried by the teller of the tale – the tattletale – rather than the told-on wrongdoer. Similarly, in womanhood we discover the strictest of the unwritten laws of patriarchy: don't tell.

I started again. This time the novel would not be a criminal investigation. It was not about finding pornographic images, examining them and then working backwards. It would focus on the devastation of a woman who discovers that the man she loves consumes pornographic images of children, but also on the pain of the girl in some of these pictures. The woman and girl were twinned, but in ways I could not yet fathom.

Years before, I had done a story for *Marie Claire* magazine about four young women, two barely eighteen, who had been duped by a man who set himself up as a model scout. He had spiked their drinks, they told me, then filmed and posted the footage. The story resulted in legal action that got the sites down and the man charged, but once images are on the internet, it is impossible to pull them all back. The words of one of those girls haunted me.

'It never stops,' she said to me. 'Even when I'm sleeping it doesn't stop. Always, someone out there is watching me.' The idea of a crime that never stops seemed to me to be the essence of trauma, repeating on an endless loop.

I never saw the actual images, but I did see the damage done to the girls, their subsequent shame and suffering. Not-seeing had been key to how I had understood their story. For a long time, I believed that if I saw the images I would understand, but I was wrong.

Seeing is believing, we are told. But what we see can also blunt our senses, what we apprehend through body-shock. There was my key to how I would tell this story – it lay in the eye of the beholder.

I had always known from my reading of *Lolita* that it is possible for a woman to be oblivious to the depraved proclivities of the man she loves. In Nabokov's novel, Lolita's mother does not realise until it is too late that the man who has seduced her has his sights on her eleven-year-old daughter.

Many perpetrators live unruffled, seemingly disassociated lives with adult women. Men who consume pornographic images of women will soon begin to search for increasingly younger objects to gaze upon to arouse them. That is how the narcotic effect works.

In the United Kingdom alone, the crime of child pornography has become so widespread that police lack the manpower to investigate and prosecute it. Investigations now follow a kind of triage; the worst cases – the men who make the images, rather than the ones who gaze – are the ones they pursue, though to me, maker and viewer form an infinite loop, like a Möbius strip.

I knew that gaze. It had penetrated me, colonising my sense of self and worth. For so many girls, it is the rite of passage to womanhood. I wanted those eyes put out. I wanted those soul-thieves dead, but I struggled to find the words to speak about those online versions of Humbert Humbert, with their casual corruption of innocent Lolitas, their poison circulating forever on the internet.

Somewhere, always, a man is raping a girl and burying her alive – as in the case I had drawn on for *Water Music*. The murderous misogyny, the connection between sex and violence that I had investigated for so long had filled my mind, poisoning everything. I needed to organise it into something that made sense: a novel.

My protagonist would be a painter, I decided, a woman concerned with the visual, whose devastating discovery would lead to madness.

'Are you having suicidal thoughts?' my sister asked me, seemingly out of the blue, in one of our regular phone conversations.

'Oh, no,' I said. 'Not at all. I'm too busy writing again.'

'I see,' said Melle, in that tone of hers which meant that she did in fact see what I was wanting her to see. 'So, tell me what you're writing about, then.'

'About this woman who loves a man, only to find out he has a conviction for possessing child porn,' I told her breezily. 'She never sees the actual images, but the thought of them – the thought of what he was looking at, looking for – drives her mad because, apart from the obvious horror of it all, it floods her with memories of what had happened to her as a child.'

'Okay, I see,' I could hear my sister's eyebrows arching. 'And?'

'Well, she's an artist, and she has a fall – in her studio. A spike goes right through her, and she's paralysed, in pain. She'd rather be dead than crippled, but because of her paralysis she can't do the deed herself. So, she has to persuade someone she trusts – a friend, her daughter – to follow through on their promise to put her down if she can't live in the way she chooses to live: active, creative, in control—'

Melle cut me short.

'So, you are writing about a woman killing herself because she can't believe her eyes?'

I could not speak, and as the silence stretched, I heard a loerie calling 'go 'way' in her Namibian garden.

'You could put it like that, yes,' I eventually said.

'That's not a book,' said my sister, 'that's a suicide note.'

After that, my sister called me every morning. The phone would ring, and I would answer. We would make coffee, though we were almost a whole line of longitude apart, and we drank it together. Phone call by phone call, Melle got me through winter and spring, and then it was summer and time for me to return to New York.

sixty-two

The heat already had a grip on the city when, at ten o'clock on the first of June, I made my way down to Tribeca, where Serkan ushered me into the Postmaster's Gallery. The cameras he had set up dissolved the walls between interior and exterior. To my right I could see an alleyway; ahead was the gallerists' office with windows onto Franklin Street; to my left, a flight of stairs leading to the apartments above.

It took me a while to decide where to sit – to decide on the vantage point of reality – but, after consideration, I set up my writing table against the back wall, placed my pen and notebooks in the centre of the table, and took stock of where I would be for the coming days. It was a relief to sit down and record fleeting glimpses: *Men off-loading a truck. A fat man heaves himself up, does things inside. The heat and the sunlight erase the street outside, but there are flashes. Two men with white shirts and jeans walk past the truck. In the alley three men are talking. Another man comes out carrying shirts. Men, more men, only men walking by. The stairs inside are quiet.*

On the opening night of *An Attempt at Exhausting a Place in New York*, the gallerist told me about a couple caught unawares by Serkan's cameras: they had stopped on the stairwell leading to their apartment, seemingly about to have sex. I wondered whether she'd felt the rail in her lower back as he leaned over her – though unseen by me, I presumed it would have been *her* back to the wall.

A man with a dog came into the gallery and the gallerist showed him around, explaining what I was doing. 'She's capturing time,' the man interrupted. He understood.

All I could do was capture fragments of what I saw, slivers of time. Time, as it passes, is chaos, but from this I selected fragments to craft meaning. The narrative of a life – its record, one's story – is created also out of what one omits, whether consciously or unconsciously: the lacunae. To capture time, which is what telling a story is, I'd have to observe myself and the world, but that is heartbreaking, because at the moment one glimpses things, they are gone. It's the same with people, I thought. You love them, then you don't. They touch you, then they don't.

Capturing time, reality, is what I have tried to do in writing this, choosing what to put in and what to leave out, weaving a narrative in an attempt to make sense of my life, our lives, how and why I do things, what we have done. Jostling in my imagination were my daughters, sister, brother, mother, father, my ex-husband. My vision was blurred, just as it was when I wrote down what I saw projected onto the gallery walls: *On Franklin Street the light a bright white stain devouring the road. Famished light. A bicycle's wheels flashed as the street was consumed. A man walked with his scrapping Peter Pan shadow at his heels. Mine sat beside me.*

I had returned here, I realised, in an attempt to heal a wound, to sit with a final span of patience to bring that time to a close. My mind quietened as the hours passed in the gallery with the city orbiting me. I had returned to New York, the site of the great severance in my life, because I needed to make sense of the impulse that had driven me, at thirty-five, to leave my girls and my home.

It would not have been possible if Aidan had not come too, I'd said at the time, everyone said it, but I was no longer sure that this was the truth. I would have come anyway, I realised, sitting in the gallery where the walls – the skin between inside and outside – had been dissolved for me by Serkan's cameras. I had been determined to escape the domestic story I'd stumbled into and been running from ever since.

My sitting there was a way to endure – or perhaps to atone for – my feeling of haunted restlessness; to exorcise it, and to find a way to feel at home in myself. Sitting there in one place imposed a sense of quiet I had lost. It was, I saw, my attempt to restore what had been shattered. I had shattered when I saw my ex-husband with his young girlfriend. The force of that blow was that it landed so soon after we'd separated, while we were meant to be seeing what could and what could not be done to salvage what had once been 'us'. A blow that had shattered the last fragile shell around the self I had brought, with all my hope and ambition, to New York in 1999 – which was when that infinite distancing had in fact begun. In the last three glacial years of our marriage and our subsequent separation, my focus had fragmented.

Now, in that gallery, I had to find a way to feel at home in myself. I had lost the ability to live in time, to maintain coherence in space, to *write*. All I could do was wait for it all to pass, to write it into the past. And so, sitting there in this unorthodox collaboration – as still as the time before everything had shattered – I wrote for hours.

On my way back to the apartment where I was staying in 21st Street, a man in the West Village asked me, 'Is Cornelia Street that way?' I said it was. Cornelia Street is the first place I'd stayed when I was in New York alone. During my first Thanksgiving here, I did not speak to a single soul for five days. When I did speak again, in class, my voice was unfamiliar. A new woman, one who could leave her children and not speak or be spoken to for five days, had moved in and occupied me. She had taken over, making iron of my will, stealing my tears, numbing my body, so that I could not feel the brush of fingertips on my skin – but I could write my books.

I harvested detail on my second day in the gallery: *A boy on a skateboard flying by; a piece of white paper tumbling down the alley; an elegant woman, her hair a sleek cascade down her back, coming down the internal staircase.* The artist achieves a sense of reality by winnowing, selecting, thereby creating a scene.

Marriage is what I had in mind as I sat there. I had believed that marriage and sex would dissolve the skin-walls of the self in the way that the cameras had broken down the walls of the gallery. I had desired that dissolution and called it love. But love makes us like children – dependent and exposed – and that I feared. Perhaps, I remember thinking, writing, the thing that had made me independent, had stolen my marriage, was my escape, enabling me to sit apart as I wrote things down. I had put many things aside in exchange for seeing more clearly.

The gallery was locked when I arrived on the third day. 'A party with a lot of vodka,' the gallerist told me, 'makes things difficult the next day.' So, I started late, my writing down of the world. The minutes slipped by faster than the previous two days. Time was slipping through my fingers, impossible to catch. The onward rush of life had taken my babies lying in my arms, their soft heads under my chin, soon to leap with brown limbs through childhood and beyond.

The gallerist asked if I needed anything. I have never known how to answer that question, so I said, 'Nothing, thank you.'

After she left, I wrote down: *A home. Love. A garden. Quiet. Company. Solitude. A horizon. Earplugs. I cannot sleep with another person unless I can block out the sound of them breathing. I cannot let my guard down unless I am completely alone, and no one is waiting for me.*

I had not known how to keep myself happy and calm and present with the person I loved. All I had known was to separate my woman-self from my work-self. I had built a wall between them so that if anyone looked at 'the woman', they could not see 'the work'. And vice versa. If they looked at 'the work', then 'the woman' was invisible. I could be either one or the other. There is a certain size that a woman can be in the world. If she works and is ambitious and fills the world, then she will not fit a man's eye. A man's desire for a woman is a narrow aperture through which he looks.

I glanced outside and saw Franklin Street had regained its shadows. *A little boy in the street with a backpack and a pink scarf around his neck comes past walking hand in hand with his mother. An old man, tall in a black cap, walking past with his shoulders down.*

He made me think of my father and his Parkinson's. He was old and I was not at home to care for him.

That night I read fragments of what I had seen, and written down, to the Manhattan art crowd who came to listen. Some of them were moved to tears, which touched me deeply. I know how hard it is to cry and the relief it offers.

I told this story a while later at my brother's dining table in Cape Town. My parents were there too – the four of us having dinner, Melle holding the fort in Windhoek – my father down to see doctors about an operation for the excruciating pain in his back; our family rallying like the clan it was. It was my father's pain I had thought of when I had seen the old man walk past the wall-dissolving cameras on Franklin Street. I had tried to convey how the light had swallowed the road and that I had felt a flash of joy in my heart and a compassion for the bravery of people, how they come and go and keep on and hold hands.

sixty-three

In September, the end of that summer, Aidan came to Oxford to see Grace; she was living with me while working on the portfolio that would get her into art school in London. The two of them were to escort Jamie to university for the start of the first semester. He was staying in a nearby guesthouse, and, on his first evening, came to fetch me before we left for dinner.

The restaurant was expensive, a glass-and-steel conservatory with olive trees in terracotta pots. The lighting was tasteful, and it was full of people like us, parents of university students. Aidan and I sat opposite each other, separated by the table – a generous square of dark wood set with candles and a small white dish containing salt flakes, bread and butter. The waiter brought water and wine, setting them down as we conducted the mannered conversation of husband and wife at dinner. Aidan spoke as if nothing had happened, and so did I. We spoke as if we went out for dinner every week, as couples with grown children do. We swapped facts about our children and our pride in them. Our hopes, our fears, our affection for these three people we had made in three different beds.

It was only after we had got all the detail about the children out of the way and had eaten the dessert – something lemon for me, panna cotta for him – that he asked me, as couples do, how I'd been.

'Heartbroken,' was the word that came out.

His eyes widened. 'I never knew.'

'How could you not know?'

'You seemed so calm. So in control.'

'I lost everything,' I said.

He left it unsaid that it was I who had made a break for it.

'I never knew,' he said.

How could you not have known? You lived with me for twenty-five years! I wanted to scream. The force it took to repress that desire was like swallowing an earthquake. Whatever it was that held me together lost its grip and there was a scraping – metal on metal – and a sharp click. The sound of my mind unhinging was unbearably loud. He did not hear it. My skull must have muffled the sound.

We settled the bill and walked back to my flat up in Summerstown, stopping to buy milk for the morning. He carried the shopping bag for me. One small burden lifted. I remembered how I'd liked that about marriage, how things were carried for you: heavy things like bags. That it had given me shelter from the storm. There had been love too, I knew. I had found the letters he'd written to me in the beginning. There was faith and trust too, but those I had lost.

Aidan returned at ten the next morning, a bag of croissants in his hand. He was to leave after breakfast. That is what I needed because my head felt strange. My mind had not reconnected during the night, and it was difficult to talk to him over coffee and pastries as couples do. Three hours went by.

'I have to work,' I said, but that was an excuse. I had reached the end of my endurance.

'Dad, we must go,' said Grace. 'We'll miss the train.'

I walked him and our daughter to the door, and it seemed to be forever before they left and I could close it on them. I shut it, knowing I was going to pass out. My head would crack like an egg if it hit the tiled floor. I had to get myself to the sofa under the window where the sun was streaming in and lie down.

When I came to, that is where I was. I was crying. It was pitch-dark. Hours had passed.

Go under, whispered a metallic voice in my head. I turned on my side. The pillow was wet. For hours, I had been adrift in this sea of grief.

Just go under. That sharp voice, scraping the inside of my skull, was new. I blocked my ears, but that made no difference. *Just go under.* It was in me, like a squatter. *Just go under* on repeat, a metronome as certain and as rigid as mathematics, and how would one argue with mathematics? It was right. I understood that, but I was too tired.

'Tomorrow,' I pleaded. 'I will do it tomorrow.' The voice went quiet, stepping back to wait in the wings.

There was no light yet, only trees steepled against a deepening blue, but I got myself up. The world was different. I felt different. Naked, with a nakedness that could not be covered no matter how many clothes I put on. I would have to move again to leave this terror behind me.

LONDON

sixty-four

The tiny flat in London I moved into in 2017 would be mine and my daughters' home for a semester – the owner away teaching in America, with three months unimaginably far into the future. The lease of my house in Cape Town paid the rent. I wrote a few articles, ghost-wrote a book about a once-famous, now-forgotten Edwardian garden painter, edited a bit, but otherwise I lived off the money I had saved for my old age: writing does not come with a pension.

Quiet, tucked away on a tree-lined loop of road on Hampstead Heath, that flat was on the ground floor, so when I undressed at night and dressed in the morning, it was as if I was dressing and undressing on the pavement. I did not care if people looked in and saw me in the tiny bedroom filled by a double bed I shared with no one, and a turquoise chest where extra blankets were stored. All I cared about was that I had a place where I could stay still.

I made that temporary sanctuary mine by rearranging the borrowed furniture, stacking the owner's books on the higher shelves, and putting my own where I could see them. I bought cushion covers in sprightly colours and removed the framed posters, leaving the walls blank and white. The living room was grand – high ceilings and an enormous bay window that looked onto the Heath, which was densely forested in this part, where no walkers ever ventured. Right in the centre of my view was an ancient oak whose thick, branching arms held up the sky. At dawn, foxes trotted across the lawn. At night I'd hear an owl call and see it fly up into the tallest of the oaks, a shadow in the moonlight. Because of the way the tall houses were angled, it felt, when I sat in the gracious living room, that I was alone in the quiet, watching woods.

I did not know what to do with myself, though. What I had written was wrong: the book I had written about the evil inflicted by the male gaze – a basilisk eye that turns its women to stone – was wrong. I'd had to tell it, but it would not sell, even though my agent submitted it to publisher after a publisher. They shot back rejection letters.

'Write something else,' she said. 'Write something funny. Write a memoir. Everyone's writing memoir.'

But I didn't manage to write anything that made sense. All I could do was draw, because that took my gaze outwards, away from the hellscape I saw when I turned my eye inwards to write about the world and myself in it.

I bought sheets of creamy paper and chalky pastels and charcoal pencils. Then I bought some lilies – the white ones that give off the sweetest of night scents – from the flower seller on the shabby high street at the end of the road. I took everything back to the flat with me, put the white lilies in a tall vase and sketched them every day, recording the curl and droop of the petals and the dropping of the pollen.

One lily opened, unfurling its night-scented flower with abandon – it would die first, I knew. The others followed in strict order, opening a few hours apart over the first few days. One held out, but it opened in the end, spreading creamy petals around erect stamens laden with ochre pollen that stained my clothes. I drew that last lily with the petals, the others lying shrivelled on the table. When I looked up from the lilies, my fingers smudged, all I could see was the garden where no one ever went and, on the other side of a tall wooden palisade, the Heath.

When I'd first moved in, the trees were a vivid green. In October they turned, and by late November spectral branches stretched into a slowly disappearing sky. In December the snow came. I drew the gnarled oak on the other side of the garden wall. There was a pillow of snow at the point where the trunk separated into branches. An owl huddled there in the day, one eye on the loudly chattering parakeets. I drew them, lime-green flashes in the winter trees. When I was drawing, I did not cry. Instead, I was recording, day by day, the external world, the existence of which I'd become increasingly uncertain.

The only new thing I bought for that apartment was a cream-coloured enamel kettle. It was the same as the kettle we'd had in our Cape Town house, and whenever it shrieked like a banshee as it boiled, I felt, for a moment, at home. More so when my daughters came to stay, to be replenished before returning to their unfolding lives.

Their presence rallied me, made me go out, meeting them for coffee or a drink. That was the best I could do as their mother at that time because of the numbness the pills had wrought.

I was taking anti-depressants again because I had frightened myself into approaching a fatigued Oxford GP with a tea stain on her white blouse for help in the ten-minute slot I was allocated. She had looked helpless and irritated, and prescribed what I had taken before. I was too ashamed of myself to tell that overworked woman they'd done me no good, and to ask for something else.

As before, it was as if some stranger, some non-person – a not-Margie – had inhabited my body. This not-Margie moved me around in my flat. I took the pills because they were meant to get my mind right, but they made me feel not myself – and what did *I* know? Maybe that's how they were meant to work – by making me not myself. This not-Margie had a strange paralysis of the hands. and writing, like any labour, is hands-on. It's an all-hands-on-deck kind of activity, but when I tried to use my hands to write, I found them hanging limp at my sides.

Who was this not-Margie who jumped me up out of my chair and chivvied me to the kitchen, where I wiped surfaces, packed dishes away, chopped things?

She drove me to the laundry basket and made me wash clothes that had barely been worn. For her I fetched the vacuum cleaner and sucked up pieces of invisible lint from the floor. She nagged me to take her to the shops to buy things I did not want or need. Because I did not want to eat, I did not want to cook. I did not want to fold or iron clothes and sheets and pillowcases.

I placated her, this not-me. I shopped and cleaned and cooked, then threw away the food I'd made. When I was dizzy, I'd eat toast for her, standing at the kitchen counter as if I wasn't eating at all. I gave up writing the stories that had earned me my place in the world. I would try to wrestle fear, fury and love into the words that had been my protection, but words had forsaken me.

I wrote things down in clandestine rushes, as if I were a prisoner trying to record, as evidence, what was being done to her, in case she died in detention. But nothing made sense. My sentences were a looped track. I was not psychotic. I knew what was going on, but it is terrifying to be so lucidly mad.

It was as if that murderous male gaze that had absorbed so much of my creative life had taken up residence in me. As if it had declared the territory of me its own – this male figment of my imagination – with boots kicking at the bone-cage that entrapped the two of us. In there, his voice had no nuance, no change of pitch, no intonation.

You are nothing, he told me. His words scorched. With him, there were no secrets, there was no feeling. Only the volleys he fired from his hideout in the base of my skull. He knotted the muscles in my scalp, rippled nausea through my belly, scratched at my skin.

He tightened the vice inside my skull, twisting my right eye. Turned me inwards to stare down the pain – migraine, despair? – but I saw him there in the shadowed part of my mind, blade glinting in one hand, all-seeing god-eye held aloft in the other. A searchlight that exposed everything uncertain and tender and joyous.

I moved around carefully when he went quiet, careful not to lure him out of his lair. Then, I could be devious, and get away with things – make love, sun myself. Hope, that most precious of a torturer's instruments, would return, but he would soon awaken and bind me. To him. I was his alone. One sinewed arm choke-holding my throat. I could not breathe, so he breathed for me. Just the two of us, his fists slamming into the solid wall that kept the inside of my head secret.

His hairless chest skin stretched tight, I have no knife, my boneless fingers inert. *And if I win*, said the voice inside my head, *what will the prize be*? So I carried him with me – this jack-booted terrorist – the only escape being absence.

Incomplete suicides is how I came to think of them: all the girls I had murdered in my novels, the dead women who bore my scars. Other forms of absence – the severances, the continual motion – had not worked. But I had a weapon. The way I could absent myself was not to be alive. Suicide was a siren calling to me.

If I died, then so would he: a murder-suicide, a domestic incident. Afterwards, everything would be quiet. Yet, whenever I sat down to write a farewell note, the cleaning woman in me, that not-Margie, that mother, would put my pen down and scurry me away to clean the bathroom yet again.

sixty-five

In the middle of one of these cleaning frenzies, on a freezing January day in 2018 when the water pipes were frozen and the snow was thick on the ground, two young friends phoned, their words tumbling out: Alice, they told me, had stepped off the edge of a station platform in front of a train.

I gasped.

They were sorry to impose, but they thought I might help them understand. 'You have a writer's insight,' one said. 'You helped me understand about many terrible things when we were together in Italy, at the residency. Can we please come over and talk to you?'

'Of course,' I said, 'come.'

As I tidied up before their arrival I thought of this girl, this woman, their Alice, and I saw her stepping out, stepping off, resolving despair with one graceful movement in front of a rushing train. I heard the brakes screaming, the driver trying to stop something that had begun long, long before, I saw her limbs sliced and crushed, bone and blood mixed with the soot lining the tunnels beneath the city.

I opened the door, seeing on their faces the stunned shock of survivors. They took off their boots and coats. I made tea and put out some scones in the warm living room. They sat close to each other, their fingers entwined.

I envied this Alice I did not know. This Alice who had stepped off. Who had left. But that was not what I said to my visitors. I let the tea draw, and I listened.

Alice was lonely, they told me. A long relationship had come to an end and she'd gone far away, to New Zealand or Canada, I no longer remember which, but it was a far-flung place.

Something happened there, something Alice hadn't spoken of, they said.

I poured tea, passed milk, sugar.

Alice's work was hard, they said, hands wrapped around warm

245

mugs. She was a teacher at the worst school in London, her class rude and unruly. And it was so cold – or so I imagined, my thoughts becoming hers – waiting for a train that gorged itself at each platform, more and more people, spitting them out onto dirty platforms where advertisements shouted: HOLIDAYS. VITAMINS. TELEPHONES. JACK DANIELS.

All those poster-people looming, Alice with her coat pulled tight and her shoulders hunched to protect her ears, but the noise was too much, and the lights were flashing, and beside her was a couple kissing. She could hear the suck and pop of their lips and feel the wet throb between the girl's legs as she embraced the boy holding onto her, so she did not fall in front of the oncoming train. She flew, free for one endless moment, arms stretched out like wings. The train screaming at her. Dismembering everything she'd ever been.

It will be weeks before her mother and her sister can take her home, said my visitors. The town where she was a little girl on a street where people all knew each other.

Alice's mum is lovely, they told me.

Then the woman smiled and said, 'Her dad's a bit quiet – but that's dads.'

The inquest people and Transport for London would investigate. They would read her scattered limbs as if they were tea leaves, revealing what had turned her into a woman who'd stepped onto a current of air that could not hold her up.

Escape. The thought had torn at my mind for months, for years, while this unknown Alice had had the courage to bring things to an end. I did not say this to those two bewildered young people, of course I didn't, but I wanted to shake them. To shout, *How can you not understand that Alice – I know her, she is me – fought until she could no longer bear it?*

Then her guard dropped, and in that split second, she was gripped by the taloned, beaked ones who know me too. They had lifted Alice up – *not me* – and dropped her – *not me* – in front of a train.

I knew them well, those carrion birds that come hop-hop-hop and take up residence. Once established, they disseminate their propaganda that the times I thought I was free to love and live, they had been there – snipers biding their time, setting their sights, taking aim.

My visitors left and I took the mugs to the sink and washed them. I did not go to a train station, but Alice was all I could think of. Her flight. Her escape. That death-feeling flooding me was taboo. I was a mother. I was not allowed to die simply because I wanted to, but the desire was there in the same way that a stone on a road is there. I saw no future, no light, and there was nothing that could reach the stone-fact – change it, chip it, shape it into something that flowed. Water. Life.

It became apparent to me that my mind was not working well, that it could work better, that if it worked better, I might work. One works so as not to starve to death. One works because it is expected of one. One works because one has this so-called talent, and it is wasteful not to use it in an era of thrift and precarity, when gifts should not be wasted.

But I could not work. I did not want to work. I did not want to use my talent. I did not want to be alive. How, though, does one go about eliminating oneself without causing a disturbance?

sixty-six

In serene, leafy Hampstead where I then lived, everyone I knew was either seeing a psychoanalyst or they were a psychoanalyst. Even the analysts, I discovered, saw other analysts. I imagined the entanglement of stories of grief and bitterness A reticulation of sorrows, variations on themes of love and unlove, which led me, via a discreet referral, to a man, tall and slender and heading for seventy, whose consulting room was at the top of a house in Belsize Park.

Up and down those steps I would go, twice a week for a year. He was not a good timekeeper, and occasionally I'd pass the person whose place I would take in the chair as she (usually) or he (sometimes) came past me. I was not sure of the etiquette of meeting the equally mad or sad on a staircase carpeted in plush red, so I kept my eyes ready, to engage or to slide by, as the situation demanded.

His door at the top of the stairs was open. In the snug little room were two identical chairs angled across opposite corners so we could face each other. On my side was a table, a vase of flowers, a box of tissues and a window, which I opened a little so that, if necessary, I might escape. In his corner was a chair and a leather-bound notebook in which he noted down my appointments and where, at the end of each month, his bills lay bundled in their manila envelopes.

There was a pretty cushion on my chair, an abstract floral in poppy red and green. Each time I went in, I plumped the cushion to get rid of the lingering warmth of the previous person, the one I might just have passed on the stairs. After that I would sit down and once I'd asked him how he was and he had said fine, he would listen as I tried to fashion words for the darkness that clutched at me, ripping my skin as if it were the flimsiest of fabrics.

I found a language, but it wasn't the right one. Madness does not lend itself to language; if anything, it breaks it down. But I told my tales, one after the other, laying them out, it felt, like trinkets on the market stall of myself.

I told him the childhood stories, and about what happened after. I found it startling that he would focus on some bit of banal brutality that to me was just the backdrop to the world I'd grown up in, where systemic injustice and racialised patriarchy had poisoned every aspect of life. That would irritate me, even though it was the kind of thing I had written about.

'That's how it was,' I would say when he made me pause and explain something that to me was obvious, yet seemed to have shocked him. This reaction of his shifted my perspective. I liked that he was on my side. I appreciated that what I had witnessed was disquieting. It gave me confidence that I might not have started out mad.

I told him that I had tried to write a suicide note, but I could not write one. Nor could I plagiarise the ones I found online, written by people more eloquent than I.

'Writer's block,' I told him. 'So far, it's kept me alive.'

I laughed at my joke, but he did not.

He looked at me over slender steepled fingers and said, 'It's what's alive in you – your writing, your creativity – that won't let you finish.'

That was not something I had considered, and it gave me pause.

sixty-seven

'I know when a man watches pornography,' I said to the psycho-analyst. 'You can feel it in his touch. It's you and then it is not you they are touching, it's not your hair they are pulling. It's not your mouth they are putting their hands over. It's some picture they have seen which erases you, this real woman trying to be human – and it's this that triggers feelings of worthlessness and self-loathing. Because in the eyes of the world, the world of men, I am worthless,' I said, not wanting to offend him, but determined to say what I knew from my skin to be true.

The kindly analyst seemed outraged by what I'd said. I appreciated that. I liked his anger on my behalf because I did not really know how to feel it myself. Perhaps it was not all men who loathed women. 'But,' I said, 'society is organised around a deep-rooted revulsion for the female body that is desire's fellow traveller. This misogyny cannot be denied or escaped. It is in every interaction, at every moment. Read the newspapers; somewhere, right now, men are raping girls and burying them alive – whether for real or for pictures.' It was fucked up, I knew, to think like that – to have one's moral sphere so contaminated by patriarchy, but there it was.

I took me a long time to tell him of a man I had loved, a man who had seduced me – an old-fashioned word right for my naivety, I'd said. 'Our paths had crossed because of the work I did. Because of the books I wrote,' I said. 'There was this professional overlap, this world we had had in common, and so I had presumed … '

He did not ask me what I had presumed, but he waited, this man I risked being alone with in a room, week after week, sitting with my eye on the door. I did not say what I had presumed because I no longer knew. Instead, I told him of waking up one morning in a guesthouse in a foreign country.

I had known, that night – the force, my spoken 'No'. But I had been helpless, not protected myself. 'I did not object – no, that's not true,' I interrupted myself, 'I tried to object. I did object but I was overruled.' I was overruled and taken and that was that and it had been awful: the man's hand over my face, the man I loved, and my unheard 'No'. He showed me my place. A piece of me remains in that room. I could not make what had happened between us what it was not.

'In the morning,' I told my analyst, sipping black coffee, able to swallow at such close quarters with another person, 'I went outside. I wrote what had happened in my notebook. Not as a record, but because I could not believe it.' He took another sip, and I went on, 'It reads like fiction, my fiction. I can't believe I'm as stupid as I was when I was twelve.' Forty years had taught me nothing. Not how to raise my hand or my voice in refusal or protest. I said to myself, I had lain there all night because I had nowhere to go, and I had no way to go. I was paralysed by his casual brutality and the fact of his impunity. He knew I would not say anything. I would make-believe and smooth it over. How could I admit to myself that a man who said he loved me, and who I loved, had done that to me?

'He did what he meant to do,' I told the analyst, 'and he did it to make me something hateful, something dirty. That's where his pleasure lay: the creation of powerlessness, erasure. Me. Erasing me.'

I took a tissue from the box on the table next to me, though I did not need it because I was not crying. The clock on the wall ticking faster.

'That desire I had to return was hope. To unhappen it. To make it not real. To make it different. To make *me* wrong so I could believe something else had in fact happened – something loving and connecting. Something good. Because,' I told the analyst while keeping my eyes on the clock as the minute hand ticked up to the end of the hour, 'if, in the eyes of another, you have been made into a receptacle of hatred, of disgust, of rubbish, then the moments and minutes and hours you were that in the eyes of the other remain in you. Your own worthlessness, nothingness is now part of you, the woman, and it casts you out of the human family. The one who did this to you, the one you were conditioned to fantasise would protect you, has made you a thing. And when I objected, I was ignored.'

'That was rape.'

The word shocked me. 'That's your word,' I said.

My analyst crossed his legs. 'It's the word for what you told me happened.'

I did not want that word. It is a word that demands policemen and courts and laws and that was impossible because it's so hard to tell the things that happen between two people, alone.

'No one will believe me,' I said. 'I don't believe myself.'

He said, 'I believe you.'

sixty-eight

The shocks in my past came unexpectedly. I had never been prepared. How could one – or should one – beware of a headmaster, a blind date, an admired acquaintance, a man who said he 'loved' me?

And there were others – a man I knew, groping me in a lift, and us both getting out on the fourth floor, him smiling, me too astonished to say a word, sitting quietly in the meeting that followed. During which he listened respectfully to my proposal for some or other feminist project. Another one – a charming old artist's calloused hands up my shirt in an art gallery. The discomfort of it. How unfunny the things are that women are meant to laugh off. Those flexes of male power that possess us, put us in our place.

Now, if a man believed me, could I begin to believe myself? Relief made me weightless, and I floated down the four flights and out into the sunny morning, where the trees were covered with colourful blossoms. It wasn't that I hadn't been believed before. I had told some of these things to my Cape Town therapist, but I had not, I realised, taken her response to heart. Of course she'd believe me, I had thought. Women believe each other. There is a kind of solidarity of the wounded.

But if a man used the word, then it could well be rape – though this was not a word I had used myself because how could a woman ever be sure? I was not sure, even though I had been there – perhaps *because* I had been there. I did not know how to be sure because it is a principle of justice – a system that often works against women – that there are two sides to every tale. But these are tales that women find hard to tell because of shame. I did not hear voices, like the ones that drove Virginia Woolf into the river with stones in her pockets. I heard silence. And everything simply got colder.

'If in the eyes of another you are worth nothing, that nothingness remains in you,' I said the next time I saw my analyst. 'It is that nothingness that inhabits me as I try to write the suicide notes I can never complete.'

I had felt that if I moved, if I spoke, if I breathed, everything I valued and everyone I loved would be destroyed. But with my analyst's belief in me, that suicide vest packed with the explosive that is shame started to loosen.

The heaviness in my chest eased, and I drew breath. The weight had not only been despair, it had been rage. Frozen rage. The ice-fire of helplessness that I had finally turned into words, clumsy words, but because they had been spoken to a man who could hear them for me, a glacier shifted, moved by the melt of tears.

It's been said that there are no monuments to rape survivors. The only memorial I can build is this one, fashioned from words.

sixty-nine

While I was going up and down the analyst's red-carpeted stairs, the #MeToo movement gathered momentum. Women, imperfect and compromised as I imagined myself to be, who had made 'bad judgements' were saying, 'Enough, we are done', refusing to participate in a game that is stacked against us.

Women were speaking of the complex mix of violence, shame, desire, hope and ambition that distorted their lives, and they were being believed. They had broken the silence that protects the powerful men who hurt them. They denounced those men and their enablers, who preached that what is done to women is a private matter, best left buried and forgotten, so as not to disrupt a fine career or a budding talent.

Despite the retaliation, women did not back down. Their anger engulfed one sector after another, particularly industries that create and sell back to us the stories of ourselves. Those #MeToo stories shifted the balance of power and let the light in.

Those women taught me how to be angry, showing me that the risk of rage was essential to life. And while cases were brought and perpetrators charged, the law and the courts were not my route. The complexity and mess of sexual violence is ill-served by the courts but well suited to writing. I had done it before, and I would do it again: write books where what I knew, what I have seen, what I fear and what I love might give others a place to call home.

Those #MeToo women gave me courage. The courage to tell my own story – to my analyst and to myself. And now here, on these pages, to you. But back then, when I started, I could not find the words to say any of this. My story sat there, a stone on my tongue.

'Take singing lessons,' said an opera-singer friend, putting me in touch with a soprano who gave lessons in her living room above a noisy pub.

I soon realised that there was a barrier at the base of my throat. The sound could not come out. I could not connect what was below in the belly – full and raw – with what was in the throat – refined and etiolated and reed-thin. This barrier, as impermeable as bullet-proof Perspex, blocked my singing just as it blocked me from telling the story I wanted to tell.

'Let your face be ugly,' my teacher would yell, her mouth wide open, sticking her tongue out as if she were Medusa.

I learned to sing with all my heart – mouth wide open and teeth bared. The power of the sound I could make astounded me.

Depression is often anger turned inwards – 'murderous impulses against others' that are redirected to oneself, as Freud suggests. So, who was it I wanted to kill? The list is long.

There was a pen in my hand. Words marched across the page. Free and furious and filled with revenge, I rewrote the novel I had failed to sell. Sure-footed as a cat, I worked – and this time, the book sold.

The stone had been lifted; I was singing.

seventy

'Light,' I instructed an estate agent in a shiny silver suit. The old couple I had rented from in Hampstead had put their flat on the market and I had to move. 'I want light. High ceilings. Big windows. Two rooms – one for me to sleep in and one for daughters. I don't care about the bathroom, and I hardly need a kitchen. But I need somewhere I can grow things.'

The agent found what I wanted in a curved street in Crouch End, a slightly less expensive yet leafy part of north London. It was the ground-floor flat of a tall townhouse, one of thousands that make up residential London. Freshly painted white, with a new carpet the colour of the sea at dawn, it had hardly any kitchen to speak of. Still, I would feed many people from the narrow galley that had been carved out of a grand old drawing room filled with light. It poured in through the bedrooms in the morning, and the living room in the afternoon.

I signed a year's lease, my possessions ferried in a single vanload and set down in my new home. I hung my three oil paintings above the sealed-off fireplace, the landscape with aloes and portraits of me and my grandmother. The living room was furnished with an antique French lounge suite I'd found on a recycling website and a few plants.

My upstairs neighbour, who turned out to be a rocket designer, was shouting cheerfully into her phone in Italian at her parents who, she later told me, sent her suitcases of olive oil and cheese because they were worried about what she ate in London.

There was a family below me with two little boys. They would argue endlessly about which dinosaurs lived in the garden, telling me one day as I hung up my washing that Stegosaurus and Brontosaurus lived in our garden, and Tyrannosaurus rex lived in the homeless shelter next door. I wasn't to worry, they said: Tyranno couldn't climb over the fence – his arms were too short.

I bought two boxes of wildflower seed mix, intending to plant them in the spring, intending to write, too, but that year the darkness welled up again, and instead of sheltering in the home I had made I went out walking. To escape myself, I walked wider and wider circles, looping through the new area, where no matter how often I walked down a street or into a café, I always felt foreign.

I found myself buying boxes of painkillers, two or three boxes only from the many pharmacies I went to, and hoarding them at home. I had stopped seeing the kind analyst man after he said he believed me. I'd found it hard to tell him anything more because after the epiphany of his belief I felt so euphoric that I was surely cured. But I was not.

Over lunch one day in a noisy café I told a friend how sad I was feeling again, and he referred me to a female psychoanalyst with an interest in psychosomatic illness and trauma. Her consulting rooms were spartan – a bay window with white venetian blinds, her chair in one corner, the patient's chair opposite, and a bed whose legs were covered with a red rug. I lay down and told her I had started buying pills, just in case, after a twenty-foot palisade was installed on the bridge above Archway Road, not far from my flat, where desperate people were known to go and jump.

As I was telling her, a migraine of an intensity I had never before experienced began. It lasted five days, and all I could do was try to get through it. My secret was out – outed by myself – but I would live because I had told my analyst that I wanted to die, and for reasons I could not fathom then, she wanted me to be alive. She wanted me to thrive. She took my part against the hostage takers in my mind, and I love her for that.

For longer and longer periods of time, the black-marabou-thoughts that beaked at me were kept at bay. One day, I hoped, they would leave me altogether. I worried about who they would turn on next, but my analyst said it did not work like that. They were my thoughts – my own mind – turning on me; it was all in my head.

I knew she was right, although I did not believe her. Together, and over many months, we attended to the fury that turned inwards and maddened me.

Five times a week: the predictable rhythm of those sessions was as close as I could get to the sanitorium I had dreamed of for so long. She was always there at the appointed time. I was never late, and I never skipped, and slowly, by some kind of alchemy, order returned. I was restored to life – and to the life I was writing.

Psychoanalysis is a collaboration, but one that depends on the braiding of a personal history. It is the taking of a history, as detectives do, although they would call it 'taking a statement'. A form of forensics, psychoanalysis assumes that every contact leaves a trace. The nature of the contact and the trace is opaque, just out of focus, and during the collaboration, what is obscured is often brought into view.

A mystery one had to accept, which I did.

seventy-one

At the end of the rectangular lawn stood an oak tree with a wooden table and chairs where I took my books whenever the sun shone. The window was open. I listened to the snap-crack of wet laundry being shaken out in the garden. Jamie was hanging up their clothes under the pale late-afternoon English sun. When those clothes were dry, they would pack them with all their other things and take their belongings, including the bed. They had graduated from Bristol University and were moving to Brixton, but their bedroom would no longer be theirs. It would be mine.

Instead of working at the dining-room table and clearing my papers away when we ate, I would have a writing room of my own once more. When they came to stay, whenever their sisters came, there would be pillows and sheets and clothes on the floor, transforming my study into a bedroom, but its occupation would be temporary, and when my daughter-guests left it would again be mine.

From the galley kitchen only big enough for one-and-a-half people came the clatter of the kettle, the tap running, the click-click of the gas, cupboards opening and shutting. The kettle boiled, they cut the steam before it began to squeal – the sound hurt their ears – and there they were in the doorway with a tray in their hands. We sat side by side on the floor, shoulders touching, and sipped tea and did a tarot card reading only partly in jest – letting the cards tell us our pasts and our futures, what was blocking us. Then they dozed off in the sun's last rays. The quiet of their sleeping presence anchored me as it had done when they were a baby.

I had always written best when my children were in my house and asleep; then, as I watched over them in my mind, the agitated rhythms of my heart would slow and sync with theirs and, without effort, the words would come. I had been mining memories of my adult life, trying to make sense of how, who, why – when, as if by magic, a scrap from infancy floated before me.

My first escape, my first disappearance, the ecstasy of being alone – it was there, intact in my mind. Afraid I would lose this first knowing of myself, the only memory I have that preceded the birth of my sister, I quickly picked up my notebook to catch the wraith. Careful not to disturb my sleeping child, I wrote:

The sun is in shards between the leaves where I crouch, thighs on potbelly, arms hugging knees, close to myself. The sunlight cuts me into pieces when it penetrates luminous hydrangea leaves that the breeze shifts and shakes. They make a sing-song of my name.

Lips clamped shut so that they will not open and answer and give me away. Smell of loam, of dry leaves on my bare feet. Rustle of beetles, the silent burrowing of earthworms below, one squashed on the path, its pink body bunched up. Blind foot kills tunnelling worm. Outside my dark-light-dark-light-dark-light shelter, where no one can find me because I am under the blue hydrangea at the gate leading to the driveway, the parents saying goodbye goodbye goodbye and kissing.

I don't like to be kissed. How to breathe? So, I ducked into this heavenly darkness with stripes of sunlight. They are calling me.

Not-answering, holding my tongue, I am filled with warmth, power. I see slices of my mother and my father on the other side of the leaves, but I don't answer because I know where I am. I am here.

I am hidden. I am alone, which is how I know myself, know I am a self – separate, apart, secret, satisfying. I could live here forever.

The calling mother-father voices fade.

In my hiding place there is the smell of dead mouse rot. The fear they will stop calling, won't find me, will go away without me rises hot in my chest and pushes me out, to shout 'Here I am!'

'There you are!' My mother, my father, my grandmother stretch out arms and lift me up as if it is a game.

It must have happened like that because games of hide-and-seek end with everyone saying, 'There you are!' but I can't be sure. The instant I left that blue-green shelter with its smell of dead mouse, I stepped off the narrow sandbank of first memory and into the time-river that had brought me to that flat in London, where the autumn sun had disappeared behind a cloud and my study felt chilly.

Jamie, stretched out on the carpet, woke, yawned, sat up, drank their cold tea and, with a smile and a 'Bye, ma, see you soon', set off on their skateboard into the city they were making their own.

It was silent after they left; even the blackbirds in the garden had stopped calling, and I reread the memory I had written down. I saw that hidden within it was loneliness – solitude's twin – and the yearning to be found, despite the cost of companionship.

seventy-two

I set out for Karen's farewell party by taxi on a clear evening in late November that year. She had been in London for some months, and I had loved having my old friend near me. She, who shared my history, who had introduced me to Aidan, and who was Grace's godmother, made me feel less foreign in London, less unfamiliar to myself. For months we had worked together at the Mews Coachworks, a women's art collective where I'd found creative companionship, calm and focus through the worst of the despair that had plagued me throughout what I thought of as my seven lost years. Having Karen there restored to me a sense of continuity with who I had once been, which helped me understand who I had become.

As the driver sedately made his way to Kentish Town, I remembered driving Karen to the University of Cape Town, she in the passenger seat as I hurtled down Main Road, speeding because I was late for a lecture. I turned up past the residences, where streams of students flowed out of the doors and up the mountainside to campus. We sailed past them jauntily, Karen beside me clutching her books as the morning sun exploded over the mountains beyond False Bay. Determined not to make us late for the first lecture of the day, I accelerated, rounding a bend, and my yellow Beetle flew off the road and over a sea of agapanthus before landing on a footpath full of students, miraculously missing them.

'God, Margie, you must slow down,' shouted Karen as we teetered on the curb, laughing because it had been marvellous to fly, and nobody had been killed. Six young men in rugby shorts rushed up and lifted our car onto their shoulders, carrying us as if we were queens in a palanquin, before setting us down on the road. We thanked them, they waved, and we sped off.

The taxi slowly pulled up outside the house where Karen's party was being held and I went in, setting down a dish of food on the buffet table. The party had been going for a while already and the house was companionably crowded. I helped myself to a drink, said hello to my eldest daughter, sitting with a glass of champagne in her hand and chatting to a handsome Catholic priest, then I circled around, greeting people, meeting people, happy to be there.

Karen came over with a wiry-looking man in tow. 'I can't believe you and Gavin don't know each other,' she said. 'You know so many of the same people. He's written a memoir. It's about boxing and politics. It's good.'

Gavin's smile – it lit up his face. He asked if I minded if he sat beside me. I did not mind. He had come late, he said, because he'd been teaching. He had thought about going straight home because he was so late, he told me, but now he was glad he had come.

I was glad, too. He was South African, but had left in 1992. Children – he had daughters the same age as mine. Books and politics. Talking to him was so easy – there was a flow and a kind of knowing. It was not love at first sight; it was recognition. He asked me what I was working on and I said a memoir. I told him about two pieces Karen had helped me shape, which were being published in *Granta* magazine. I said I'd send them to him, and I did. When we met up in the freezing first week of January 2019, he said, 'I loved the essay about your childhood.'

A good place to start with a writer – telling them you love something they've written. I had read his memoir, but I confessed I'd skipped over the boxing to get to the arc of his life and his politics. 'It was illuminating,' I told him, 'I could see what you'd left out.'

'That's the trouble with writers,' he replied.

The pub had emptied; the bar staff were already stacking glasses, and by the time I watched him speed away on his bike, I knew: this is a man with whom I can be true.

seventy-three

The first time Gavin visited my house he followed me into my kitchen, where there wasn't room for two people. 'Why do you have that kettle?' he asked.

I picked up my enamel kettle, though I did not intend to fill it. I had bought it because of its pleasing colour, cream the shade of farm milk – just like the one I used to leave on the stove in my Cape Town house.

'Why don't you have an electric kettle?' he asked.

'I don't like wires,' I said. 'I don't like things cluttering the counter. I like the sound the gas makes when you light it. I like how the kettle wails when it boils. It doesn't stop until you stop what you are doing and attend to it. I like that it reminds me I want tea.' I put the kettle back on the hob.

'I love my kettle,' Gavin said. 'It's black. Smart.'

He's afraid, I thought to myself. If I came to live with him in his house, he's afraid I'd bring my kettle and the whistling and the rushing to the kitchen to stop the scream, furious and insistent. It's true that I don't like wires and things on the counter, but it's also true that I don't care about kettles.

We went into the garden, and I cut his hair for the first time in the bright spring sunshine.

seventy-four

When I went to my favourite café for the first time after Covid lockdowns ended, I placed my order and waited for it at the table in the bay window. The street was not as empty as before, but people were keeping their distance, even though the pandemic's threat had receded. I had found the lockdown strangely calming. For the first time in my life I could not go anywhere. I could no longer bolt about because I had been caged, as we all were, by a virus and government decree, for our own good. It had certainly done me good, that enforced stillness. It had homed me, settled my mind, and made me productive. Knowing that the impossible book would be published in 2022 as *The Eye of the Beholder* had restored my confidence. It helped, too, that I'd successfully completed a PhD by publication at the University of East Anglia. Though this was two decades after my scholarship years in New York, the doctoral research I had done at the time nevertheless nourished my first five novels. My professor was right – I had wanted and needed, then, to be out and about in the world. But I eventually circled back, having reflected deeply on what I had learned through the process of writing my southern African novels.

I defended my dissertation, titled 'Nostalgia for the Future', on Zoom during lockdown in May 2020. I was now officially Dr Orford.

'A proper doctor!' my sister had crowed when I'd phoned her. 'Not one of those rubbish medical ones!'

The barista put down my coffee and asked if I was okay. 'I am,' I said. 'How about you?'

'I'm fine,' he smiled, but there were tears in his eyes. 'Nobody I loved died.'

'Me neither,' I replied.

I walked on to Gavin's house, which had been my destination all along. I'd bought a blue-and-white toothbrush from the corner shop to leave in his bathroom the second time I spent the night there. It was obvious to me that I meant to keep returning, and I had. But, despite that territorial marker, there were occasions when I walked to his house simply because I wanted to be with him, only to find, when I got there, that I was unable to knock. Who would I be inside? What would happen? If I went in, how would I get out? My heart would pound, and I'd turn around and slip away.

Once, he'd found me there on his doorstep, then taken me in his arms and coaxed me inside. I felt foolish because I couldn't explain myself, but he'd made me stay and we sat on the couch for a while and played with the kitten until he said, 'Come to bed,' and it was fine. I wanted to be able to sleep in his bed, warm and contented. I sensed that my being harmed would never be a precondition for this man's pleasure.

If I could not sleep, I lay there, awake. It was rude to leave in the middle of the night, even to escape the dread vibrating through my body, as if each cell were a restless bee humming along with all the other bees, ready to swarm. I could not get the humming cells – the molecules, the electrons – to stop looking for an exit when no exit was needed. I was learning to wait them out and not to flee. To make it easier when my nerve cracked at two in the morning, I took the taxi apps off my phone, stopping myself from calling a cab. Although I suspect the truth was that the measured rationality of my psychoanalyst, who'd continued her sessions with me over the phone, curbed my impulse to flee.

I walked, as I had so many evenings during the loneliness and peace of the lockdowns, towards Gavin's house. When the marabou-thoughts of annihilation circled back, he would chase them off, despite the sharpness of their beaks and the wounds they inflict.

His narrow garden opened onto an enormous park, where at night, owls called out to each other in the oak trees. Anticipation and trust were edging out the shadows in my mind. My desire-rhythm-joy – I don't know if there is a single word that describes the capacity to be open to love – had not been crushed. Instead, it had gone underground and waited until, under cover of the contentment I had found, it seemed safe to return.

The feeling of being present in my body so that things around me felt real had been gone so long that I had forgotten it. But we only forget things we have known, so it was something I *had* known, and I believed I could know it again. Back through the years I went, back and back I went until I came across myself at fourteen.

I am lying curled up with a boy in his room with Deep Purple's 'Smoke on the Water', boy music if ever there was, looped forever around that suspended moment. I see, with the hindsight that telescopes aeons-long childhood into seconds, that this is only a year after I'd escaped the grip of that predatory headmaster. But there I am, nose-to-nose with a dark-haired boy, the two of us transfixed by a feeling for which we do not yet have a name.

Just the two of us in the whole wide world. His button-up shirt smelled of his mother's soap, different to my mother's, and of sweat and dust. His breathing swelled his narrow chest, tightening his white school shirt. I breathed with him, and that matched breath set me on fire and burned the hurt child out of my body. I was flying with the joy of his body, the one I had chosen. The backs of his hands brushed my breasts. My hands were folded between us, but they wanted to map out his smooth, hairless chest, so I let them.

A month or two later, I went away to boarding school. I returned after my first term, but the routine of our school, which had thrown us together and made our inarticulate pairing possible, was gone. And then things happened – the ones I have written about in this book – and they buried the ease and certainty I'd had with that boy.

But now I remembered I had once known how to be with someone without wanting to escape. I understood that I had loved him, and he had loved me, for the duration of an afternoon, and that this feeling of bodily presence and pleasure had endured, lasting a lifetime.

I opened the gate, walked through Gavin's garden, which I had started reshaping, and knocked on his green door. The optimistic man whose face I liked so much, this weather-beaten marathon runner, opened it and ushered me in. He held my face between his eyes and searched my eyes – looking for the demons that so often got me in their grip.

But they were not there. I did not know where they had gone, but it was so peaceful without them jack-booting around on the inside of my skull that it was as if they had never existed.

Gavin had made his house ready for me. There were flowers on the table and the food was cooked. I was ravenous; I ate everything he put on my plate. I drank all the champagne he offered to me. He was celebrating me signing up to write this book.

'It will bring your confidence back,' he who loved my writing said, 'which will get you back after your being so sad for so long. That's worth celebrating, isn't it?'

'It is,' I said, sipping the champagne he'd poured for me.

seventy-five

And that is where this book was meant to end, with that moment of unfurling, of healing, of love, and of hope. I had written myself to the edge of what I thought might be the future. I had found a way to begin again. And I had finished this memoir, after a fashion, on Thursday the eleventh of November 2021. So I spent the morning cutting, pruning, winnowing – the real work of writing.

I left my desk at 13:28 – the time recorded on my saved manuscript – and walked to the living room. Jamie, back with me for a while because of the disruptions of the pandemic, sat working at the dining table, and I was about to ask what they wanted for lunch.

Before I could speak, my silenced phone alongside the sofa flashed. My mother calling me at 1:30 pm on a chilly winter afternoon.

When she called, it was always in the morning or at night.

A tightening in my belly as I picked up.

'Melle.' My mother's voice was low and tense. She repeated my sister's name, 'Melle.'

'What—'

'She had a bleed.'

'Where—'

'On the brain,' she said before I could finish my question.

'Okay—'

'It's very serious, Margie.'

I felt my mother's fear. She told me more things, but I don't know what they were. I was listening to the throb of the hospital. My father's voice in the background, flat and desperate.

'Okay, Mum. I'm coming.' I looked up at Jamie's face. It was white. 'It's Dede,' I said. 'She's in the hospital.'

The bones in my legs were no longer there when I walked to the tiny kitchen and poured a glass of water I could not drink. I phoned my travel agent. She booked me a ticket via Addis Ababa to Windhoek for the next day. I could fly only if I tested negative for Covid.

I went to the pharmacy for a test. The one that dispensed my HRT – which my sister and I had once discussed. She'd been plagued by menopause. Couldn't sleep from the heat that surged through her and she was so enraged sometimes she could have killed someone. Another time she'd mentioned that maybe it was just the future she wasn't able to picture. Going on getting up, going to work, looking after our parents.

Our father has changed, she'd said. He's frailer, fading. That was her word. He was fading and she was so afraid he would die. She cried when she told me. She loved him so, even if he drove her crazy going on about shares and Darwin and gut microbes. She cared for my parents. Dropped in at their house every day. Kept them company. Organised their lives for them, as they kept telling me: car licences, documents, computers gone wrong.

I'd told Melle I should come now – I hadn't seen them all for eighteen months, but she'd laughed and said, 'You're always flying around, wrecking the planet. Come at Christmas.'

So that was what we had planned.

The Covid result arrived. Next day, I'd fly.

seventy-six

My sister died. I write this – I'd written that – and my pen stops. I try again. My sister died. I do not know what to write after. My mind won't take in the termination. I am lopsided. The world is out of kilter. I don't know what comes after that sentence. I don't know what comes next. But that is the sentence I must write because her death is a fact and, even though I don't know what to do with a fact like this, facts are what we must stick with. The reason I started writing fiction was to hack my way through a thicket of facts about death and dying to get to the truth of loss and love and resilience. It has not stood me in good stead.

I don't know what to do with the fact that my sister died. I don't know what to do with the other fact, which is that I did not die. What killed her will not kill me – something else will, for sure, but not the vein-bomb that exploded in her head, erasing her mind before it destroyed her brain.

The swelling crushed the brainstem, the sunburned doctor who had treated her told me. He used his left fist to demonstrate her brainstem and his right hand, spread out, closing on his fist – Melle's brainstem – to show why heart-beating and lung-breathing stopped.

Her dying took place over four long days in the second week of November – Thursday, when I knew. Friday, when I flew. Saturday and Sunday, when I sat beside her and ate the KitKats my daughters had bought at the airport for fortification during the journey.

Our hands on her arm were made hot by her heart, which was kept beating, blood circulating, by the machine ensuring that her chest rose and fell in unreal ventilator breaths. My sister, who used to twist and turn her small dolphin body around mine in the oval swimming pool in the house in Windhoek where we grew up, the house where everyone gathered together.

I can't deny the fact my sister died. It is incontrovertible. I was there when it happened. I saw it with my own eyes. Heard it with my own ears. Smelled it. Felt it. Volker, the bewildered man she had been with for seventeen years, who loved her – and still does – was there. We both were. Another undeniable fact. Two of my cousins were there, too. Xandi and Cate had driven from Botswana to be with her because they, too, love her. Loved her. Love her. The grammar of love and death is impossible.

This doctor had – when my father asked if there was any chance, if there was no chance, if there was a chance he was wrong – injected ice-cold water into her brain through her ear, but there was not the slightest dilation of a pupil. This had to be told to our old parents, stunned beyond comprehension by this blow, this loss, this dismemberment of their days, their lives, their heart-child.

'Yes,' we replied when the question was asked for the last time, the final time, the official time.

'For the record,' said the doctor in charge of procedures.

The test, a primitive one in my view, was apparently done so that the ventilator could be legally switched off and my sister – who was 'brain-dead', this same doctor told us – could stop having her lungs inflated with oxygen she could no longer do anything with. I still can't believe that this is how it was done, despite knowing this is what was said and done.

Afterwards I did not know where to turn my mind, or why. The invisible architecture of my future had collapsed. The end of my life had always involved my sister. She and I had always said that when we were old and finished with all our husbands and lovers, we would live in a hotel by the sea and smoke cigarettes, drink champagne and talk about everyone we knew. This had been our lifelong joke. Now she was dead, I understood it had been my only plan.

I could not stitch her death into my life, which is not in Namibia where she lived and died and where the night air was cool on my skin when I awoke at three o'clock each morning. In the liminal pre-dawn when I felt her alive with me, I edited my novel, *The Eye of the Beholder*, the writing of which had cured me of my death-wish madness only because my sister, who was afraid for me but never of me, had phoned – getting me up, keeping me writing from one day to the next, until she was sure I'd keep myself alive.

I drank coffee and watched the stars fade, hearing the first bulbul's liquid call as the night departed. The bird seemed surprised to be alive. To be piercing the sleeping silence. But I had long been awake, startled from the deep vanishing that sleep became in this time after my sister died. That nonsensical sentence again. The death sentence.

The heat of the rising sun returned the unbelievable fact of her absence. But because my life went nonsensically on, I wrote more sentences. These sentences: *The morning fills with apricot light and there are so many birds singing. I don't know their names, but I am not sure I want to. I prefer their calls to slip untaxonomied into my ears. This sound that is always the same and always new. As if this dawn chorus is an orchestra that plays the same piece of music, 'Ode to Joy', say, that one knows, recognising that this is how each morning is stitched onto the previous night. There are new rhythms, new orders of things, but despite the daily repeat, what was yesterday is irretrievably gone.*

We put her into her grave dressed in clothes my daughters and I picked out for her – pale-pink embroidered cardigan, white shirt, khaki pants, the ancient and hideous trainers we'd argued about. The daughters said their aunt needed those shoes because that's what she wore. They said that at her wedding Dede wore her farm boots and Father Christmas socks under her exquisite gold silk wedding dress because she decided not to get wedding shoes. She didn't approve of buying things that would only be worn once. We put the battered trainers and a pair of socks into the bag to take to the funeral home.

I thought about her body all the time.

In an abstract way, I knew what was happening to her body – for my novels I'd read many books on decomposition, as I needed to know about the process of bodily decay. Whenever I think of Melle and her body, I feel a strange tingling in my lip, a numbness on the left side of my face, cheek, nose, where it settles – as it does now, while I'm writing.

Exposed to the unblinking eye of the summer sun, I wrote mourning pages, the words unspooling to stitch the tear in time. I wrote to find a way to go on with the life I could not get back. But what exactly was it that I'd been doing? Writing a memoir. A personal record, the story coming in a rush, in a shape I lost. I had once written about going to New York, but all I remembered now was my sister coming to visit me there in the summer of 2000. How things came to vivid life with her eyes on my life. Shopping at Macy's, where she had stripped off her clothes, much to the delighted horror of a small boy, who clung to a rail and stared at her bare breasts.

'Melle,' I'd exclaimed, 'go to the changeroom.'

'It's fine here,' she'd said, pulling on a pink silk skirt. She had a white wrap shirt to try on too, but as she did so, a platoon of shop assistants – young men – beetled towards us in their dark suits. She lifted her arms, flashing the bush of black hair in her armpits, and they turned on their heels and retreated. 'Hair scare,' she had said in triumph. 'Always works,' and without further molestation, she put on the shirt.

I remembered this when, after we had buried her, Volker said I might want to have some of Melle's clothes. I found that fancy Macy's blouse, unworn for years. The fabric was fragile, and it ripped down the back when I put it on.

'I'll stitch that up,' I had said. 'Keep it with me.'

I take Melle's white shirt out of my cupboard sometimes and hold it because it reminds me of her and how happy I was when she visited me.

In the hell weeks after my sister's death, Gavin's voice in the darkness guided me home. I would phone him after midnight when I collapsed into bed – me in Windhoek, him in London, separated by yet another lockdown. He was not afraid of me when I cried the tears dammed up during the frenzy of family needs that took – thank god they did – my attention during the day. Gavin was able to withstand the ice storm of my grief.

'Let's get engaged,' I said to him deep into one of those nights. 'Permanently engaged. Like Trotsky's idea of permanent revolution. I could do that. I could live with engagement.'

His 'Yes' in the darkness, an anchor.

An aneurysm killed her, she was shot in the head as if by sniper fire while she sat drinking coffee with my father. The bullet, the trigger, the tripwire in her brain, in the base of her skull – there was, unbeknown to any of us, a kink, a bulge, an off-ramp in the highway of veins taking blood from her big loving heart to her brain. It exploded. Only when it happened did we know it had been there, lying in wait all the time.

The same radiologist who had scanned my sister checked my head twenty days after the vein in her head gave way. Melle was conscious then, Volker had told me, nauseous, moaning in pain, wanting it to stop, to get out of the machine shooting waves that were unbearably loud, creating the medical resonance image so that the inside of her head could be read.

She hated loud noises, my sister.

My daughter watched me go in for the scan. I was shown a room and told to take off my clothes and to put on a blue hospital gown with ribbons that tied at the back. I took off my gold bracelets and locked them into a cubicle together with my phone and my handbag and my shoes. I kept on the gold ring – a thick band with 'Melle 24–9–87' engraved on the inside: her name and the date of her 21st birthday.

'It's my sister's ring,' I told the nurse.

She'd had to take it off in ICU, and the night she died Volker gave it to me and said, 'Please wear this. Melle always did.'

I promised him I would never take it off.

With tear-filled eyes, the nurse said I could keep it on – she knew my sister; Windhoek is a small town, so everyone knew her. The nurse guided me into the chamber where the MRI machine was and told me to lie down. I lay with my hands crossed on my belly. This was the last thing my sister was conscious of – lying in this white tube.

Her ring began to vibrate as the hum of the machine found its way to the gold on my left hand. The vibration became stronger and stronger until it resonated through my hands, my arms, my whole body. I could have lived with Melle in that white tube forever. I know it was all sound waves, molecules, science – but I also know it was a visitation.

The radiologist found no kinks in the veins and arteries carrying blood in and out of my head.

This would not be my death.

seventy-seven

Reader, I married him. Our five daughters gave us away and I wore a red silk dress. Starlings swirled above when I said my vows. She's here! I thought. My sister is here as my witness. Grief flared in my chest – but then Gavin spoke. His voice in the darkness had guided me home, which is now the tiny house above his that I bought and moved into after our wedding. I can't imagine being two and becoming one, so I live upstairs and he downstairs. We have two front doors, but we knocked an opening into the wall dividing our hallways and put in a glass door to connect us. We took down the fence separating the two narrow gardens and made them one. In the centre, surrounded by roses and wildflowers, is the magnolia Gavin and our daughters planted for my sister. I watch it grow, and I feel her here, with me, where I have learned to live again.

Acknowledgements

A book, like a life, is made up of the labour and love of many people. I am grateful, firstly, for my daughters, who shape me into the woman I am always becoming; also, I am grateful to my parents and my brother and sister, not only for loving me, but for championing me.

Thank you to my community of readers – Karen Martin, Gavin Evans (who read more drafts than I can count), Josh Cohen, Jean McNeil, Julia Bell, Marina Benjamin, Volker Schubert, Kate Burling, Joost Nijsen and Pumla Dineo Gqola – for their attention, candour, patience and rigour.

Abigail Schama and the Mews Coachworks – a community of creative women – where I wrote much of this book, gave me the space I needed to think and write, as did the Institute for Advanced Studies in the Humanities (IASH) at Edinburgh University, where I was a Community Fellow. Thank you to all the people who gave me shelter and a bed for a night, or several nights, in the unsettled years I spent in transit.

I am so grateful to Nicole Duncan, my editor at Jonathan Ball, for coaxing me back to the manuscript a year after my sister's death. Word by word, week by week, she got me writing again. Lynda Gilfillan, who I was thrilled to work with again as she edited all my Clare Hart novels, has done her exacting and elegant copy-editing best. Thanks to the team at Jonathan Ball who have, from the beginning, supported me and my work. My thanks also to Nkanyezi Tshabalala for seeing the potential of this memoir, and to my agent, Cath Summerhayes of Curtis Brown.

This book, in which I have wrestled with my private life, is sprinkled with references to other books, to lectures, to art performances

– to all the things that have made up my public life. Readers who wish to know more are welcome to visit my website, www.margieorford. net; here, they may also view *An Attempt at Exhausting a Place in New York* – my all-time favourite work.

I am indebted to a multitude of writers and thinkers who have not only shaped my thinking but also compelled my actions. On p. 254 I reference Judith Herman: 'There is no public monument for rape survivors', *Trauma and Recovery: The Aftermath of Violence – from Domestic Abuse to Political Terror* (1992), while the epigraph references Louise Bourgeois, No. 8 of 9, from the series, 'What is the Shape of This Problem?' (1999).

About the author

MARGIE ORFORD is an internationally acclaimed writer and an award-winning journalist. Her five Clare Hart novels have been widely translated, leading to her being described as the 'queen of South African crime-thriller writers' (*The Weekender*). Her most recent novel is *The Eye of the Beholder* (2022), while *Common Purpose* is due to be published in 2025.

A Fulbright Scholar, she has a Master's in Comparative Literature from the City University of New York and a PhD in English Literature from the University of East Anglia. An honorary fellow of St Hugh's College, Oxford, she was also an executive board member of PEN International and is currently President Emerita of PEN South Africa. In addition, she has served as a patron of Rape Crisis in Cape Town.

Born in England to South African parents, she has lived in Namibia and South Africa, and is now based in London.